Taste of Home *made from* SCRATCH

TASTE OF HOME BOOKS • RDA ENTHUSIAST BRANDS, LLC • MILWAUKEE, WI

©2025 RDA Enthusiast Brands, LLC.
1610 N. 2nd St., Suite 102,
Milwaukee WI 53212-3906

All rights reserved. Taste of Home is a registered trademark of RDA Enthusiast Brands, LLC.

Visit us at tasteofhome.com for other Taste of Home books and products.

International Standard Book Number:
979-8-88977-112-8

Chief Content Officer:
Jason Buhrmester
Content Director:
Mark Hagen
Creative Director:
Raeann Thompson
Associate Creative Director:
Jami Geittmann
Deputy Editor:
Adila Matra
Senior Editors:
Christine Rukavena, Simrran Gill
Editor:
Hazel Wheaton
Associate Editor:
Smita Mustafi
Senior Art Director:
Courtney Lovetere
Manager, Production Design:
Satyandra Raghav
Assistant Art Director (Production):
Jogesh Antony
Print Publication Designer:
Akash Christopher
Deputy Editor, Copy Desk:
Ann M. Walter
Copy Editor:
Rayan Naqash

**Cover Photography
Photographer:**
Mark Derse
Set Stylist:
Stacey Genaw
Food Stylist:
Josh Rink

Pictured on front cover:
Best Lasagna, page 126;
Caesar Salad, p. 159;
Mom's Italian Bread, p. 191;
Shortbread Lemon Tart, p. 212

Pictured on back cover:
Oven-Baked Brisket, p. 115;
Cream Cheese Blueberry Pie, p. 234;
The Best Beef Stew, p. 105;
The Best Marinara Sauce, p. 133;
Millionaire Shortbread Bars, p. 254

Printed in China
1 3 5 7 9 10 8 6 4 2

APPLE PIE, PAGE 215

CONTENTS

INTRODUCTION 4

BREAKFAST & BRUNCH 6

APPETIZERS & SNACKS 40

SOUPS & STEWS 74

MAIN COURSES 108

SIDES & SALADS 144

BREADS, BISCUITS & MORE 170

CAKES & PIES 208

BROWNIES, BARS & COOKIES 244

DESSERTS & SWEETS 280

INDEX 316

BEST CINNAMON ROLLS, PAGE 29

RELISH THE BENEFITS OF A FROM-SCRATCH KITCHEN

Sit back, relax and savor the unbeatable goodness of a hearty homemade dinner just as Mom and Grandma used to prepare. Think you don't have time with today's busy schedules? Let this keepsake cookbook show you how easy, rewarding and downright delicious from-scratch cooking can be!

Whether you're craving cheesy casseroles, savory stews, buttery biscuits or the old-fashioned cakes and pies you remember most, the 279 finger-licking recipes found here are sure to fill the bill. Best of all, they feature the homemade flair today's cooks are looking for.

Pare down fat, sodium and carbohydrates when you decrease convenience items and start preparing foods from scratch. In fact, you will find a complete set of nutrition facts with each dish, so you know exactly what you're feeding your family. Step-by-step photos, clear instructions and common ingredients make it easier than ever to serve wholesome foods without taxing your time in the kitchen.

You'll even discover no-fuss recipes for homemade mayonnaise, flavored butters, sauces, seasonings, peanut butter, basic pastry dough and more. These simple sensations are sure to become favorites in your home and save money at the grocery store too. Simply see the book's back-cover flap for a complete listing of these specialties.

In addition, reader reviews, Test Kitchen tips and hints, incredible photography and spaces for your own notes and comments make this one book you can't do without.

Want to surprise the gang with a hearty breakfast? Consider all the options inside. Need a flavorful snack without all the salt and calories of packaged treats? There are numerous options to consider. For everything from appetizers and entrees to breads and brownies, you'll always find the perfect dish here. Take a peek inside and you'll quickly realize that this colorful collection of homemade dishes is one you'll reach for time and again.

SUNDAY PORK ROAST, PAGE 125

from scratch
BREAKFAST & BRUNCH

BRIOCHE FRENCH TOAST, PAGE 32

PIZZA RUSTICA (EASTER PIE)

My grandma shared this recipe and always supervised when I made it for Easter. My husband and brother love it so much! You can make the dough ahead to save time and choose just about any deli meat for the filling, but we always come back to Grandma's original recipe. If pressed for time, eliminate the dough portion by purchasing refrigerated pie dough.
—Kristy Pianoforte, Brooklyn, NY

PREP: 20 MIN. + CHILLING • **BAKE:** 1¼ HOURS + COOLING • **MAKES:** 8 SERVINGS

- 3½ cups all-purpose flour
- ¾ tsp. salt
- ½ tsp. pepper
- 1 cup shortening
- 8 to 10 Tbsp. ice water

FILLING
- 9 large eggs, divided use
- 1 container (15 oz.) whole-milk ricotta cheese
- 1 lb. shredded mozzarella cheese (4 cups)
- 2 cups cubed dry salami
- ¼ lb. thinly sliced hard salami, chopped
- ¼ lb. diced provolone cheese
- 4 thin slices prosciutto, chopped

1. In a large bowl, mix flour, salt and pepper; cut in shortening until crumbly. Gradually add ice water, 1 Tbsp. at a time, tossing with a fork until the dough holds together when pressed. Divide dough into two-thirds and one-third sized pieces. Shape each into a disk; wrap and refrigerate 1 hour or overnight.

2. Preheat the oven to 350°. On a lightly floured surface, roll the larger piece of the dough to a 12-in. circle; line bottom and press up the side of a greased 9-in. springform pan. For filling, in a large bowl, beat 8 eggs and ricotta until smooth. Stir in the mozzarella, salamis, provolone and prosciutto. Pour into the crust. Roll the remaining dough to an 11-in. circle. Place over the filling. Trim and seal edge. Cut slits in top.

3. In a small bowl, whisk remaining egg; brush over crust.

4. Bake until crust is golden brown and a knife inserted in the center comes out clean, 1¼ to 1½ hours. Loosen side from pan with a knife; remove rim. Let cool 1-1½ hours. Serve warm or at room temperature.

1 PIECE 1010 cal., 69g fat (27g sat. fat), 312mg chol., 1928mg sod., 47g carb. (4g sugars, 2g fiber), 48g pro.

EGGS BENEDICT CASSEROLE

Here's a casserole as tasty as eggs Benedict, but without the hassle. Simply assemble the ingredients ahead, and bake it the next morning for an elegant breakfast or brunch.
—Sandie Heindel, Liberty, MO

PREP: 25 MIN. + CHILLING • **BAKE:** 45 MIN. • **MAKES:** 12 SERVINGS (1⅔ CUPS SAUCE)

- 12 oz. Canadian bacon, chopped
- 6 English muffins, split and cut into 1-in. pieces
- 8 large eggs
- 2 cups 2% milk
- 1 tsp. onion powder
- ¼ tsp. paprika

HOLLANDAISE SAUCE
- 4 large egg yolks
- ½ cup heavy whipping cream
- 2 Tbsp. lemon juice
- 1 tsp. Dijon mustard
- ½ cup butter, melted
- Minced chives, optional

1. Place half the bacon in a greased 3-qt. or 13x9-in. baking dish; top with English muffin pieces and remaining bacon. In a large bowl, whisk the eggs, milk and onion powder; pour over the top. Refrigerate, covered, overnight.

2. Preheat the oven to 375°. Remove casserole from refrigerator while oven heats. Sprinkle top with paprika. Bake, covered, 35 minutes. Uncover; bake 10-15 minutes longer or until a knife inserted in center comes out clean.

3. For the sauce, in top of a double boiler or a metal bowl over simmering water, whisk the egg yolks, cream, lemon juice and mustard until blended; cook until mixture is just thick enough to coat a metal spoon and temperature reaches 160°, whisking constantly. Reduce heat to very low. Very slowly drizzle in warm melted butter, whisking constantly. Serve sauce immediately with casserole. If desired, sprinkle with chives.

1 PIECE WITH ABOUT 2 TBSP. SAUCE
286 cal., 19g fat (10g sat. fat), 256mg chol., 535mg sod., 16g carb. (4g sugars, 1g fiber), 14g pro.

FLUFFY WAFFLES

A friend shared the recipe for these light and delicious waffles. The cinnamon cream syrup is a nice change from maple syrup, and it keeps quite well in the fridge. Our kids also like it on toast.
—Amy Gilles, Ellsworth, WI

PREP: 25 MIN. • **COOK:** 20 MIN. • **MAKES:** 10 WAFFLES (6½ IN.) AND 1⅔ CUPS SYRUP

- 2 cups all-purpose flour
- 1 Tbsp. sugar
- 2 tsp. baking powder
- ½ tsp. salt
- 3 large eggs, separated
- 2 cups 2% milk
- ¼ cup canola oil

CINNAMON CREAM SYRUP
- 1 cup sugar
- ½ cup light corn syrup
- ¼ cup water
- 1 can (5 oz.) evaporated milk
- 1 tsp. vanilla extract
- ½ tsp. ground cinnamon
  Mixed fresh berries, optional

1. In a bowl, combine the flour, sugar, baking powder and salt. Combine the egg yolks, milk and oil; stir into the dry ingredients just until moistened. In a small bowl, beat egg whites until stiff peaks form; fold into batter. Bake in a preheated waffle maker according to manufacturer's directions.

2. Meanwhile, for syrup, combine sugar, corn syrup and water in a saucepan. Bring to a boil over medium heat; cook and stir for 2 minutes or until thickened. Remove from the heat; stir in the milk, vanilla and cinnamon. Serve with the waffles, with fresh berries if desired.

FREEZE OPTION Cool waffles on wire racks. Freeze between layers of waxed paper in a freezer container. Reheat the waffles in a toaster on medium setting. Or microwave each waffle on high 30-60 seconds or until heated through.

1 WAFFLE WITH 2½ TBSP. SYRUP 424 cal., 12g fat (4g sat. fat), 94mg chol., 344mg sod., 71g carb. (41g sugars, 1g fiber), 9g pro.

LOADED BREAKFAST BURGER

This recipe is a twist on your traditional breakfast sandwich!
I use ground turkey for a leaner option and Sriracha mayo for heat.
To make your own maple bacon, brush one side of regular bacon with
maple syrup before cooking, then flip halfway and brush with a bit more.
—Gabriella DiSanto, Lancaster, PA

PREP: 25 MIN. • **COOK:** 15 MIN. • **MAKES:** 4 SERVINGS

¼ cup mayonnaise
2 tsp. Sriracha chili sauce
¼ tsp. lemon juice
¼ tsp. salt
⅛ tsp. pepper

BURGERS
¼ cup dry bread crumbs
1 Tbsp. mayonnaise
1 tsp. salt
1 tsp. onion powder
½ tsp. garlic powder
½ tsp. pepper
1 lb. ground turkey
1 Tbsp. canola oil
4 slices cheddar cheese
1 Tbsp. butter
4 large eggs
½ cup cubed medium ripe avocado, peeled
½ tsp. lemon juice
4 English muffins, split and toasted
8 cooked maple bacon strips

1. In a small bowl, combine the first 5 ingredients.

2. In a large bowl, combine the bread crumbs, mayonnaise, salt, onion powder, garlic powder and pepper. Add turkey; mix lightly but thoroughly. Shape into four 3-in.-thick patties.

3. In a large nonstick skillet, heat oil over medium heat. Add burgers; cook until a thermometer reads 160°, 2-3 minutes on each side. Top each burger with 1 slice cheese; cover and cook until the cheese is melted, 1-2 minutes longer. Remove and keep warm. Wipe pan clean.

4. Heat butter in the same skillet over medium-high heat. Break eggs, 1 at a time, into pan; reduce heat to low. Cook until whites are set and yolks begin to thicken, turning once if desired.

5. In a small bowl, mash avocado with lemon juice; spread over English muffin bottoms. Place the burger, egg and bacon on each. Spread the Sriracha mayonnaise over the inside of tops. Replace tops.

1 SERVING 831 cal., 54g fat (17g sat. fat), 325mg chol., 1929mg sod., 37g carb. (3g sugars, 3g fiber), 50g pro.

---

made from scratch
HOMEMADE MAYONNAISE

Did you know America's top-selling condiment and go-to dressing for chicken, tuna and potato salad can be prepared right in your own kitchen with only a handful of everyday pantry items? It's a cinch with this handy recipe.
—Taste of Home *Test Kitchen*

TAKES: 25 MIN. • **MAKES:** 1¼ CUPS

2 large egg yolks
2 Tbsp. water, divided
2 Tbsp. lemon juice
½ tsp. salt
Dash white pepper
1 cup olive oil

1. In a double boiler or heatproof bowl over simmering water, constantly whisk the egg yolks, 1 Tbsp. water and lemon juice until mixture reaches 160°, 30-40 seconds. While whisking, quickly place the bottom of the pan or the heatproof bowl in a bowl of ice water; continue whisking until cooled, 1-2 minutes.

2. Transfer to a 2-cup glass measuring cup or other narrow container. Add salt and pepper. Using an immersion blender, process mixture while gradually adding the oil in a steady stream. Whisk in remaining 1 Tbsp. water if desired. Cover and refrigerate for up to 7 days.

1 TBSP. 84 cal., 9g fat (1g sat. fat), 17mg chol., 50mg sod., 0 carb. (0 sugars, 0 fiber), 0 pro. **DIABETIC EXCHANGES** 2 fat.

LOUKOUMADES (GREEK DOUGHNUTS WITH HONEY)

These Greek doughnuts are easy enough to make at home but taste as if they're fresh from the bakery! Consisting of fluffy, fried dough soaked in a sweet honey syrup, they're the perfect bite-sized treats to pop in your mouth one after the other.
—Risa Lichtman, Portland, OR

PREP: 25 MIN. + RISING • **COOK:** 5 MIN./BATCH • **MAKES:** 2 DOZEN

- 1 pkg. (¼ oz.) active dry yeast
- ½ cup warm water (110° to 115°)
- ½ cup warm 2% milk (110° to 115°)
- ¼ cup olive oil
- 1¾ cups all-purpose flour
- 2 Tbsp. sugar
- ½ tsp. salt
- ¼ tsp. ground cinnamon
- Oil for deep-fat frying
- ½ cup honey
- 4½ tsp. lemon juice
- 1 Tbsp. hot water
- Chopped walnuts

1. In a large bowl, dissolve yeast in warm water. Let stand until foamy, 5-10 minutes. Beat in milk and olive oil. Combine flour, sugar, salt and cinnamon; gradually stir into yeast mixture to form a soft dough (dough will be sticky). Cover and let rise in a warm place until doubled, 1-1½ hours.

2. Stir dough down. In an electric skillet, deep fryer or Dutch oven, heat the oil to 375°. Drop the batter by tablespoonfuls, a few at a time, into the hot oil. Fry until golden brown, about 2 minutes on each side. Drain on paper towels.

3. In a small bowl, whisk honey, lemon juice and hot water; drizzle over warm doughnuts. Sprinkle with the walnuts. Serve immediately.

1 DOUGHNUT 111 cal., 6g fat (1g sat. fat), 0 chol., 52mg sod., 14g carb. (7g sugars, 0 fiber), 1g pro.

NOTES

HEAVENLY CHEESE DANISH

This tempting cheese Danish is baked to flaky perfection and made to shine with a simple egg wash gloss. It tastes just as decadent as any breakfast pastry you'd find in a bakery or coffee shop.
—*Josephine Triton, Lakewood, OH*

PREP: 50 MIN. + CHILLING • **BAKE:** 15 MIN. • **MAKES:** 16 ROLLS

2 pkg. (¼ oz. each) active dry yeast
½ cup warm water (110° to 115°)
4 cups all-purpose flour
⅓ cup sugar
2 tsp. salt
1 cup cold butter, cubed
1 cup 2% milk
4 large egg yolks, room temperature

ASSEMBLY
3 tsp. ground cinnamon
12 oz. cream cheese, softened
⅓ cup sugar
1 large egg, separated
1 Tbsp. water
2 Tbsp. maple syrup

1. Dissolve yeast in the warm water. In another bowl, mix flour, sugar and salt; cut in butter until crumbly. Add the milk, egg yolks and yeast mixture; stir to form a soft dough (dough will be sticky). Cover and refrigerate 8-24 hours.

2. To assemble, punch down the dough; divide into 4 portions. On a lightly floured surface, pat each portion into a 9x4-in. rectangle; sprinkle each with ¾ tsp. cinnamon. Cut each rectangle lengthwise into four 9x1-in. strips. Twist each strip, then loosely wrap strip around itself to form a coil; tuck end under and pinch to seal. Place 3 in. apart on greased baking sheets.

3. Beat cream cheese, sugar and egg yolk until smooth. Press an indentation in center of each roll; fill with 1 rounded Tbsp. cream cheese mixture. Cover; let rise in a warm place until doubled, about 45 minutes. Preheat oven to 350°.

4. Whisk egg white with water; brush over rolls. Bake until golden brown, 15-20 minutes. Remove to wire racks; brush with syrup. Serve warm. Refrigerate leftovers.

1 ROLL 359 cal., 21g fat (12g sat. fat), 111mg chol., 468mg sod., 37g carb. (12g sugars, 1g fiber), 7g pro.

DELECTABLE GRANOLA

Here's a great make-ahead recipe! Be sure to remove the granola from the cookie sheets within 20 minutes, or it may stick to the pans.
—*Lori Stevens, Riverton, UT*

PREP: 20 MIN. • **BAKE:** 25 MIN. + COOLING • **MAKES:** 11 CUPS

8 cups old-fashioned oats
1 cup finely chopped almonds
1 cup finely chopped pecans
½ cup sweetened shredded coconut
½ cup packed brown sugar
½ cup canola oil
½ cup honey
¼ cup maple syrup
2 tsp. ground cinnamon
1½ tsp. salt
2 tsp. vanilla extract
Plain yogurt, optional

1. In a large bowl, combine the oats, almonds, pecans and coconut. In a small saucepan, combine the brown sugar, oil, honey, maple syrup, cinnamon and salt. Heat 3-4 minutes over medium heat until sugar is dissolved. Remove from heat; stir in vanilla. Pour over the oat mixture; stir to coat.

2. Transfer to two 15x10x1-in. baking pans coated with cooking spray. Bake at 350° for 25-30 minutes or until crisp, stirring every 10 minutes. Cool in pans on wire racks. Store in an airtight container. Serve with yogurt if desired.

½ CUP 288 cal., 15g fat (2g sat. fat), 0 chol., 170mg sod., 36g carb. (15g sugars, 4g fiber), 6g pro. **DIABETIC EXCHANGES** 2½ starch, 2 fat.

BREAKFAST & BRUNCH

HOMEMADE FROSTED STRAWBERRY TOASTER PASTRIES

I love this classic childhood treat! Homemade toaster pastries are not just awesome for breakfast, they are also a satisfying dessert, like hand pies. These pastries are worth the extra effort.
—*Andrea Potischman, Menlo Park, CA*

PREP: 45 MIN. + CHILLING • **BAKE:** 15 MIN. + COOLING • **MAKES:** 8 SERVINGS

- 2 cups all-purpose flour
- 2 Tbsp. sugar
- Dash salt
- 1 cup cold unsalted butter, cubed
- 1 large egg, room temperature
- 2 to 4 Tbsp. 2% milk
- ½ tsp. vanilla extract

FILLING
- ½ cup seedless strawberry jam
- 1 Tbsp. cornstarch
- ¼ tsp. vanilla extract
- 1 large egg

FROSTING
- 1¼ cups confectioners' sugar
- 2 Tbsp. 2% milk
- Nonpareils, optional

CAN YOU FREEZE HOMEMADE FROSTED STRAWBERRY TOASTER PASTRIES?

Before frosting, cool pastries. Freeze unfrosted pastries in freezer containers. To use, thaw at room temperature or, if desired, microwave each pastry on high until heated through, 20-30 seconds. Frost as directed.

1. Place flour, sugar and salt in a food processor; pulse until blended. Add butter; pulse until butter is the size of peas. In a small bowl, whisk egg, 2 Tbsp. milk and vanilla. While pulsing, add egg mixture to form moist crumbs. If needed, add the remaining milk, 1 tsp. at a time, to form moist crumbs. Divide dough in half. Shape each into a disk; wrap and refrigerate 1 hour or overnight.

2. For the filling, in a small bowl, combine the jam, cornstarch and vanilla extract.

3. Preheat the oven to 375°. On a lightly floured surface, roll half the dough into a 12x8-in. rectangle. Cut into eight 4x3-in. rectangles. Transfer to a parchment-lined baking sheet. Whisk egg; brush over rectangles all the way to edges. Spoon about 1 Tbsp. filling onto each pastry to within ½ in. of edges. Roll the remaining dough into a 12x8-in. rectangle; cut into eight 4x3-in. rectangles and place over filling. Press edges with a fork to seal.

4. Bake until edges are golden brown and filling is bubbly, 15-18 minutes. Remove from baking sheet to a wire rack to cool. For the frosting, mix the confectioners' sugar and milk until smooth. Spread on the pastries. Sprinkle with nonpareils if desired. Let stand until set.

1 PASTRY 475 cal., 24g fat (15g sat. fat), 97mg chol., 40mg sod., 60g carb. (34g sugars, 1g fiber), 5g pro.

CINNAMON ROLL BISCUITS

When my grandchildren visit, this is their favorite breakfast-at-Grammy's-house treat. If you're not a nut lover, these biscuits are also delicious without the pecans.
—Joyce Conway, Westerville, OH

PREP: 25 MIN. • **BAKE:** 20 MIN. • **MAKES:** 14 BISCUITS

2½ cups all-purpose flour
3 tsp. baking powder
1 tsp. salt
¼ tsp. baking soda
1 cup buttermilk
¼ cup canola oil
1 tsp. vanilla extract
¼ cup butter, softened
½ cup sugar
¾ tsp. ground cinnamon
¼ tsp. ground cardamom
½ cup chopped pecans, optional

GLAZE
1 cup confectioners' sugar
1 tsp. vanilla extract
3 to 4 tsp. 2% milk

1. In a large bowl, combine flour, baking powder, salt and baking soda. Combine buttermilk, oil and vanilla; stir into dry ingredients just until moistened (dough will be sticky).

2. Turn onto a well-floured surface; knead 8-10 times. Roll out dough into a 15x9-in. rectangle. Spread butter to within ½ in. of edges. Combine sugar, cinnamon, cardamom and, if desired, pecans; sprinkle over the butter. Roll up jelly-roll style, starting with a long side; pinch the seam to seal. Cut into about 1-in. slices.

3. Place 1 in. apart on a parchment-lined baking sheet. Bake at 400° until lightly browned, 20-25 minutes.

4. Meanwhile, in a small bowl, combine confectioners' sugar, vanilla and enough milk to achieve a drizzling consistency. Drizzle over the warm biscuits. Serve immediately.

1 BISCUIT 217 cal., 8g fat (3g sat. fat), 10mg chol., 355mg sod., 34g carb. (17g sugars, 1g fiber), 3g pro.

COPYCAT STARBUCKS EGG BITES

These are quick, easy and delicious—perfect for easy breakfasts. You can swap Gruyere for Swiss cheese and ham for bacon, or add small-cut veggies. I also like baking them in small Mason jars for fun, single-portion servings. Serve with avocado slices and fresh fruit for a healthy breakfast.

—*Maria Morelli, West Kelowna, BC*

PREP: 10 MIN. • **BAKE:** 25 MIN. • **MAKES:** 6 SERVINGS

- 6 large eggs
- ¼ cup 4% cottage cheese
- ¼ tsp. salt
- ¼ tsp. pepper
- ½ cup shredded Swiss cheese
- 3 cooked bacon strips, chopped

CAN YOU MAKE COPYCAT STARBUCKS EGG BITES AHEAD OF TIME?

Not only can you freeze cooked eggs, but they actually taste better when reheated than cooked eggs stored in the refrigerator. On the weekend, you can meal prep these Copycat Starbucks Egg Bites and toss them into the freezer. Then, thaw them overnight in the refrigerator for an on-the-go breakfast.

1. Arrange an oven rack at the lowest rack setting; place a second rack in middle of oven. Place an oven-safe skillet on bottom oven rack; preheat oven and skillet to 300°. Meanwhile, in a small saucepan, bring 2 cups water to a boil.

2. In a blender, puree the first 4 ingredients until smooth, about 20 seconds. Line 6 muffin cups with foil liners. Divide Swiss cheese and bacon among the muffin cups. Pour the egg mixture over top.

3. Wearing oven mitts, place muffin tin on top rack. Pull bottom rack out 6-8 in.; add boiling water to skillet. (Work quickly and carefully, pouring water away from you. Don't worry if some water is left in the saucepan.) Carefully slide bottom rack back into place; quickly close the door to trap steam in oven.

4. Bake until the eggs puff and are cooked to desired degree of doneness, 25-30 minutes. Serve immediately.

1 EGG BITE 143 cal., 10g fat (4g sat. fat), 201mg chol., 311mg sod., 1g carb. (1g sugars, 0 fiber), 12g pro.

BUTTERMILK PANCAKES

You just can't beat a basic buttermilk pancake for a down-home country breakfast.
Paired with sausage and fresh fruit, these pancakes are just like the ones you get at Cracker Barrel.
—*Betty Abrey, Imperial, SK*

PREP: 10 MIN. • **COOK:** 5 MIN./BATCH • **MAKES:** 2½ DOZEN

4 cups all-purpose flour
¼ cup sugar
2 tsp. baking soda
2 tsp. salt
1½ tsp. baking powder
4 large eggs, room temperature
4 cups buttermilk

1. In a large bowl, combine flour, sugar, baking soda, salt and baking powder. In another bowl, whisk eggs and buttermilk until blended; stir into dry ingredients just until moistened.

2. Pour batter by ¼ cupfuls onto a lightly greased hot griddle; turn when bubbles form on top. Cook until second side is golden brown.

FREEZE OPTION Freeze the cooled pancakes between layers of waxed paper in a freezer container. To use, place the pancakes on an ungreased baking sheet, cover with foil and reheat in a preheated 375° oven 6-10 minutes. Or place a stack of 3 pancakes on a microwave-safe plate and microwave on high until heated through, 45-90 seconds.

3 PANCAKES 270 cal., 3g fat (1g sat. fat), 89mg chol., 913mg sod., 48g carb. (11g sugars, 1g fiber), 11g pro.

PECAN APPLE PANCAKES To the flour mixture, stir in 1¾ tsp. ground cinnamon, ¾ tsp. ground ginger, ¾ tsp. ground mace and ¾ tsp. ground cloves. To batter, fold in 2½ cups shredded peeled apples and ¾ cup chopped pecans.

BLUEBERRY PANCAKES Fold in 1 cup fresh or frozen blueberries.

BANANA WALNUT PANCAKES Fold in 2 finely chopped ripe bananas and ⅔ cup finely chopped walnuts.

made from scratch PANCAKE SYRUP

My husband has fond memories of this recipe. His dad would get up early every Sunday to make these pancakes and syrup for the family. They didn't have much, but the kids never knew that. What they do remember is that their dad always made their Sundays extra special.
—*Lorrie McCurdy, Farmington, NM*

TAKES: 10 MIN. • **MAKES:** 2 CUPS

1 cup packed brown sugar
1 cup sugar
1 cup water
1 tsp. maple flavoring

In a small saucepan, combine the sugars and water. Bring to a boil; cook and stir 2 minutes. Remove from heat; stir in maple flavoring. Refrigerate leftovers.

2 TBSP. 102 cal., 0 fat (0 sat. fat), 0 chol., 4mg sod., 26g carb. (26g sugars, 0 fiber), 0 pro.

LEMON & CORIANDER GREEK YOGURT

You'll be surprised how easy it is to make homemade Greek yogurt.
Flavored with lemon and coriander, it is simply amazing.
—Taste of Home *Test Kitchen*

PREP: 5 MIN. + CHILLING • **COOK:** 20 MIN. + STANDING • **MAKES:** ABOUT 3 CUPS

2 qt. pasteurized whole milk
2 Tbsp. plain yogurt with live active cultures
2 tsp. grated lemon zest
1 tsp. ground coriander
Honey, optional

1. In a Dutch oven, heat the milk over medium heat until a thermometer reads 200°, stirring occasionally to prevent the milk from scorching. Remove from the heat; let stand until a thermometer reads 112°-115°, stirring occasionally. (If desired, place the pan in an ice-water bath for faster cooling.)

2. Whisk 1 cup warm milk into yogurt until smooth; return all to pan, stirring gently. Stir in lemon zest and coriander. Transfer mixture to warm, clean jars, such as 1-qt. canning jars.

3. Cover jars; place in oven, turn on oven light to keep mixture warm, about 110°. Let stand, undisturbed, 6-24 hours or until yogurt is set, tilting jars gently to check. (Yogurt will become thicker and more tangy as it stands.)

4. Cover; refrigerate until cold. Store in refrigerator up to 2 weeks. If desired, serve with honey.

½ CUP 203 cal., 11g fat (6g sat. fat), 33mg chol., 142mg sod., 16g carb. (16g sugars, 0 fiber), 10g pro.

HOME FRIES

When I was little, my dad and I would get up early on Sundays and make these for the family.
The rest of the gang would be awakened by the tempting aroma.
—*Teresa Koide, Manchester, CT*

PREP: 25 MIN. • **COOK:** 15 MIN./BATCH. • **MAKES:** 8 SERVINGS

1 lb. bacon, chopped
8 medium potatoes (about 3 lbs.), peeled and cut into ½-in. pieces
1 large onion, chopped
1 tsp. salt
½ tsp. pepper

1. In a large skillet, cook the chopped bacon over medium-low heat until crisp. Remove bacon from pan with a slotted spoon; drain on paper towels. Reserve the bacon drippings.

2. Working in batches, add ¼ cup bacon drippings, potatoes, onion, salt and pepper to pan; toss to coat. Cook and stir over medium-low heat until potatoes are golden brown and tender, 15-20 minutes, adding more drippings as needed. Stir in cooked bacon; serve immediately.

1 CUP 349 cal., 21g fat (8g sat. fat), 33mg chol., 681mg sod., 31g carb. (3g sugars, 2g fiber), 10g pro.

CINNAMON SUGAR DOUGHNUTS

No need for the deep fryer with this recipe! Just mix the batter, bake in doughnut pans and roll the doughnuts in cinnamon sugar for a sweet start to your day.
—Taste of Home *Test Kitchen*

TAKES: 30 MIN. • **MAKES:** 1 DOZEN

- 1 cup all-purpose flour
- ½ cup sugar
- ½ tsp. baking powder
- ½ tsp. baking soda
- ¼ tsp. salt
- ½ tsp. ground cinnamon
- ¼ tsp. ground nutmeg
- 1 large egg, room temperature, lightly beaten
- ⅔ cup buttermilk
- 1 Tbsp. canola oil
- ½ tsp. vanilla extract

CINNAMON SUGAR COATING
- ½ cup sugar
- 1 Tbsp. ground cinnamon

1. Preheat oven to 350°. In a small bowl, combine the first 7 ingredients. Combine egg, buttermilk, oil and vanilla; stir into the dry ingredients just until moistened. Pipe or spoon into 2 greased 6-cavity doughnut pans, filling the cavities three-fourths full.

2. Bake until a toothpick inserted in the center comes out clean, 10-12 minutes. Cool for 5 minutes before removing from pans to wire racks.

3. In a small bowl, combine coating ingredients. Roll warm doughnuts in coating.

1 DOUGHNUT 98 cal., 2g fat (0 sat. fat), 16mg chol., 154mg sod., 18g carb. (10g sugars, 0 fiber), 2g pro.

BREAKFAST & BRUNCH 23

GRUYERE SPINACH QUICHE

Versatile and comforting, this creamy blend of Gruyere cheese and hearty spinach is perfect any time of day. With a sprinkle of shallots and a crisp crust complementing the egg base, you can't stop at just one slice!
—Taste of Home *Test Kitchen*

PREP: 30 MIN. • **BAKE:** 45 MIN. + STANDING • **MAKES:** 6 SERVINGS

Dough for single-crust pie (9 in.)
- 1 large shallot, chopped
- 1 Tbsp. butter
- 8 cups fresh baby spinach
- 1 cup shredded Gruyere cheese
- 4 large eggs
- 1½ cups heavy whipping cream
- ½ tsp. salt
- ½ tsp. pepper

1. Line a deep-dish 9-in. pie plate with the dough. Trim and flute edge. Line the unpricked pastry shell with a double thickness of heavy-duty foil. Fill with pie weights, dried beans or uncooked rice. Bake at 450° for 5 minutes. Remove foil and weights; bake 5 minutes longer. Place on a wire rack. Reduce heat to 350°.

2. In a skillet, saute the shallot in butter until tender. Stir in spinach; cook until wilted. Remove from the heat. Sprinkle cheese into the crust; top with spinach mixture. In a bowl, beat eggs. Add cream, salt and pepper; mix well. Carefully pour into the crust.

3. Bake at 350° for 45-50 minutes or until a knife inserted in the center comes out clean. Let stand for 10 minutes before cutting.

1 PIECE 590 cal., 48g fat (29g sat. fat), 258mg chol., 649mg sod., 25g carb. (3g sugars, 2g fiber), 16g pro.

AUNT BETTY'S
BLUEBERRY MUFFINS

My Aunt Betty bakes many items each Christmas, but I look forward to these mouthwatering muffins the most.
—*Sheila Raleigh, Kechi, KS*

PREP: 15 MIN. • **BAKE:** 20 MIN. • **MAKES:** ABOUT 1 DOZEN

½ cup old-fashioned oats
½ cup orange juice
1 large egg, room temperature
½ cup canola oil
½ cup sugar
1½ cups all-purpose flour
1¼ tsp. baking powder
½ tsp. salt
¼ tsp. baking soda
1 cup fresh or frozen blueberries

TOPPING
2 Tbsp. sugar
½ tsp. ground cinnamon

1. In a large bowl, combine oats and orange juice; let stand for 5 minutes. Beat in the egg, oil and sugar until blended. Combine the flour, baking powder, salt and baking soda; stir into oat mixture just until moistened. Fold in blueberries.

2. Fill greased or paper-lined muffin cups two-thirds full. Combine topping ingredients; sprinkle over batter. Bake at 400° until a toothpick inserted in the center comes out clean, 20-25 minutes. Cool for 5 minutes before removing from pan to a wire rack. Serve warm.

NOTE If using frozen blueberries, use without thawing to avoid discoloring the batter.

1 MUFFIN 208 cal., 10g fat (1g sat. fat), 18mg chol., 172mg sod., 28g carb. (13g sugars, 1g fiber), 3g pro.

made from scratch
HONEY CINNAMON BUTTER

This is a simple but special spread for toast and muffins. The sweetness of honey pairs well with the warm spice of cinnamon.
—*Sue Seymour, Valatie, NY*

TAKES: 5 MIN.
MAKES: ABOUT 1⅓ CUPS

1 cup butter, softened
½ cup honey
1 tsp. ground cinnamon

Beat all the ingredients until smooth. Store, tightly covered, in the refrigerator.

1 TBSP. 107 cal., 9g fat (6g sat. fat), 24mg chol., 73mg sod., 7g carb. (7g sugars, 0 fiber), 0 pro.

CHEESY BACON & GRITS CASSEROLE

I was craving grits, so I created this masterpiece with fresh corn and leftover bacon. Serve with avocado and hot sauce.
—Rebecca Yankovich, Springfield, VA

PREP: 30 MIN. • **BAKE:** 35 MIN. + STANDING • **MAKES:** 8 SERVINGS

- 6 bacon strips, chopped
- 3 cups water
- 1 cup 2% milk
- ¾ tsp. salt
- 1 cup uncooked old-fashioned grits
- 2 cups shredded Colby-Monterey Jack cheese, divided
- 2 large eggs, lightly beaten
- 1 cup fresh or frozen corn, thawed
- ¼ tsp. pepper
- Sliced avocado, optional

1. Preheat oven to 350°. In a large skillet, cook bacon over medium heat until crisp, stirring occasionally. Remove with a slotted spoon; drain on paper towels.

2. Meanwhile, in a Dutch oven, bring water, milk and salt to a boil. Slowly stir in grits. Reduce heat to low; cook, covered, until thickened, 15-20 minutes, stirring occasionally. Remove from the heat. Stir in 1½ cups cheese until melted. Slowly stir in the eggs until blended. Stir in the bacon, corn and pepper. Transfer to a greased 2-qt. baking dish. Sprinkle with remaining ½ cup cheese.

3. Bake, uncovered, until edges are golden brown and cheese is melted, 35-40 minutes. Let casserole stand 10 minutes before serving. If desired, serve with avocado.

FREEZE OPTION Cool unbaked casserole; cover and freeze. To use, partially thaw in refrigerator overnight. Remove casserole from refrigerator 30 minutes before baking. Preheat oven to 350°. Bake as directed until heated through and a thermometer inserted in center reads 165°, increasing time to 45-55 minutes.

¾ CUP 261 cal., 13g fat (8g sat. fat), 81mg chol., 534mg sod., 23g carb. (3g sugars, 1g fiber), 13g pro.

BREAKFAST & BRUNCH   27

BEST CINNAMON ROLLS

Surprise a neighbor with a batch of oven-fresh cinnamon rolls slathered in cream cheese frosting. These breakfast treats make Christmas morning or any special occasion even more memorable.
—*Shenai Fisher, Topeka, KS*

PREP: 40 MIN. + RISING • **BAKE:** 20 MIN. • **MAKES:** 16 ROLLS

- 1 pkg. (¼ oz.) active dry yeast
- 1 cup warm 2% milk (110° to 115°)
- ½ cup sugar
- ⅓ cup butter, melted
- 2 large eggs, room temperature
- 1 tsp. salt
- 4 to 4½ cups all-purpose flour

FILLING
- ¾ cup packed brown sugar
- 2 Tbsp. ground cinnamon
- ¼ cup butter, melted, divided

FROSTING
- ½ cup butter, softened
- ¼ cup cream cheese, softened
- ½ tsp. vanilla extract
- ⅛ tsp. salt
- 1½ cups confectioners' sugar

WHY DID MY CINNAMON ROLLS NOT RISE?

In general, sweet doughs take longer to rise because the sugar soaks up the liquid that feeds the yeast. To counteract this, allow sweet doughs, like cinnamon rolls, plenty of time to rise. Also, when kneading the dough, do not add too much flour. Else, the dough becomes tough and dry, causing the yeast to not work properly.

1. Dissolve yeast in the warm milk. In another bowl, combine sugar, butter, eggs, salt, yeast mixture and 2 cups flour; beat on medium speed until smooth. Stir in enough remaining flour to form a soft dough (dough will be sticky).

2. Turn out the dough onto a floured surface; knead until smooth and elastic, 6-8 minutes. Place in a greased bowl, turning once to grease top. Cover and let rise in a warm place until doubled, about 1 hour.

3. Mix brown sugar and cinnamon. Punch down dough; divide in half. On a lightly floured surface, roll out 1 portion into an 11x8-in. rectangle. Brush with 2 Tbsp. butter; sprinkle with half the brown sugar mixture to within ½ in. of edges. Roll up jelly-roll style, starting with a long side; pinch seam to seal. Cut into 8 slices; place in a greased 13x9-in. pan, cut side down. Cover with a kitchen towel. Repeat with remaining dough and filling. Let rise in a warm place until doubled, about 1 hour. Preheat oven to 350°.

4. Bake until golden brown, 20-25 minutes. Cool on wire racks.

5. For frosting, beat the butter, cream cheese, vanilla and salt until blended; gradually beat in confectioners' sugar. Spread over tops. Refrigerate leftovers.

1 ROLL 364 cal., 15g fat (9g sat. fat), 66mg chol., 323mg sod., 53g carb. (28g sugars, 1g fiber), 5g pro.

BREAKFAST & BRUNCH

SHEET-PAN YELLOW BELLS & EGGS

This recipe is healthy and versatile—just add your favorite veggies or even fruit. I love sweet potato and apple tossed into the mix.
—Marina Castle Kelley, Canyon Country, CA

PREP: 15 MIN. • **BAKE:** 20 MIN. • **MAKES:** 2 SERVINGS

- ½ medium zucchini, halved lengthwise and cut into ¼-in. slices
- 1 cup fresh sliced Brussels sprouts
- 1 shallot, sliced
- ¼ tsp. salt
- ¼ tsp. pepper
- 2 Tbsp. olive oil
- 1 large sweet yellow pepper, cut into 4 rings
- 4 large eggs
- ¼ cup shredded Parmesan cheese

1. Preheat oven to 350°. Place the first 5 ingredients in a large bowl. Drizzle with oil; toss to coat. Place pepper rings on a baking sheet. Arrange vegetable mixture around peppers. Bake for 12 minutes.

2. Break and slip an egg into the center of each pepper ring; sprinkle with the Parmesan. Bake until whites are set and yolks begin to thicken, 8-10 minutes.

2 PEPPER RINGS WITH 1½ CUP VEGETABLES 373 cal., 26g fat (7g sat. fat), 379mg chol., 626mg sod., 16g carb. (3g sugars, 3g fiber), 20g pro.

READER REVIEW

"This was so good! It didn't need more than a pinch of salt to make it perfect. So simple, yet so delicious!"

—MARIA8572, TASTEOFHOME.COM

BUBBLE & SQUEAK LEFTOVER POTATO CAKES

Nothing gets wasted in my kitchen, including leftover mashed potatoes. This classic British breakfast recipe is traditionally fried as one dish, but I love individual portions.
—*Jas Brechtl, South Bend, IN*

PREP: 15 MIN. + CHILLING. • **COOK:** 20 MIN. • **MAKES:** 4 SERVINGS

- 1 Tbsp. canola oil
- 2 cups thinly sliced Brussels sprouts
- ½ cup diced carrots, optional
- 3 to 4 cups leftover mashed potatoes (with added milk and butter)
- 4 green onions, thinly sliced
- 1 tsp. ground cumin, optional
- ½ tsp. salt
- ½ tsp. pepper
- 3 Tbsp. all-purpose flour
  Oil for frying
  Optional: Poached or fried eggs, bacon, sausage and additional sliced green onions

1. In a large skillet, heat oil over medium heat. Add Brussels sprouts and carrots if desired; cook and stir for 5 minutes or until tender. Remove from skillet.

2. In a large bowl, combine mashed potatoes and cooled Brussels sprouts mixture. Add the green onion, cumin if desired, salt and pepper until blended.

3. Divide the mixture and form into eight 1-in. cakes, packing well. Place on a large plate; cover. Chill until firm, 30 minutes.

4. Dip each cake into flour to lightly coat. In a deep cast-iron or electric skillet, heat ¼ in. oil to 375°. Working in batches, place a few cakes at a time in hot oil. Fry until golden brown, 3-4 minutes on each side. Drain on paper towels.

5. If desired, serve with eggs, bacon or breakfast sausage and sprinkle with sliced green onion.

2 POTATO CAKES 339 cal., 22g fat (5g sat. fat), 17mg chol., 808mg sod., 33g carb. (4g sugars, 5g fiber), 5g pro.

BREAKFAST & BRUNCH

BRIOCHE FRENCH TOAST

If you prefer a sweeter breakfast to a savory one, this brioche French toast will hit the spot. Using soft, buttery, sweet brioche bread instead of regular Texas toast creates a heavenly, decadent bite.
—Taste of Home *Test Kitchen*

TAKES: 15 MIN. • **MAKES:** 4 SERVINGS

- 1½ cups 2% milk
- 3 large eggs
- 2 Tbsp. sugar
- 2 tsp. vanilla extract
- ¼ tsp. salt
- 8 slices day-old brioche bread (1 in. thick)
- Optional toppings: Butter, maple syrup, fresh berries and confectioners' sugar

Make your own Pancake Syrup. Recipe on p. 21.

1. In a shallow dish, whisk together the first 5 ingredients. Preheat a greased griddle over medium heat.

2. Dip bread into egg mixture, letting it soak 5 seconds on each side. Cook on griddle until golden brown on both sides. Serve with toppings as desired.

2 PIECES 437 cal., 16g fat (10g sat. fat), 189mg chol., 657mg sod., 58g carb. (20g sugars, 2g fiber), 14g pro.

NOTES

_____
_____
_____
_____
_____

CINNAMON COFFEE CAKE

I love the excellent texture of this old-fashioned streusel-topped coffee cake. Always a crowd-pleaser, its lovely vanilla flavor enriched by sour cream may remind you of brunch at Grandma's!
—*Eleanor Harris, Cape Coral, FL*

PREP: 20 MIN. • **BAKE:** 1 HOUR + COOLING • **MAKES:** 20 SERVINGS

- 1 cup butter, softened
- 2¾ cups sugar, divided
- 4 large eggs, room temperature
- 2 tsp. vanilla extract
- 3 cups all-purpose flour
- 1 tsp. baking soda
- 1 tsp. salt
- 2 cups sour cream
- 2 Tbsp. ground cinnamon
- ½ cup chopped walnuts

1. In a large bowl, cream butter and 2 cups sugar until light and fluffy, 5-7 minutes. Add eggs, 1 at a time, beating well after each addition. Beat in vanilla. Combine flour, baking soda and salt; add alternately with the sour cream, beating just enough after each addition to keep batter smooth.

2. Spoon a third of the batter into a greased 10-in. tube pan. Combine the cinnamon, nuts and remaining ¾ cup sugar; sprinkle one-third of mixture over batter in pan. Repeat layers twice. Bake at 350° until a toothpick inserted in the center comes out clean, 60-65 minutes. Cool for 15 minutes before removing from pan to a wire rack to cool completely.

1 PIECE 340 cal., 16g fat (9g sat. fat), 83mg chol., 299mg sod., 44g carb. (28g sugars, 1g fiber), 5g pro.

WHY IS MY CAKE DRY?

If your coffee cake is dry, it may have been overbaked. Always bake to the minimum cooking time and check for doneness. Also, measuring flour properly is key! Before measuring, stir the flour with a spoon or whisk. Spoon it into a dry measuring cup until heaping, then level it with the flat side of a knife. For the right texture, we suggest weighing the flour.

GREEN SHAKSHUKA

Start your day with a protein-packed breakfast featuring eggs, feta and healthy green vegetables, elevated by the flavor of Italian parsley. If you can, make this dish with lemon-infused olive oil.
—*Carrie Dault, Harriman, TN*

PREP: 20 MIN. • **COOK:** 20 MIN. • **MAKES:** 4 SERVINGS

- 1 Tbsp. olive oil
- ½ lb. fresh Brussels sprouts, quartered
- 1 medium green pepper, chopped
- 1 tsp. kosher salt, divided
- ¼ cup reduced-sodium chicken broth or vegetable broth, divided
- 3 garlic cloves, minced
- 1 small bunch kale, trimmed and chopped (about 8 cups)
- 9 oz. fresh baby spinach, chopped (about 7 cups)
- ¼ cup fresh parsley leaves, minced
- 4 large eggs
- ¼ cup crumbled feta cheese
- 1 tsp. grated lemon zest

Make your own Homemade Chicken Broth. Recipe on p. 92.

1. In a large skillet, heat the oil over medium-high heat. Add the Brussels sprouts, green pepper and ½ tsp. salt; cook and stir until lightly browned, 10-12 minutes. Add 2 Tbsp. broth and garlic; cook 1 minute longer. In batches if needed, add kale, spinach and parsley; cook and stir until wilted, 3-4 minutes. Stir in remaining 2 Tbsp. broth and ½ tsp. salt.

2. With back of spoon, make 4 wells in vegetable mixture; break an egg into each well. Sprinkle with feta and lemon zest. Cook, covered, until egg whites are completely set and yolks begin to thicken but are not hard, 4-6 minutes.

1 EGG WITH 1 CUP VEGETABLE MIXTURE 209 cal., 10g fat (3g sat. fat), 190mg chol., 756mg sod., 18g carb. (2g sugars, 6g fiber), 15g pro. **DIABETIC EXCHANGES** 1 starch, 1 medium-fat meat, ½ fat.

BREAKFAST & BRUNCH 35

ZUCCHINI FRITTATA

When we travel by car, I make frittata the night before, stuff it into pita bread in the morning and microwave for a minute or two. I wrap them in a towel, so down the road we can enjoy a still-warm breakfast!
—*Carol Blumenberg, Lehigh Acres, FL*

TAKES: 20 MIN. • **MAKES:** 2 SERVINGS

3 large eggs
¼ tsp. salt
1 tsp. canola oil
½ cup chopped onion
1 cup coarsely shredded zucchini
½ cup shredded Swiss cheese
   Coarsely ground pepper, optional

1. Preheat oven to 350°. Whisk together eggs and salt; set aside.

2. In an 8-in. ovenproof skillet coated with cooking spray, heat oil over medium heat; saute onion and zucchini until onion is crisp-tender. Pour in egg mixture; cook until almost set, 5-6 minutes. Sprinkle with cheese.

3. Bake, uncovered, until the cheese is melted, 4-5 minutes. If desired, sprinkle with pepper.

1 SERVING 261 cal., 18g fat (8g sat. fat), 304mg chol., 459mg sod., 7g carb. (3g sugars, 1g fiber), 18g pro.

NOTES

BREAKFAST & BRUNCH

HOMEMADE BISCUITS & MAPLE SAUSAGE GRAVY

I remember digging into flaky, gravy-smothered biscuits on Christmas morning and other special occasions when I was a child. What a satisfying way to start the day!
—Jenn Tidwell, Fair Oaks, CA

PREP: 30 MIN. • **BAKE:** 15 MIN. • **MAKES:** 8 SERVINGS

2 cups all-purpose flour
3 tsp. baking powder
1 Tbsp. sugar
1 tsp. salt
¼ tsp. pepper, optional
3 Tbsp. cold butter, cubed
1 Tbsp. shortening
¾ cup 2% milk

SAUSAGE GRAVY
1 lb. bulk maple pork sausage
¼ cup all-purpose flour
3 cups 2% milk
2 Tbsp. maple syrup
½ tsp. salt
¼ tsp. ground sage
¼ tsp. coarsely ground pepper

1. Preheat oven to 400°. In a large bowl, whisk flour, baking powder, sugar, salt and, if desired, pepper. Cut in butter and shortening until the mixture resembles coarse crumbs. Add milk; stir just until moistened. Turn onto a lightly floured surface; knead gently 8-10 times.

2. Pat or roll dough to 1-in. thickness; cut with a floured 2-in. biscuit cutter. Place 1 in. apart on an ungreased baking sheet. Bake until golden brown, 15-17 minutes.

3. Meanwhile, in a large skillet, cook sausage over medium heat until no longer pink, 6-8 minutes, breaking into crumbles. Stir in flour until blended; gradually stir in milk. Bring to a boil, stirring constantly; cook and stir until sauce is thickened, 4-6 minutes. Stir in remaining ingredients. Serve with warm biscuits.

1 BISCUIT WITH ½ CUP GRAVY 371 cal., 19g fat (8g sat. fat), 41mg chol., 915mg sod., 38g carb. (11g sugars, 1g fiber), 11g pro.

TURKEY BREAKFAST SAUSAGE

These hearty sausage patties are loaded with flavor but contain a fraction of the sodium and fat found in commercial breakfast links.
—Judy Culbertson, Dansville, NY

TAKES: 20 MIN. • **MAKES:** 8 SERVINGS

1 lb. lean ground turkey
¾ tsp. salt
½ tsp. rubbed sage
½ tsp. pepper
¼ tsp. ground ginger

1. Crumble the turkey into a large bowl. Add the salt, sage, pepper and ginger; mix lightly but thoroughly. Shape into eight 2-in. patties.

2. In a greased cast-iron or other heavy skillet, cook the patties over medium heat until a thermometer reads 165° and juices run clear, 4-6 minutes on each side.

1 PATTY 85 cal., 5g fat (1g sat. fat), 45mg chol., 275mg sod., 0 carb. (0 sugars, 0 fiber), 10g pro. **DIABETIC EXCHANGES** 1 lean meat, ½ fat.

BASIC CREPES

This simple crepe recipe is a favorite. It is best to make the batter at least 30 minutes ahead, so the flour can absorb all the moisture before you cook the crepes.
—Taste of Home *Test Kitchen*

PREP: 10 MIN. + CHILLING • **COOK:** 20 MIN. • **MAKES:** 20 CREPES

- 4 large eggs, room temperature
- 1½ cups 2% milk
- 1 cup all-purpose flour
- 1½ tsp. sugar
- ⅛ tsp. salt
- 8 tsp. butter

1. In a small bowl, whisk the eggs and milk. In another bowl, mix flour, sugar and salt; add to egg mixture and mix well. Refrigerate, covered, 1 hour.

2. Melt 1 tsp. butter in an 8-in. nonstick skillet over medium heat. Stir batter. Fill a ¼-cup measure halfway with the batter; pour into center of pan. Quickly lift and tilt pan to coat bottom evenly. Cook until top appears dry; turn crepe over and cook until bottom is cooked, 15-20 seconds longer. Remove to a wire rack. Repeat with the remaining batter, adding butter to skillet as needed. When cool, stack crepes between pieces of waxed paper or paper towels.

1 CREPE 61 cal., 3g fat (2g sat. fat), 43mg chol., 50mg sod., 6g carb. (1g sugars, 0 fiber), 3g pro.

SHRIMP CREPES Preheat oven to 350°. In a large skillet, cook 4½ cups chopped fresh broccoli, 6 chopped green onions, 2 tsp. minced garlic, ½ tsp. salt, ¼ tsp. pepper and ¼ tsp. Worcestershire sauce in 3 Tbsp. melted butter for 7-9 minutes or until broccoli is crisp-tender. Remove and set aside. In same skillet, saute 1 pound peeled deveined uncooked shrimp in ¼ cup white wine until shrimp turn pink. Return broccoli to skillet and combine. Spoon filling down the center of 16 crepes; roll up. Place in an ungreased 15x10x1-in. baking pan. Bake, uncovered, 15-20 minutes or until heated through. Meanwhile, prepare 1 envelope bearnaise sauce according to package directions. Serve over crepes. Yield: 8 servings.

CREAMY STRAWBERRY CREPES In a large bowl, beat 1 pkg. (8 oz.) softened cream cheese, 1¼ cups confectioners' sugar, 1 Tbsp. lemon juice, 1 tsp. grated lemon zest and ½ tsp. vanilla extract until smooth. Fold in 2 cups each sliced fresh strawberries and whipped cream. Spoon about ⅓ cup filling down the center of 14 crepes; roll up. Garnish with additional sliced berries. Yield: 7 servings.

BANANA CREPES In a small skillet, bring ⅔ cup sugar, ⅔ cup orange juice, ½ cup butter and 4 tsp. grated orange zest to a boil. Remove from heat. Peel 6 medium firm bananas and cut in half lengthwise. Add them to orange sauce; cook over medium heat until heated through, about 1 minute. Place 1 banana half in center of 12 crepes; roll up. Place seam side down on a plate; drizzle with the orange sauce. Yield: 6 servings.

BREAKFAST & BRUNCH

from scratch
APPETIZERS & SNACKS

BEST BACON-WRAPPED SHRIMP, PAGE 63

HOMEMADE TORTILLA CHIPS

I serve these tortilla chips with salsa and guac—the chipotle adds a nice kick. If you prefer, skip the chipotle and just sprinkle with salt after frying. For a Tajin flavor, add a squeeze of lime to your chips right before serving.
—*David Ross, Spokane Valley, WA*

TAKES: 25 MIN. • **MAKES:** 4 SERVINGS

¾ tsp. salt
½ tsp. ground chipotle pepper
10 corn tortillas (6 in.)
  Canola or corn oil for deep-fat frying

1. In a small bowl, mix salt and chipotle powder. Cut each tortilla into 4 wedges. In an electric skillet, heat 1 in. oil to 350°. Fry the tortilla wedges, several at a time, 2-3 minutes on each side or until golden brown. Drain on paper towels.

2. Transfer chips to a large bowl; sprinkle with salt mixture and gently toss to coat.

10 CHIPS 183 cal., 8g fat (1g sat. fat), 0 chol., 479mg sod., 27g carb. (1g sugars, 4g fiber), 3g pro.

made from scratch NACHO CHEESE SAUCE

Ooey-gooey cheddar cheese meets cumin and chili powder for a thick and creamy queso dip with a little kick. It's perfect for dipping tortilla chips and drizzling over loaded nachos for a cheesy finish.
—*Dianna Smith, Newport, TN*

TAKES: 10 MIN. **MAKES:** 3 CUPS

2 Tbsp. butter
2 Tbsp. all-purpose flour
1½ cups whole milk
1 tsp. chili powder
½ tsp. ground cumin
½ tsp. salt
2 cups shredded cheddar cheese

In a small saucepan, melt butter over medium heat. Stir in flour until smooth; gradually whisk in milk. Stir in chili powder, cumin and salt. Bring to a boil, stirring constantly; cook and stir until thickened, 1-2 minutes. Reduce heat to low. Add cheese; stir until melted.

¼ CUP 120 cal., 9g fat (5g sat. fat), 27mg chol., 208mg sod., 3g carb. (2g sugars, 0 fiber), 6g pro.

BACON CHEDDAR POTATO SKINS

Both crisp and hearty, this restaurant-quality snack is one that my family requests often.
—*Trish Perrin, Keizer, OR*

TAKES: 30 MIN. • **MAKES:** 8 SERVINGS

- 4 large baking potatoes, baked
- 3 Tbsp. canola oil
- 1 Tbsp. grated Parmesan cheese
- ½ tsp. salt
- ¼ tsp. garlic powder
- ¼ tsp. paprika
- ⅛ tsp. pepper
- 8 bacon strips, cooked and crumbled
- 1½ cups shredded cheddar cheese
- ½ cup sour cream
- 4 green onions, sliced

1. Preheat oven to 475°. Cut potatoes in half lengthwise; scoop out pulp, leaving a ¼-in. shell (save pulp for another use). Place the potato skins on a greased baking sheet.

2. Combine oil with next 5 ingredients; brush over both sides of skins.

3. Bake until crisp, about 7 minutes on each side. Sprinkle bacon and cheddar cheese inside skins. Bake until cheese is melted, about 2 minutes longer. Top with the sour cream and green onion. Serve immediately.

1 POTATO SKIN 350 cal., 19g fat (7g sat. fat), 33mg chol., 460mg sod., 34g carb. (2g sugars, 4g fiber), 12g pro.

SMART SWAPS

- In Europe, Parmesan and Parmigiano-Reggiano are the same, but in the U.S., Parmesan can be a generic term. For a richer flavor with fewer calories, use authentic Parmigiano-Reggiano in smaller amounts.

- Canola oil is low in saturated fats and high in heart-healthy monounsaturated fats. Olive oil is another excellent choice, offering a similar healthy fat profile and a richer flavor.

AIR-FRYER MOZZARELLA STICKS

Deep-fried mozzarella sticks are one of our favorite appetizers, and I figured out how to make them at home without the deep fryer. Make sure to double-bread each one for a crunchy outside and to keep the cheese from oozing out as the sticks get warm.
—Mary Merchant, Barre, VT

PREP: 15 MIN. + FREEZING • **COOK:** 10 MIN. • **MAKES:** 1 DOZEN

- 2 cups dry bread crumbs
- 3 Tbsp. all-purpose flour
- 3 large eggs
- 2 Tbsp. water
- 1 Tbsp. Italian seasoning
- 1 tsp. garlic powder
- ¼ tsp. pepper
- 12 sticks string cheese
  Cooking spray
- 1 cup marinara sauce or meatless pasta sauce, warmed
  Chopped fresh basil, optional

1. In a small skillet, toast bread crumbs until lightly browned, 1-2 minutes. Cool completely.

2. Place the flour in a shallow bowl. In another shallow bowl, beat eggs and water. In a third shallow bowl, combine bread crumbs, Italian seasoning, garlic powder and pepper. Coat cheese sticks with flour, then dip into egg mixture and coat with bread crumb mixture. Repeat egg and bread crumb coatings. Cover and freeze for 8 hours or overnight.

3. Preheat air fryer to 400°. Place the cheese in a single layer on a greased tray in air-fryer basket; spritz with cooking spray. Cook until golden brown and heated through, 6-8 minutes, turning halfway through cooking and spritzing with additional cooking spray. Let stand 3-5 minutes before serving. Serve with marinara or pasta sauce for dipping. If desired, sprinkle with basil.

NOTE Cook times vary dramatically among brands of air fryers. Refer to your air-fryer manual for general cook times and adjust if necessary.

1 PIECE 148 cal., 8g fat (4g sat. fat), 46mg chol., 384mg sod., 10g carb. (2g sugars, 1g fiber), 11g pro.

THE BEST HUMMUS

Hummus is my go-to appetizer when I need something quick, easy and impressive. Over the years I've picked up a number of tricks that make this the best hummus you'll ever have.
—*James Schend, Pleasant Prairie, WI*

PREP: 25 MIN. + CHILLING • **COOK:** 20 MIN. • **MAKES:** 1½ CUPS

- 1 can (15 oz.) garbanzo beans or chickpeas, rinsed and drained
- ½ tsp. baking soda
- ¼ cup fresh lemon juice
- 1 Tbsp. minced garlic
- ½ tsp. kosher salt
- ½ tsp. ground cumin
- ½ cup tahini
- 2 Tbsp. extra virgin olive oil
- ¼ cup cold water
- Optional: Olive oil, roasted garbanzo beans, toasted sesame seeds, ground sumac

READER REVIEW

"The flavor of this hummus is great, and peeling the chickpeas gives it a silky smooth texture."
—CURLYLIS85, TASTEOFHOME.COM

1. Place garbanzo beans in a large saucepan; add water to cover by 1 in. Gently rub beans together to loosen outer skin. Pour off water and any skins that are floating. Repeat 2-3 times until no skins float to surface; drain. Return to saucepan; add baking soda and enough water to cover by 1 in. Bring to a boil; reduce the heat. Simmer, uncovered, until beans are very tender and just starting to fall apart, 20-25 minutes.

2. Meanwhile, in a blender, process the lemon juice, garlic and salt until almost a paste. Let stand for 10 minutes; strain, discarding solids. Return to the blender; add cumin. In a small bowl, stir together tahini and olive oil.

3. Drain beans and add to blender; add cold water. Loosely cover and process until completely smooth. With blender running, slowly add tahini mixture, scraping side as needed. Adjust the seasoning with additional salt and cumin if desired.

4. Transfer the mixture to a serving bowl; cover and refrigerate at least 30 minutes. Top with additional olive oil and optional toppings if desired.

¼ CUP 250 cal., 19g fat (3g sat. fat), 0 chol., 361mg sod., 15g carb. (2g sugars, 5g fiber), 7g pro.

APPETIZERS & SNACKS

HOMEMADE CHEEZ-ITS

Bring some childhood magic back to your kitchen with this homemade Cheez-Its recipe. It's a fun and delicious weekend baking project the whole family can enjoy (and subsequently devour).
—Lauren Habermehl, Pewaukee, WI

PREP: 30 MIN. + CHILLING • **BAKE:** 15 MIN./BATCH + COOLING • **MAKES:** 12 DOZEN

- 8 oz. cheddar cheese, cubed
- 1 cup all-purpose flour
- 1 tsp. cornstarch
- 1 tsp. kosher salt
- ½ tsp. ground mustard
- ½ tsp. paprika
- 4 Tbsp. cold unsalted butter
- 2 Tbsp. ice water
- 1 large egg, beaten
- Flaky sea salt, optional

1. In a food processor, pulse cheese until finely chopped; transfer to a large bowl. Stir in flour, cornstarch, salt, mustard and paprika. Cut in butter until mixture resembles coarse crumbs. Gradually add ice water, tossing with a fork until dough holds together when pressed. Shape into a disk; wrap and refrigerate 1 hour or overnight.

2. Preheat oven to 350°. On a lightly floured surface, roll dough to ⅛-in. thickness. Using a fluted pastry wheel, pizza cutter or sharp knife, cut the dough into 1-in. squares. Transfer to parchment-lined baking sheets. Using a toothpick or skewer, poke a hole in center of each square. Brush with the beaten egg; sprinkle with salt if desired.

3. Bake until crisp and lightly golden around the edges, 15-18 minutes. Cool completely on baking sheets.

1 CRACKER 13 cal., 1g fat (1g sat. fat), 2mg chol., 24mg sod., 1g carb. (0 sugars, 0 fiber), 0 pro.

EASY SHRIMP COCKTAIL

Tender, well-cooked shrimp is paired with a flavorful sauce of sweet ketchup, tart lemon juice, sharp horseradish and savory Worcestershire sauce for an easy and delicious dish. The best part—it takes only 30 minutes to make!
—Taste of Home *Test Kitchen*

TAKES: 30 MIN. • **MAKES:** 32 SERVINGS

1 cup ketchup
2 Tbsp. lemon juice
2 Tbsp. prepared horseradish
2 tsp. Worcestershire sauce
 Dash hot pepper sauce, optional
3 qt. water
1 small onion, sliced
½ medium lemon, sliced
2 sprigs fresh parsley
2 tsp. salt
5 whole peppercorns
1 bay leaf
¼ tsp. dried thyme
2 lbs. uncooked shell-on shrimp
 (26-30 per lb.)

1. In a small bowl, combine the ketchup, lemon juice, horseradish, Worcestershire sauce and, if desired, hot pepper sauce.

2. In a large saucepan, combine water, onion, lemon, parsley, salt, peppercorns, bay leaf and thyme; bring to a boil. Add shrimp. Cook just until shrimp turn pink, 1-2 minutes. Drain; immediately drop the shrimp into a bowl of ice water. Discard onion, lemon, parsley, peppercorns and bay leaf. Drain the shrimp. Peel shrimp, leaving tails on. Devein if needed. Serve shrimp with sauce.

1 OZ. COOKED SHRIMP WITH ABOUT 2 TSP. SAUCE 42 cal., 1g fat (0 sat. fat), 44mg chol., 193mg sod., 3g carb. (3g sugars, 0 fiber), 6g pro.

EFFORTLESS GUACAMOLE

This super easy classic is so delicious you'll keep coming back to it.
I've been making this recipe since I started cooking, and that was a long time ago!
—*DeAnn Lokvam, Tijeras, NM*

TAKES: 15 MIN. • **MAKES:** 1 CUP

2 medium ripe avocados, peeled
2 green onions, chopped
1 Tbsp. salsa
1 Tbsp. mayonnaise
2 to 3 tsp. lime juice, optional
½ tsp. ground cumin
½ tsp. chili powder
¼ tsp. garlic salt
 Tortilla chips

In a small bowl, mash the avocados. Stir in green onion, salsa, mayonnaise, lime juice if desired, cumin, chili powder and garlic salt. Serve with the chips.

¼ CUP 175 cal., 16g fat (2g sat. fat), 1mg chol., 159mg sod., 9g carb. (1g sugars, 6g fiber), 2g pro.

READER REVIEW

"This might be the best guacamole I have ever made—creamy and delicious. I wanted to eat the whole bowl by myself!"

—SEMINOLES, TASTEOFHOME.COM

APPETIZERS & SNACKS

CINNAMON SPICED PECANS

This easy recipe is perfect for a holiday party or as a gift from your kitchen. If you're making many batches for gifts, you may want to use peanuts instead of pecans—they're just as tasty and easier on the budget.
—*Brenda Schneider, Armington, IL*

PREP: 10 MIN. • **BAKE:** 20 MIN. + COOLING • **MAKES:** ABOUT 6 CUPS

½ cup sugar
3 tsp. ground cinnamon
½ tsp. salt
1 large egg white
1 lb. large pecan halves

1. Preheat oven to 300°. In a small bowl, combine sugar, cinnamon and salt. In a large bowl, lightly beat egg white. Add pecans; stir until coated. Sprinkle with sugar mixture; mix well.

2. Spread in a single layer on a greased baking sheet. Bake until lightly browned, 20-25 minutes, stirring once. Remove nuts from the baking sheet to cool on waxed paper.

⅓ CUP 198 cal., 18g fat (2g sat. fat), 0 chol., 69mg sod., 9g carb. (7g sugars, 3g fiber), 3g pro.

NOTES

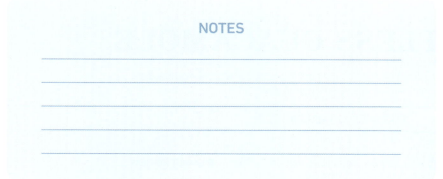

BAKED CHORIZO CORN DIP

This spicy dip is a family favorite for any occasion. Not only is it addictive, but it's super versatile. You can keep it in your freezer and just heat it before serving.
—Cindy Nerat, Menominee, MI

PREP: 20 MIN. • **BAKE:** 30 MIN. • **MAKES:** 9 CUPS

- 1 lb. fresh chorizo or spicy bulk pork sausage
- 2 cans (15¼ oz. each) whole kernel corn, drained
- ½ cup finely chopped sweet red pepper
- 1 cup finely chopped seeded jalapeno pepper (about 4 peppers)
- 6 green onions, chopped
- 1 cup mayonnaise
- ½ cup grated Parmesan cheese
- 1½ tsp. chili powder
- 1 garlic clove, minced
- 3 cups shredded Monterey Jack cheese
  Tortilla chips

1. Preheat the oven to 350°. In a large skillet, cook chorizo over medium heat until cooked through, 6-8 minutes, breaking into crumbles; drain.

2. In a large bowl, combine the cooked chorizo and next 9 ingredients. Transfer to an ungreased 10-in. cast-iron skillet or 13x9-in. baking dish.

3. Bake until heated through, 30-35 minutes. Serve warm, with tortilla chips.

FREEZE OPTION Freeze unbaked chorizo mixture in freezer containers. To use, partially thaw in refrigerator overnight. Bake as directed, increasing time as necessary.

NOTE Wear disposable gloves when cutting hot peppers; the oils can burn skin. Avoid touching your face.

¼ CUP 141 cal., 12g fat (4g sat. fat), 23mg chol., 334mg sod., 3g carb. (2g sugars, 1g fiber), 6g pro.

EASY CHEESE-STUFFED JALAPENOS

A few years ago, I saw a man in the grocery store buying a big bag of jalapeno peppers. Curious, I asked what he intended to do with them, and he gave me this fabulous recipe for stuffed jalapenos right there!
—Janice Montiverdi, Sugar Land, TX

PREP: 30 MIN. • **BAKE:** 5 MIN. • **MAKES:** 4 DOZEN

- 24 medium fresh jalapeno peppers
- 1 pkg. (8 oz.) cream cheese, softened
- 3 cups finely shredded cheddar cheese
- 1½ tsp. Worcestershire sauce
- 4 bacon strips, cooked and crumbled

1. Preheat oven to 400°. Cut jalapenos in half lengthwise; remove seeds and membranes. In a large saucepan, boil peppers in water for 5-10 minutes (the longer you boil peppers, the milder they become). Drain and rinse in cold water.

2. In a small bowl, beat cream cheese, cheddar cheese and Worcestershire sauce until smooth. Spoon 2 tsp. mixture into each jalapeno; sprinkle with bacon. Arrange on greased baking sheets. Bake until filling is warmed, 3-5 minutes.

NOTE Wear disposable gloves when cutting hot peppers; the oils can burn skin. Avoid touching your face.

1 PIECE 141 cal., 12g fat (8g sat. fat), 39mg chol., 200mg sod., 3g carb. (0 sugars, 1g fiber), 6g pro.

WHAT PAIRS WELL WITH JALAPENO PEPPERS?

Jalapeno peppers shine in a Mexican-style appetizer spread. Pair them with taco cups, tortilla chips, guacamole and queso for a flavorful combination. Their spicy kick adds depth to the dish, complementing creamy and crunchy textures perfectly.

COPYCAT BLOOMIN' ONION

No one can resist the crunchy goodness of a bloomin' onion. Plus, the dipping sauce makes this copycat recipe an irresistible replica of the restaurant version.
—Taste of Home *Test Kitchen*

PREP: 30 MIN. + CHILLING • **COOK:** 5 MIN. • **MAKES:** 4 SERVINGS

1 cup all-purpose flour
1½ tsp. salt
1 tsp. garlic powder
1 tsp. onion powder
½ tsp. paprika
½ tsp. dried oregano
½ tsp. dried thyme, optional
½ tsp. pepper
¼ tsp. cayenne pepper
  Oil for deep-fat frying
1 large egg, lightly beaten
½ cup 2% milk
1 large sweet onion

1. In a shallow bowl, combine flour and seasonings. In an electric skillet or deep fryer, heat oil to 375°. In another shallow bowl, whisk egg and milk. Using a sharp knife, slice ½ in. off the top of the onion; peel onion. Cut into 16 wedges to within ½ in. of root end. Gently spread the onion petals apart.

2. Hold onion over dry ingredients. Spoon flour mixture over and around the onion petals; shake off excess. Hold onion over egg mixture. Spoon over and around the onion petals, allowing excess to drip off. Again, hold onion over dry ingredients. Spoon flour mixture over and around the onion petals; shake off excess.

3. Fry onion cut-side down, 3 minutes. Flip and fry until golden brown, about 3 minutes longer. Drain on paper towels; sprinkle with additional salt.

1 SERVING 442 cal., 31g fat (4g sat. fat), 59mg chol., 1203mg sod., 35g carb. (7g sugars, 2g fiber), 7g pro.

made from scratch
COPYCAT BLOOMING ONION SAUCE

This zippy sauce absolutely completes homemade onion rings. I usually use a beer batter for the onion rings and dip them in this easy-to-make sauce.
—*Sherri Melotik, Oak Creek, WI*

TAKES: 10 MIN. **MAKES:** ⅔ CUP

½ cup mayonnaise
2 Tbsp. prepared horseradish
2 tsp. ketchup
¼ tsp. garlic powder
¼ tsp. smoked paprika
⅛ tsp. salt
⅛ tsp. dried oregano
  Dash cayenne pepper
  Dash pepper

Combine all the ingredients in a small bowl. Cover and refrigerate at least 2 hours before serving.

2 TBSP. 75 cal., 8g fat (1g sat. fat), 4mg chol., 111mg sod., 1g carb. (1g sugars, 0 fiber), 0 pro.

APPETIZERS & SNACKS

TERIYAKI BEEF JERKY

Jerky is a portable, chewy snack, and you can make your own with our recipe. The meat has a savory flavor and a bit of heat.
—Taste of Home Test Kitchen

PREP: 40 MIN. + MARINATING • **BAKE:** 3 HOURS + COOLING • **MAKES:** 8 SERVINGS

- 1 beef flank steak (1½ to 2 lbs.)
- ⅔ cup reduced-sodium soy sauce
- ⅔ cup Worcestershire sauce
- ¼ cup honey
- 3 tsp. coarsely ground pepper
- 2 tsp. onion powder
- 2 tsp. garlic powder
- 1½ tsp. crushed red pepper flakes
- 1 tsp. liquid smoke

1. Trim all visible fat from steak. Freeze, covered, until firm, about 30 minutes. Slice steak along the grain into long ⅛-in.-thick strips.

2. Transfer beef to a large resealable container. In a small bowl, whisk the remaining ingredients; add to beef. Seal the container and turn to coat. Refrigerate 2 hours or overnight, turning occasionally.

3. Transfer beef and marinade to a large saucepan; bring to a boil. Reduce heat; simmer 5 minutes. Using tongs, remove beef from marinade. Drain on paper towels; pat dry. Discard marinade.

4. Preheat oven to 170°. Arrange beef strips in a single layer on wire racks placed on 15x10x1-in. baking pans. Dry in oven until beef becomes dry and leathery, 3-4 hours, rotating pans occasionally. (Or use a commercial dehydrator or smoker, following the manufacturer's directions.)

5. Remove from oven; cool completely. Using paper towels, blot any beads of oil from jerky. Store the jerky, covered, in refrigerator or freezer.

1 OZ. COOKED BEEF 132 cal., 6g fat (3g sat. fat), 40mg chol., 139mg sod., 2g carb. (1g sugars, 0 fiber), 17g pro. **DIABETIC EXCHANGES** 2 lean meat.

DEHYDRATE IN A SMOKER When using a smoker, omit liquid smoke. Follow steps 1-3, then proceed with the recipe following the manufacturer's directions for temperature and time. We cooked ours at 170° for 2 hours.

MOM'S PICKLED CARROTS

My mother is the only other person I've known to make this recipe. In fact, when I take it to a potluck or picnic, no one has ever heard of pickled carrots. But once they try them, they are hooked.
—*Robin Koble, Fairview, PA*

PREP: 15 MIN. + CHILLING • **COOK:** 20 MIN. • **MAKES:** 6 CUPS

- 2 lbs. carrots, cut lengthwise into ¼-in.-thick strips
- 1½ cups sugar
- 1½ cups water
- 1½ cups cider vinegar
- ¼ cup mustard seed
- 3 cinnamon sticks (3 in.)
- 3 whole cloves

1. Place carrots in a large saucepan; add enough water to cover. Bring to a boil. Cook, covered, until crisp-tender, 3-5 minutes. Drain. Transfer carrots to a large bowl. In another large saucepan, combine remaining ingredients. Bring to a boil. Reduce heat; simmer, uncovered, 20 minutes. Pour mixture over carrots. Refrigerate, covered, overnight to allow flavors to blend.

2. Transfer mixture to jars. Cover and refrigerate up to 1 month.

¼ CUP 30 cal., 0 fat (0 sat. fat), 0 chol., 170mg sod., 7g carb. (6g sugars, 1g fiber), 1g pro.

AIR-FRYER EGGPLANT FRIES

My kids love this snack, and I like that it's healthy. Coated with Italian seasoning, Parmesan cheese and garlic salt, these veggie sticks are air-fried, not deep-fried, so there's no guilt when you crunch into them.
—*Mary Murphy, Atwater, CA*

PREP: 15 MIN. • **COOK:** 10 MIN./BATCH • **MAKES:** 6 SERVINGS

- 2 large eggs
- ½ cup grated Parmesan cheese
- ½ cup toasted wheat germ
- 1 tsp. Italian seasoning
- ¾ tsp. garlic salt
- 1 medium eggplant (about 1¼ lbs.) Cooking spray
- 1 cup meatless pasta sauce, warmed

1. Preheat air fryer to 375°. In a shallow bowl, whisk eggs. In another shallow bowl, mix cheese, wheat germ and seasonings.

2. Trim ends of eggplant; cut eggplant lengthwise into ½-in.-thick slices. Cut the slices lengthwise into ½-in. strips. Dip eggplant in eggs, then coat with cheese mixture.

3. In batches, arrange the eggplant in a single layer on a greased tray in air-fryer basket; spritz with cooking spray. Cook until golden brown, 4-5 minutes. Turn; spritz with cooking spray. Cook until golden brown, 4-5 minutes. Serve immediately with pasta sauce.

1 SERVING 135 cal., 5g fat (2g sat. fat), 68mg chol., 577mg sod., 15g carb. (6g sugars, 4g fiber), 9g pro. **DIABETIC EXCHANGES** 1 vegetable, ½ starch.

APPETIZERS & SNACKS 57

CHEWY SOFT PRETZELS

These homemade pretzels never last long around our house. My kids love to make them and eat them! I serve them to company with dips such as pizza sauce, ranch dressing, spinach dip or hot mustard.
—*Elvira Martens, Aldergrove, BC*

PREP: 1 HOUR + RISING • **BAKE:** 15 MIN. • **MAKES:** 1 DOZEN

- 1 pkg. (¼ oz.) active dry yeast
- 1½ cups warm water (110° to 115°)
- 1 Tbsp. sugar
- 2 tsp. salt
- 4 to 4¼ cups all-purpose flour
- 8 cups water
- ½ cup baking soda
- 1 large egg, lightly beaten
- Optional toppings: Kosher salt, sesame seeds, poppy seeds and grated Parmesan cheese

HOW DO YOU KNEAD PRETZEL DOUGH?
Be careful not to add too much flour while mixing or kneading the dough; keep it fairly sticky. Else, it will be harder to roll out, and the pretzels will not hold their shape. If you knead the dough with gloves on, the dough will not stick to your hands. As you keep kneading, the flour will hydrate, and the dough will naturally firm up without needing extra flour.

1. Dissolve the yeast in warm water. In a large bowl, combine sugar, salt, yeast mixture and 2 cups flour; beat on medium speed until smooth. Stir in enough remaining flour to form a stiff dough.

2. Turn dough onto a floured surface; knead until smooth and elastic, about 5 minutes. Place dough in a greased bowl, turning once to grease the top. Cover and let rise in a warm place until doubled, about 1 hour.

3. Punch down dough; divide and shape into 12 balls. Roll each into a 22-in. rope; shape into a pretzel.

4. Preheat oven to 425°. Place water and baking soda in a large saucepan; bring to a boil. Place pretzels, 1 at a time, in boiling water for 30 seconds. Remove; drain on paper towels that have been lightly coated with cooking spray.

5. Place the pretzels on greased baking sheets. Brush with egg; top as desired. Bake until golden brown, 12-14 minutes. Remove them from pans to wire racks; serve warm.

1 PRETZEL 164 cal., 1g fat (0 sat. fat), 16mg chol., 400mg sod., 33g carb. (1g sugars, 1g fiber), 5g pro.

BACK PORCH MEATBALLS

This idea came to me while sitting on my back porch. The combination of meats and ingredients in the sauce produces meatballs unlike any I've ever had.
—Justin Boudreaux, Walker, LA

PREP: 30 MIN. • **COOK:** 3 HOURS • **MAKES:** 6 DOZEN

- 2 large eggs, lightly beaten
- 2 cups seasoned bread crumbs
- 2 cups salsa
- ½ cup grated onion
- ⅔ lb. ground turkey
- ⅔ lb. ground pork
- ⅔ lb. ground beef

SAUCE
- 3 cups tomato sauce
- 1 medium onion, grated
- 1 cup beef stock
- 1 cup mixed fruit jelly
- 1 cup molasses
- ½ cup packed brown sugar
- ½ cup canola oil
- ½ cup red wine vinegar
- ⅓ cup prepared mustard
- ⅓ cup Worcestershire sauce
- 1 tsp. salt

1. Preheat oven to 400°. In a large bowl, combine eggs, bread crumbs, salsa and onion. Add the turkey, pork and beef; mix lightly but thoroughly. Shape into 1½-in. balls. Place meatballs on greased racks in two 15x10x1-in. baking pans. Bake until browned, 18-22 minutes.

2. In a 6-qt. slow cooker, combine sauce ingredients. Add meatballs; gently stir to coat. Cook, covered, on low 3-4 hours or until meatballs are cooked through.

FREEZE OPTION Freeze cooled meatballs and sauce in freezer containers. To use, partially thaw in refrigerator overnight. Microwave, covered, on high in a microwave-safe dish until heated through, gently stirring; add water if necessary.

1 MEATBALL 87 cal., 3g fat (1g sat. fat), 13mg chol., 195mg sod., 11g carb. (8g sugars, 0 fiber), 3g pro.

CHUNKY TOMATO SALSA

Our college-age daughter, two of her friends and a nephew ate a quart of this salsa with chips in one sitting. They loved it so much that they each took a quart home.
—Carol Carpenter, Jansen, NE

PREP: 45 MIN. • **COOK:** 1¼ HOURS + CHILLING • **MAKES:** 4 CUPS

- 3½ cups peeled chopped tomatoes (about 4 large)
- 1 large green pepper, chopped
- 1 medium onion, chopped
- 1 serrano pepper, seeded and chopped
- 1 jalapeno pepper, seeded and chopped
- 1 Tbsp. sugar
- 2¼ tsp. salt
- 1 garlic clove, minced
- ¾ tsp. ground cumin
- 1 can (6 oz.) tomato paste
- ¼ cup white vinegar
- 2 Tbsp. lemon juice
- Baked tortilla chip scoops

In a large saucepan, combine the first 9 ingredients. Stir in the tomato paste, vinegar and lemon juice. Bring to a boil. Reduce the heat; simmer, uncovered, 1 hour, stirring frequently. Cool to room temperature. Cover and refrigerate until chilled. Serve with chips.

NOTE Wear disposable gloves when cutting hot peppers; the oils can burn skin. Avoid touching your face.

¼ CUP 28 cal., 0 fat (0 sat. fat), 0 chol., 344mg sod., 6g carb. (4g sugars, 1g fiber), 1g pro. **DIABETIC EXCHANGES** 1 vegetable.

HOW CAN YOU PACK MORE HEAT?
The right peppers make all the difference. If serrano and jalapeno fall short, add a tablespoon chopped habanero or, if you dare, ghost pepper. For a more subtle heat, simply double the amount of serrano or jalapeno in the recipe.

APPETIZERS & SNACKS

BEST BACON-WRAPPED SHRIMP

Bacon and shrimp make a terrific team in this super-easy party appetizer.
—Taste of Home *Test Kitchen*

PREP: 15 MIN. + MARINATING • **BROIL:** 10 MIN. • **MAKES:** 1½ DOZEN

- ¼ cup sugar
- ¼ cup lemon juice
- 2 Tbsp. olive oil
- 3 tsp. paprika
- 1 tsp. each salt, garlic powder and pepper
- 18 uncooked shrimp (16-20 per lb.), peeled and deveined, tails on
- 9 bacon strips, halved lengthwise
  Optional: Ranch dip and lemon wedges

Make your own Ranch Dressing. Recipe on p. 146.

1. In a small bowl, combine sugar, lemon juice, oil and seasonings. Pour ¼ cup marinade into a large shallow dish; add shrimp. Let stand 15 minutes. Cover and refrigerate remaining marinade for basting.

2. Preheat broiler. Drain the shrimp; discard marinade. Wrap each shrimp with a piece of bacon and secure with a toothpick.

3. Place on a greased rack of a broiler pan. Broil 4 in. from heat until shrimp turn pink, 3-4 minutes on each side, basting frequently with the remaining marinade after turning. If desired, serve with ranch dip and lemon wedges.

1 APPETIZER 93 cal., 7g fat (2g sat. fat), 40mg chol., 189mg sod., 2g carb. (2g sugars, 0 fiber), 6g pro.

NOTES

APPETIZERS & SNACKS

SWEET CURRY ROASTED PISTACHIOS

I was looking for a way to spice up plain pistachios and came up with this winning flavor combination. They're great for snacking anytime. When I have a batch on hand, I like sharing them with the guys at work—they can't stop eating them!

—*Redawna Kalynchuk, Rochester, AB*

PREP: 15 MIN. • **BAKE:** 15 MIN. + COOLING • **MAKES:** 3 CUPS

- 2 Tbsp. curry powder
- 2 Tbsp. coconut oil or canola oil
- 1 Tbsp. maple syrup
- ½ tsp. salt
- ⅛ tsp. cayenne pepper
- 3 cups shelled roasted and salted pistachios
- 3 Tbsp. brown sugar

1. Preheat the oven to 300°. In a small saucepan, combine first 5 ingredients. Cook and stir over low heat until fragrant and oil is absorbed. Remove from heat; stir in the pistachios. Spread into a 15x10x1-in. baking pan lined with parchment.

2. Bake until pistachios are lightly toasted and appear dry, 15-18 minutes, stirring occasionally. Sprinkle with the brown sugar; toss to coat. Cool completely. Store in an airtight container.

⅓ CUP 288 cal., 22g fat (5g sat. fat), 0 chol., 309mg sod., 18g carb. (9g sugars, 5g fiber), 9g pro.

COURTSIDE CARAMEL CORN

Guests can't stop eating my caramel corn. For our basketball party, I fix enough to fill a big red tin decorated with the University of Arizona logo. The delectable syrup coats the popcorn well but isn't sticky.

—*Sharon Landeen, Tucson, AZ*

PREP: 15 MIN. • **BAKE:** 45 MIN. + COOLING • **MAKES:** ABOUT 5½ QT.

- 6 qt. popped popcorn
- 2 cups packed brown sugar
- 1 cup butter, cubed
- ½ cup corn syrup
- 1 tsp. salt
- 3 tsp. vanilla extract
- ½ tsp. baking soda

1. Place popcorn in a large bowl and set aside. In a large saucepan, combine the brown sugar, butter, corn syrup and salt; bring to a boil over medium heat, stirring constantly. Boil for 5 minutes, stirring occasionally.

2. Remove from the heat. Stir in vanilla and baking soda; mix well. Pour over popcorn and stir until well coated. Pour into 2 greased 13x9-in. baking pans.

3. Bake, uncovered, at 250° for 45 minutes, stirring every 15 minutes. Cool completely. Store in airtight containers.

1 CUP 230 cal., 12g fat (6g sat. fat), 22mg chol., 343mg sod., 32g carb. (23g sugars, 1g fiber), 1g pro.

PIMIENTO CHEESE

I've always loved pimiento cheese but never made my own—this was a fun challenge! Serve cold on crackers or sandwiches. Drizzle with honey for added flavor; I used hot honey, which was terrific!
—Darla Andrews, Boerne, TX

TAKES: 10 MIN. • **MAKES:** 3 CUPS

- 1 pkg. (8 oz.) cream cheese, softened
- 2 green onions, chopped
- 2 Tbsp. mayonnaise
- ½ tsp. salt
- ½ tsp. onion powder
- ½ tsp. garlic powder
- ½ tsp. smoked paprika
- ¼ tsp. pepper
- 1 jar (4 oz.) diced pimientos, drained
- 2 cups shredded cheddar cheese
- Hot chile-infused honey, optional

Place the first 8 ingredients in a food processor. Process until smooth. Add pimientos and cheddar cheese. Pulse until combined. If desired, drizzle with honey before serving.

2 TBSP. 81 cal., 7g fat (4g sat. fat), 19mg chol., 147mg sod., 1g carb. (1g sugars, 0 fiber), 3g pro.

MOREISH MIX-INS

Shake up the flavors! You can add diced pickles for a tangy-sweet freshness, bacon bits for smoky richness or a squeeze of lemon juice for a bright tang. For a burst of umami, stir in Worcestershire sauce.

BEST DEVILED EGGS

Herbs lend amazing flavor, making these the best deviled eggs ever!
—*Jesse and Anne Foust, Bluefield, WV*

TAKES: 25 MIN. • **MAKES:** 2 DOZEN

- ½ cup mayonnaise
- 2 Tbsp. 2% milk
- 1 tsp. dried parsley flakes
- ½ tsp. dill weed
- ½ tsp. minced chives
- ½ tsp. ground mustard
- ¼ tsp. salt
- ¼ tsp. paprika
- ⅛ tsp. garlic powder
- ⅛ tsp. pepper
- 12 hard-boiled large eggs
  Minced fresh parsley and additional paprika

In a small bowl, combine the first 10 ingredients. Cut eggs lengthwise in half; remove yolks and set whites aside. In another bowl, mash yolks; add to mayonnaise mixture, mixing well. Spoon or pipe filling into egg whites. Sprinkle with parsley and additional paprika. Refrigerate until serving.

1 STUFFED EGG HALF 73 cal., 6g fat (1g sat. fat), 108mg chol., 81mg sod., 0 carb. (0 sugars, 0 fiber), 3g pro.

BACON DEVILED EGGS To mayonnaise, mix in 3 crumbled cooked bacon strips, 3 Tbsp. finely chopped red onion, 3 Tbsp. sweet pickle relish and ¼ tsp. smoked paprika.

SMOKIN' HOT DEVILED EGGS To mayonnaise, mix in 3 finely chopped chipotle peppers in adobo sauce, 1 Tbsp. drained capers, 1 Tbsp. stone-ground mustard, ¼ tsp. salt and ¼ tsp. white pepper. Sprinkle the stuffed eggs with minced fresh cilantro.

CRABBY DEVILED EGGS Increase mayonnaise to ⅔ cup. Mix in 1 cup finely chopped imitation crabmeat, ½ cup finely chopped celery, ½ cup chopped slivered almonds, 2 Tbsp. finely chopped green pepper and ½ tsp. salt.

HONEY-MUSTARD CHICKEN WINGS

For a change from spicy Buffalo sauce, try these sweet and sticky wings. There's a good chance they'll become your new favorite!
—Susan Seymour, Valatie, NY

PREP: 15 MIN. • **BAKE:** 1 HOUR • **MAKES:** ABOUT 3 DOZEN

- 4 lbs. chicken wings
- ½ cup spicy brown mustard
- ½ cup honey
- ¼ cup butter, cubed
- 2 Tbsp. lemon juice
- ¼ tsp. ground turmeric

1. Preheat oven to 400°. Line two 15x10x1-in. baking pans with foil or parchment; grease foil or parchment. Using a sharp knife, cut through the 2 chicken wing joints; discard wing tips. Place remaining wings in prepared pans.

2. In a small saucepan, combine the remaining ingredients; bring to a boil, stirring frequently. Pour over wings, turning to coat. Bake 30-40 minutes on each side or until wings are glazed and chicken juices run clear. If desired, serve with additional honey mustard.

1 PIECE 85 cal., 5g fat (2g sat. fat), 19mg chol., 59mg sod., 4g carb. (4g sugars, 0 fiber), 5g pro.

GRILLED BRUSCHETTA

This is my go-to summer appetizer with fresh garden tomatoes and basil. The balsamic glaze takes it over the top, and while I like using a Tuscan herb or basil-infused olive oil for this, plain olive oil works well too.

—Brittany Allyn, Mesa, AZ

PREP: 30 MIN. • **GRILL:** 5 MIN. • **MAKES:** 16 SERVINGS

- ½ cup balsamic vinegar
- 1½ cups chopped and seeded plum tomatoes
- 2 Tbsp. finely chopped shallot
- 1 Tbsp. minced fresh basil
- 2 tsp. plus 3 Tbsp. olive oil, divided
- 1 garlic clove, minced
- 16 slices French bread baguette (½ in. thick)
  Sea salt
  Grated Parmesan cheese

1. In a small saucepan, bring vinegar to a boil; cook until liquid is reduced to 3 Tbsp., 8-10 minutes. Remove from heat. Meanwhile, combine tomatoes, shallot, basil, 2 tsp. olive oil and garlic. Cover and refrigerate until serving.

2. Brush the remaining 3 Tbsp. olive oil over both sides of the baguette slices. Grill, uncovered, over medium heat until golden brown on both sides.

3. Top toasts with the tomato mixture. Drizzle with balsamic syrup; sprinkle with sea salt and Parmesan. Serve immediately.

1 PIECE 58 cal., 3g fat (0 sat. fat), 0 chol., 49mg sod., 7g carb. (3g sugars, 0 fiber), 1g pro. **DIABETIC EXCHANGES** ½ starch, ½ fat.

TASTY SALMON CROQUETTES

These golden brown salmon croquettes have a nice crunch from red and green peppers. They're crispy on the outside and soft on the inside.

—Taste of Home *Test Kitchen*

PREP: 20 MIN. + MARINATING • **COOK:** 10 MIN./BATCH • **MAKES:** 12 SERVINGS

- 1 large egg, lightly beaten
- ¼ cup panko bread crumbs
- ¼ cup finely chopped sweet red pepper
- 2 green onions, chopped
- 2 Tbsp. mayonnaise
- 1 Tbsp. all-purpose flour
- 1 tsp. Worcestershire sauce
- ½ tsp. salt
- ¼ tsp. pepper
- ¼ tsp. garlic powder
- 2 pouches (5 oz. each) boneless skinless pink salmon
- ¼ cup canola oil
  Optional: Tartar sauce and lemon wedges

Make your own Classic Tartar Sauce. Recipe on p. 123.

1. In a large bowl, combine egg, panko, red pepper, green onions, mayonnaise, flour, Worcestershire sauce, salt, pepper and garlic powder. Fold in the salmon. Refrigerate, covered, at least 30 minutes.

2. Shape 2 Tbsp. salmon mixture into ½-in.-thick patty. Repeat with remaining mixture In a large skillet, heat the oil over medium heat. Add croquettes in batches; cook until golden brown, 3-4 minutes on each side. If desired, serve with tartar sauce and lemon wedges.

1 CROQUETTE 97 cal., 8g fat (1g sat. fat), 25mg chol., 241mg sod., 2g carb. (0 sugars, 0 fiber), 5g pro.

CAN YOU AIR FRY SALMON CROQUETTES?

Absolutely! Preheat the air fryer to 400° and spray the basket with oil. Placing a few croquettes in the basket, cook 8-10 minutes, then flip them. If needed, spray with a little more oil and cook for another 4-6 minutes until they are a rich golden brown.

APPETIZERS & SNACKS

CHEESE PUFFS

I adapted this recipe from one of my mother's old cookbooks and updated the flavor with cayenne and mustard. Tasty and quick to make, these tender, golden puffs go together in minutes and simply disappear at parties!
—Jamie Wetter, Boscobel, WI

PREP: 15 MIN. • **BAKE:** 15 MIN./BATCH • **MAKES:** 4½ DOZEN

1 cup water
2 Tbsp. butter
½ tsp. salt
⅛ tsp. cayenne pepper
1 cup all-purpose flour
4 large eggs, room temperature
1¼ cups shredded Gruyere or Swiss cheese
1 Tbsp. Dijon mustard
¼ cup grated Parmesan cheese

1. In a large saucepan, bring the water, butter, salt and cayenne to a boil. Add flour all at once and stir until a smooth ball forms. Remove from the heat; let stand for 5 minutes. Add eggs, 1 at a time, beating well after each addition. Continue beating until mixture is smooth and shiny. Stir in Gruyere and mustard.

2. Drop by 1-in. balls 2 in. apart on greased baking sheets. Sprinkle with Parmesan cheese. Bake at 425° for 15-20 minutes or until golden brown. Serve warm or cold.

1 PUFF 30 cal., 2g fat (1g sat. fat), 18mg chol., 62mg sod., 2g carb. (0 sugars, 0 fiber), 2g pro.

HOW DO YOU SERVE CHEESE PUFFS?

Elevate Cheese Puffs by splitting them open and filling them with a delicious filling such as ham salad or smoked trout pate. For an even heartier option, do as the Parisians do—pipe the fillings into larger bun-sized puffs and fill them with roasted chicken or your favorite deli meats. They make a sophisticated and delicious sandwich!

HOMEMADE POTATO CHIPS

Forget buying the bag of potato chips at the grocery store when you can make these at home. This quick and easy recipe will delight everyone in the family.
—Taste of Home *Test Kitchen*

PREP: 30 MIN. + SOAKING • **COOK:** 5 MIN./BATCH • **MAKES:** 8½ CUPS

7 unpeeled medium potatoes (about 2 lbs.)
2 qt. ice water
5 tsp. salt
2 tsp. garlic powder
1½ tsp. celery salt
1½ tsp. pepper
Oil for deep-fat frying

1. Using a vegetable peeler or metal cheese slicer, cut potatoes into very thin slices. Place in a large bowl; add ice water and salt. Soak for 30 minutes.

2. Drain potatoes; place on paper towels and pat dry. In a small bowl, combine the garlic powder, celery salt and pepper; set aside.

3. In a cast-iron or other heavy skillet, heat 1½ in. oil to 375°. Fry potatoes in batches until golden brown, 3-4 minutes, stirring frequently.

4. Remove with a slotted spoon; drain on paper towels. Immediately sprinkle with seasoning mixture. Store in an airtight container.

¾ CUP 176 cal., 8g fat (1g sat. fat), 0 chol., 703mg sod., 24g carb. (1g sugars, 3g fiber), 3g pro.

CARAMELIZED ONION SPINACH DIP

Spinach dip is at the top of nearly everyone's list of favorite party foods. I make it extra special with caramelized onions and a splash of white wine, so this is a recipe you can feel excited about serving.
—*Corrine Rupp, Statesville, NC*

PREP: 10 MIN. • **COOK:** 40 MIN. • **MAKES:** 2½ CUPS

2 Tbsp. olive oil
1 sweet onion, chopped
3 garlic cloves, minced
¼ cup reduced-sodium chicken broth
¼ cup white wine or additional reduced-sodium chicken broth
2 cups fat-free sour cream
1 pkg. (10 oz.) frozen chopped spinach, thawed and squeezed dry
¾ tsp. salt
Tortilla chips and assorted fresh vegetables

1. In a large skillet, heat oil over medium heat. Add onion; cook and stir until tender, 6-8 minutes. Add garlic; cook 1 minute longer.

2. Stir in broth and wine. Reduce heat to medium low; cook for 25-30 minutes or until onion is golden brown and liquid is evaporated, stirring occasionally.

3. Transfer to a bowl. Stir in sour cream, spinach and salt. Serve dip with tortilla chips and vegetables. Refrigerate leftovers.

¼ CUP 89 cal., 3g fat (0 sat. fat), 1mg chol., 251mg sod., 7g carb. (5g sugars, 1g fiber), 4g pro. **DIABETIC EXCHANGES** ½ starch, ½ fat.

PEPPY PEACH SALSA

Garden-fresh salsas are one of my favorite condiments. So when I saw a recipe for peach salsa in the newspaper, I couldn't think of anything that sounded better.
—*Jennifer Abbott, Moraga, CA*

TAKES: 20 MIN. • **MAKES:** 1¼ CUPS

- 2 Tbsp. lime juice
- 1 Tbsp. honey
- ½ tsp. minced garlic
- ⅛ tsp. ground ginger
- 2 fresh peaches, peeled and diced
- ½ green serrano chile pepper, seeded and minced
- ½ red serrano chile pepper, seeded and minced
- ½ small yellow chile pepper, seeded and minced
- 2 tsp. minced fresh cilantro
- Tortilla chips

In a small bowl, combine the lime juice, honey, garlic and ginger; let stand for 5 minutes. Stir in the peaches, peppers and cilantro. Serve with chips. Refrigerate leftovers.

NOTE Wear disposable gloves when cutting hot peppers; the oils can burn skin. Avoid touching your face.

¼ CUP 30 cal., 0 fat (0 sat. fat), 0 chol., 1mg sod., 8g carb. (6g sugars, 1g fiber), 0 pro.

READER REVIEW

"Bright and refreshing, this salsa is so easy to make in a jiffy. I can't wait to try it with falafel."

—RENEEMURBY, TASTEOFHOME.COM

APPETIZERS & SNACKS

from scratch SOUPS & STEWS

THE ULTIMATE CHICKEN NOODLE SOUP, PAGE 89

BURGOO

A Kentucky Derby favorite, this hearty, comforting meat-and-vegetable stew will feed a large crowd. It takes a bit of effort but is worth it.
—Taste of Home *Test Kitchen*

PREP: 30 MIN. • **COOK:** 2½ HOURS • **MAKES:** 24 SERVINGS (7½ QT.)

- 3 Tbsp. olive oil, divided
- 2 lbs. boneless pork shoulder butt roast, cut into 1½-in. cubes
- 2 lbs. boneless beef chuck roast, cut into 1½-in. cubes
- 2 lbs. bone-in chicken thighs
- 3 medium carrots, cut into 1-in. pieces
- 2 celery ribs, cut into 1-in. pieces
- 1 large onion, chopped
- 1 large green pepper, chopped
- 3 garlic cloves, minced
- 2 cartons (32 oz. each) reduced-sodium beef broth
- 1 can (28 oz.) crushed tomatoes
- 3 bay leaves
- 2 tsp. salt
- 2 tsp. dried thyme
- 1 tsp. pepper
- 2 medium potatoes, peeled and cubed
- 2½ cups frozen lima beans (about 12 oz.)
- 2½ cups frozen corn (about 12 oz.)
- 2 cups finely chopped cabbage
- ¼ cup Worcestershire sauce
- 3 Tbsp. cider vinegar
  Hot pepper sauce, optional

Make your own Homemade Beef Broth. Recipe on p. 103.

1. In a large stockpot, heat 2 Tbsp. oil over medium heat. Brown the pork in batches; remove and set aside. Repeat with beef and chicken. In the same pan, heat remaining 1 Tbsp. oil over medium heat. Add the carrots, celery, onion and green pepper; cook and stir until tender, 5-7 minutes. Add garlic; cook 1 minute longer.

2. Add broth, stirring to loosen browned bits from pan. Add tomatoes, bay leaves, salt, thyme and pepper. Return pork, beef and chicken to pan. Bring to a boil. Reduce heat; cover and simmer until meat is very tender, about 2 hours.

3. Remove chicken to a plate. When cool enough to handle, remove meat from the bones; discard skin and bones. Using 2 forks, shred the meat into bite-sized pieces. Return meat to stockpot.

4. Add potatoes, lima beans, corn and cabbage; cover and cook 30 minutes. Discard the bay leaves. Stir in the Worcestershire sauce and vinegar. If desired, serve with hot sauce.

1¼ CUPS 265 cal., 13g fat (4g sat. fat), 67mg chol., 404mg sod., 15g carb. (4g sugars, 3g fiber), 22g pro.

QUICK CREAM OF MUSHROOM SOUP

My daughter-in-law, a gourmet cook, served this soup as the first course for a holiday dinner. She received the recipe from her mom and graciously shared it with me. Now I'm happy to share it with my own friends and family.
—*Anne Kulick, Phillipsburg, NJ*

TAKES: 30 MIN. • **MAKES:** 6 SERVINGS

- 2 Tbsp. butter
- ½ lb. sliced fresh mushrooms
- ¼ cup chopped onion
- 6 Tbsp. all-purpose flour
- ½ tsp. salt
- ⅛ tsp. pepper
- 2 cans (14½ oz. each) chicken broth
- 1 cup half-and-half cream
  Chopped chives, optional

Make your own Homemade Chicken Broth. Recipe on p. 92.

1. In a large saucepan, heat butter over medium-high heat; saute mushrooms and onion until tender.

2. Mix flour, salt, pepper and 1 can broth until smooth; stir into the mushroom mixture. Stir in the remaining can of broth. Bring to a boil; cook and stir until thickened, about 2 minutes. Reduce the heat; stir in the half-and-half. Simmer, uncovered, until flavors are blended, about 15 minutes, stirring occasionally. If desired, top with chives.

1 CUP 136 cal., 8g fat (5g sat. fat), 33mg chol., 842mg sod., 10g carb. (3g sugars, 1g fiber), 4g pro.

MINT LAMB STEW

The lamb here isn't just tender—it melts in your mouth! This recipe is an adaptation of a stew my mother used to make when I was growing up in England. Now I round it out with local root vegetables.
—*Maureen Evans, Rancho Cucamonga, CA*

PREP: 40 MIN. • **COOK:** 6 HOURS • **MAKES:** 6 SERVINGS (2¼ QT.)

- ½ cup all-purpose flour
- ½ tsp. salt
- ¼ tsp. pepper
- 1½ lbs. lamb stew meat, cubed
- 2 shallots, sliced
- 2 Tbsp. olive oil
- ½ cup red wine
- 2 cans (14½ oz. each) beef broth
- 2 medium potatoes, cubed
- 1 large sweet potato, peeled and cubed
- 2 large carrots, cut into 1-in. pieces
- 2 medium parsnips, peeled and cubed
- 1 garlic clove, minced
- 1 Tbsp. mint jelly
- 4 bacon strips, cooked and crumbled
  Minced fresh mint, optional

1. In a large shallow dish, combine flour, salt and pepper. Add meat, a few pieces at a time, and turn to coat. In a large skillet, brown meat and shallots in oil in batches.

2. Transfer to a 5- or 6-qt. slow cooker. Add wine to the skillet, stirring to loosen browned bits from pan. Bring to a boil. Reduce heat; simmer, uncovered, for 1-2 minutes. Add to slow cooker.

3. Stir in the broth, potatoes, sweet potato, carrots, parsnips and garlic. Cover and cook on low 6-8 hours or until meat is tender. Stir in the jelly; sprinkle with bacon. Sprinkle with fresh mint before serving if desired.

1½ CUPS 442 cal., 13g fat (4g sat. fat), 79mg chol., 1016mg sod., 46g carb. (11g sugars, 5g fiber), 31g pro.

NOTES

_____
_____
_____
_____
_____

SOUPS & STEWS

SEAFOOD GUMBO

Gumbo is a signature dish of Louisiana cuisine, and living across the border in Texas, we can't get enough of this traditional Cajun dish. While this recipe calls for seafood, you could also use chicken, duck or sausage.

—Ruth Aubey, San Antonio, TX

PREP: 20 MIN. • **COOK:** 30 MIN. • **MAKES:** 24 SERVINGS (6 QT.)

- 1 cup all-purpose flour
- 1 cup canola oil
- 4 cups chopped onion
- 2 cups chopped celery
- 2 cups chopped green pepper
- 1 cup sliced green onions
- 4 cups chicken broth
- 8 cups water
- 4 cups sliced okra
- 2 Tbsp. paprika
- 1 Tbsp. salt
- 2 tsp. oregano
- 1 tsp. ground black pepper
- 6 cups small shrimp, rinsed and drained, or seafood of your choice
- 1 cup minced fresh parsley
- 2 Tbsp. Cajun seasoning

1. In a heavy Dutch oven, combine flour and oil until smooth. Cook over medium-high heat 5 minutes, stirring constantly. Reduce heat to medium. Cook and stir until mixture is reddish brown, about 10 minutes longer.

2. Add the onion, celery, green pepper and green onion; cook and stir 5 minutes. Add chicken broth, water, okra, paprika, salt, oregano and pepper. Bring to boil; reduce the heat and simmer, covered, 10 minutes.

3. Add the shrimp and parsley. Simmer, uncovered, until shrimp or other seafood is done, about 5 minutes longer. Remove from heat; stir in Cajun seasoning.

1 CUP 166 cal., 10g fat (1g sat. fat), 96mg chol., 900mg sod., 10g carb. (2g sugars, 2g fiber), 10g pro.

made from scratch
HOMEMADE CAJUN SEASONING

We in Louisiana love seasoned foods. I use this in gravy, over meats and with salads. It also makes an excellent gift for teachers, and many have asked for the recipe.

—*Onietta Loewer, Branch, LA*

TAKES: 5 MIN.
MAKES: ABOUT 3½ CUPS

- 1 carton (26 oz.) salt
- 2 containers (1 oz. each) cayenne pepper
- ⅓ cup pepper
- ⅓ cup chili powder
- 3 Tbsp. garlic powder

Combine all ingredients; store in airtight containers. Use to season pork, chicken, seafood, steaks or vegetables.

¼ TSP. 1 cal., 0 fat (0 sat. fat), 0 chol., 433mg sod., 0 carb. (0 sugars, 0 fiber), 0 pro.

SOUPS & STEWS

THE BEST CHICKEN & DUMPLINGS

Chicken and dumplings hearken back to my childhood and chilly days when we devoured those cute little balls of dough swimming in hot, rich broth.
—Erika Monroe-Williams, Scottsdale, AZ

PREP: 25 MIN. • **COOK:** 1 HOUR 10 MIN. • **MAKES:** 8 SERVINGS (3 QT.)

- ¾ cup all-purpose flour, divided
- ½ tsp. salt
- ½ tsp. freshly ground pepper
- 1 broiler/fryer chicken (about 3 lbs.), cut up
- 2 Tbsp. canola oil
- 1 large onion, chopped
- 2 medium carrots, chopped
- 2 celery ribs, chopped
- 3 garlic cloves, minced
- 6 cups chicken stock
- ½ cup white wine or apple cider
- 2 tsp. sugar
- 2 bay leaves
- 5 whole peppercorns

DUMPLINGS
- 1⅓ cups all-purpose flour
- 2 tsp. baking powder
- ¾ tsp. salt
- ⅔ cup 2% milk
- 1 Tbsp. butter, melted

SOUP
- ½ cup heavy whipping cream
- 2 tsp. minced fresh parsley
- 2 tsp. minced fresh thyme
- Additional salt and pepper to taste

1. In a shallow bowl, mix ½ cup flour, salt and pepper. Add chicken, 1 piece at a time, and toss to coat; shake off excess. In a 6-qt. stockpot, heat oil over medium-high heat. Brown chicken in batches on all sides; remove from pan.

2. Add onion, carrots and celery to same pan; cook and stir 6-8 minutes or until onion is tender. Add garlic; cook and stir 1 minute longer. Stir in ¼ cup flour until blended. Gradually add stock, stirring constantly. Stir in wine, sugar, bay leaves and peppercorns. Return chicken to pan; bring to a boil. Reduce heat; simmer, covered, 20-25 minutes or until chicken juices run clear.

3. For dumplings, in a bowl, whisk flour, baking powder and salt. In another bowl, whisk milk and butter until blended. Add to flour mixture; stir just until moistened (do not overmix). Drop dough by rounded tablespoonfuls onto a parchment-lined baking sheet; set aside.

4. Remove chicken from stockpot; cool slightly. Discard bay leaves and skim fat from soup. Remove skin and bones from the chicken and discard. Using 2 forks, coarsely shred the meat into 1-to-1½-in. pieces; return to soup. Cook, covered, on high until mixture reaches a simmer.

5. Drop dumplings on top of simmering soup, a few at a time. Reduce heat to low; cook, covered, 15-18 minutes or until a toothpick inserted in center of dumplings comes out clean (do not lift cover while simmering). Gently stir in cream, parsley and thyme. Season with additional salt and pepper to taste.

1½ CUPS 470 cal., 24g fat (8g sat. fat), 104mg chol., 892mg sod., 29g carb. (5g sugars, 2g fiber), 32g pro.

"BONE" APPETIT!
If the butcher includes a backbone with your chicken, don't throw it away. Simmer the bone with the chicken and vegetables to add flavor and body to the gravy. Make sure to remove it before adding dumplings.

TURKEY CABBAGE STEW

Chock-full of ground turkey, cabbage, carrots and tomatoes, this stew delivers down-home comfort food fast!
—Susan Lasken, Woodland Hills, CA

TAKES: 30 MIN. • **MAKES:** 6 SERVINGS

- 1 lb. lean ground turkey
- 1 medium onion, chopped
- 3 garlic cloves, minced
- 4 cups chopped cabbage
- 2 medium carrots, sliced
- 1 can (28 oz.) diced tomatoes, undrained
- ¾ cup water
- 1 Tbsp. brown sugar
- 1 Tbsp. white vinegar
- 1 tsp. salt
- 1 tsp. dried oregano
- ¼ tsp. dried thyme
- ¼ tsp. pepper

1. Cook turkey, onion and garlic in a large saucepan over medium heat until meat is no longer pink, 5-7 minutes, breaking turkey into crumbles; drain.

2. Add the remaining ingredients. Bring to a boil; cover and simmer until the vegetables are tender, 12-15 minutes.

FREEZE OPTION Freeze cooled stew in freezer containers. To use, partially thaw in refrigerator overnight. Heat through in a saucepan, stirring occasionally; add water if necessary.

1 CUP 180 cal., 6g fat (2g sat. fat), 52mg chol., 674mg sod., 16g carb. (10g sugars, 5g fiber), 17g pro. **DIABETIC EXCHANGES** 2 vegetable, 2 lean meat.

SOUPS & STEWS

CLASSIC FRENCH ONION SOUP

Enjoy my signature soup the way my granddaughter Becky does: I make it for her in a French onion soup bowl complete with garlic croutons and gobs of melted Swiss cheese on top.
—Lou Sansevero, Ferron, UT

PREP: 20 MIN. • **COOK:** 2 HOURS • **MAKES:** 12 SERVINGS (2¼ QT.)

- 5 Tbsp. olive oil, divided
- 1 Tbsp. butter
- 8 cups thinly sliced onions (about 3 lbs.)
- 3 garlic cloves, minced
- ½ cup port wine or dry sherry
- 2 cartons (32 oz. each) beef broth
- ½ tsp. pepper
- ¼ tsp. salt
- 24 slices French bread baguette (½ in. thick)
- 2 large garlic cloves, peeled and halved
- ¾ cup shredded Gruyere or Swiss cheese

1. In a Dutch oven, heat 2 Tbsp. oil and butter over medium heat. Add the onions; cook and stir until softened, 10-13 minutes. Reduce heat to medium low; cook, stirring occasionally, until deep golden brown, 30-40 minutes. Add minced garlic; cook 2 minutes longer.

2. Stir in wine. Bring to a boil; cook until liquid is reduced by half. Add the broth, pepper and salt; return to a boil. Reduce the heat. Simmer, covered, stirring occasionally, 1 hour.

3. Meanwhile, preheat oven to 400°. Place baguette slices on a baking sheet; brush both sides with remaining 3 Tbsp. oil. Bake until toasted, 3-5 minutes on each side. Rub toasts with halved garlic.

4. To serve, ladle the soup into twelve 8-oz. broiler-safe bowls or ramekins on baking sheets; place 2 toasts in each. Top with cheese. Broil 4 in. from heat until cheese is melted.

¾ CUP SOUP WITH 2 PIECES BREAD AND 1 TBSP. CHEESE 195 cal., 10g fat (3g sat. fat), 9mg chol., 765mg sod., 21g carb. (4g sugars, 2g fiber), 6g pro.

MANCHESTER STEW

While studying abroad at the University of Manchester, I was a vegetarian, and my favorite meal was Beans Burgundy. It inspired me to create this version after I returned to the States. As it simmers in the slow cooker, the enticing aroma always takes me back to my time in England!
—*Kimberly Hammond, Kingwood, TX*

PREP: 25 MIN. • **COOK:** 8 HOURS • **MAKES:** 6 SERVINGS (2½ QT.)

- 2 Tbsp. olive oil
- 2 medium onions, chopped
- 2 garlic cloves, minced
- 1 tsp. dried oregano
- 1 cup dry red wine
- 1 lb. small red potatoes, quartered
- 1 can (16 oz.) kidney beans, rinsed and drained
- ½ lb. sliced fresh mushrooms
- 2 medium leeks (white portions only), sliced
- 1 cup fresh baby carrots
- 2½ cups water
- 1 can (14½ oz.) no-salt-added diced tomatoes
- 1 tsp. dried thyme
- ½ tsp. salt
- ¼ tsp. pepper
- Fresh basil leaves

1. In a large skillet, heat oil over medium-high heat. Add onions; cook and stir until tender, 2-3 minutes. Add the garlic and oregano; cook and stir 1 minute longer. Stir in wine. Bring to a boil; cook until liquid is reduced by half, 3-4 minutes.

2. Transfer to a 5- or 6-qt. slow cooker. Add potatoes, beans, mushrooms, leeks and carrots. Stir in the water, tomatoes, thyme, salt and pepper. Cook, covered, on low 8-10 hours or until potatoes are tender. Top with basil.

1⅔ CUPS 221 cal., 5g fat (1g sat. fat), 0 chol., 354mg sod., 38g carb. (8g sugars, 8g fiber), 8g pro. **DIABETIC EXCHANGES** 2 starch, 1 vegetable, 1 fat.

VEGAN CARROT SOUP

Yukon Gold potatoes—instead of cream—make a smooth carrot soup vegan and add a mild sweetness. If you don't have Yukon Golds on hand, use russet potatoes.
—Taste of Home *Test Kitchen*

TAKES: 30 MIN. • **MAKES:** 6 SERVINGS

1 medium onion, chopped
2 celery ribs, chopped
1 Tbsp. canola oil
4 cups vegetable broth
1 lb. carrots, sliced
2 large Yukon Gold potatoes, peeled and cubed
1 tsp. salt
¼ tsp. pepper
Fresh cilantro leaves, optional

1. In a large saucepan, saute onion and celery in oil until tender. Add the broth, carrots and potatoes; bring to a boil. Reduce heat; cover and simmer 15-20 minutes or until the vegetables are tender. Remove from heat; cool slightly.

2. Transfer to a blender; cover and process until smooth. Return to pan; stir in salt and pepper. Heat through. If desired, sprinkle with cilantro.

1 CUP 176 cal., 3g fat (0 sat. fat), 0 chol., 710mg sod., 35g carb. (7g sugars, 4g fiber), 4g pro. **DIABETIC EXCHANGES** 2 starch, ½ fat.

made from scratch
HOMEMADE VEGETABLE BROTH

The flavor of celery and mushrooms comes through in this homemade vegetable broth. You can use it as a substitute for chicken broth.
—Taste of Home *Test Kitchen*

PREP: 45 MIN. • **COOK:** 1¾ HOURS • **MAKES:** 5½ CUPS

2 Tbsp. olive oil
2 medium onions, cut into wedges
2 celery ribs, cut into 1-in. pieces
1 whole garlic bulb, separated into cloves and peeled
3 medium leeks, white and light green parts only, cleaned and cut into 1-in. pieces
3 medium carrots, cut into 1-in. pieces
8 cups water
½ lb. fresh mushrooms, quartered
1 cup packed fresh parsley sprigs
4 sprigs fresh thyme
1 tsp. salt
½ tsp. whole peppercorns
1 bay leaf

1. Heat oil in a stockpot over medium heat until hot. Add onions, celery and garlic. Cook and stir 5 minutes or until tender. Add the leeks and carrots; cook and stir 5 minutes. Add water, mushrooms, parsley, thyme, salt, peppercorns and bay leaf; bring to a boil. Reduce the heat; simmer, uncovered, 1 hour.

2. Remove from heat. Strain through a cheesecloth-lined colander; discard the vegetables. If using immediately, skim fat. Or refrigerate 8 hours or overnight; remove fat from surface. The broth can be covered and refrigerated up to 3 days or frozen up to 6 months.

1 CUP 15 cal., 0 fat (0 sat. fat), 0 chol., 105mg sod., 3g carb. (2g sugars, 1g fiber), 1g pro.

THE ULTIMATE CHICKEN NOODLE SOUP

My first Wisconsin winter was so cold, all I wanted to eat was soup. This recipe is in heavy rotation from November to April at our house.
—Gina Nistico, Denver, CO

PREP: 15 MIN. • **COOK:** 45 MIN. + STANDING • **MAKES:** 10 SERVINGS (ABOUT 3½ QT.)

- 2½ lbs. bone-in chicken thighs
- ½ tsp. salt
- ½ tsp. pepper
- 1 Tbsp. canola oil
- 1 large onion, chopped
- 1 garlic clove, minced
- 10 cups chicken broth
- 4 celery ribs, chopped
- 4 medium carrots, chopped
- 2 bay leaves
- 1 tsp. minced fresh thyme or ¼ tsp. dried thyme
- 3 cups uncooked kluski or other egg noodles (about 8 oz.)
- 1 Tbsp. chopped fresh parsley
- 1 Tbsp. lemon juice
- Optional: Additional salt and pepper

1. Pat chicken dry with paper towels; sprinkle with salt and pepper. In a 6-qt. stockpot, heat oil over medium-high heat. Add the chicken in batches, cook until dark golden brown, 3-4 minutes. Remove chicken from the pan; discard all but 2 Tbsp. drippings.

2. Add onion to drippings; cook and stir over medium-high heat until tender, 4-5 minutes. Add garlic; cook 1 minute longer. Add the broth, stirring to loosen browned bits from pan. Bring to a boil. Return chicken to pan. Add the celery, carrots, bay leaves and thyme. Reduce heat; simmer, covered, until the chicken is tender, 25-30 minutes.

3. Transfer chicken to a plate. Remove soup from heat. Add noodles; let stand, covered, until the noodles are tender, 20-22 minutes.

4. Meanwhile, when chicken is cool enough to handle, remove meat from bones; discard bones. Shred meat into bite-sized pieces. Return meat to the stockpot. Stir in the parsley and lemon juice. If desired, adjust seasoning with additional salt and pepper. Discard the bay leaves.

1⅓ CUPS 239 cal., 12g fat (3g sat. fat), 68mg chol., 1176mg sod., 14g carb. (3g sugars, 2g fiber), 18g pro.

ROASTED TOMATO SOUP WITH FRESH BASIL

Roasting really brings out the flavor of the tomatoes in this wonderful soup. It has a slightly chunky texture that indicates it's fresh and homemade.
—*Marie Forte, Raritan, NJ*

PREP: 20 MIN. • **BAKE:** 25 MIN. • **MAKES:** 6 SERVINGS (1½ QT.)

3½ lbs. tomatoes (about 11 medium), halved
1 small onion, quartered
2 garlic cloves, peeled and halved
2 Tbsp. olive oil
2 Tbsp. fresh thyme leaves
1 tsp. salt
¼ tsp. pepper
12 fresh basil leaves
Optional: Salad croutons and thinly sliced fresh basil

1. Preheat oven to 400°. Place tomatoes, onion and garlic in a greased 15x10x1-in. baking pan; drizzle with oil. Sprinkle with thyme, salt and pepper; toss to coat. Roast until tender, 25-30 minutes, stirring once. Cool slightly.

2. Working in batches, process tomato mixture and basil leaves in a blender until smooth. Transfer to a large saucepan; heat through. If desired, top with croutons and fresh basil.

1 CUP 107 cal., 5g fat (1g sat. fat), 0 chol., 411mg sod., 15g carb. (9g sugars, 4g fiber), 3g pro. **DIABETIC EXCHANGES** 1 starch, 1 fat.

QUICK HAM & BEAN SOUP

If you like ham and bean soup but don't want to spend hours in the kitchen, this timely version is the one for you. It is delicious and takes just 30 minutes from start to finish.
—Taste of Home *Test Kitchen*

TAKES: 30 MIN. • **MAKES:** 7 SERVINGS

2 medium carrots, sliced
2 celery ribs, chopped
½ cup chopped onion
2 Tbsp. butter
4 cans (15½ oz. each) great northern beans, rinsed and drained
4 cups chicken broth
2 cups cubed fully cooked ham
1 tsp. chili powder
½ tsp. minced garlic
¼ tsp. pepper
1 bay leaf

In a large saucepan, saute the carrots, celery and onion in butter until tender. Stir in remaining ingredients. Bring to a boil. Reduce heat; cook for 15 minutes or until heated through. Discard bay leaf.

1 CUP 300 cal., 6g fat (3g sat. fat), 32mg chol., 1383mg sod., 40g carb. (2g sugars, 13g fiber), 22g pro.

BAY FOR FRESHNESS

Fresh bay leaves, available in the herb section of large supermarkets, are more aromatic than dried. You can finely mince them to season kabobs and Mediterranean dishes. To preserve leftover bay leaves, rinse and pat them dry, freeze quickly in a single layer and store in a freezer container to use for soups.

BEER-BRAISED STEW

Friends and family will never guess that the secret ingredient in this wonderful stew is beer! What a nice meal to come home to—just cook the noodles and dinner is ready.
—*Geri Faustich, Appleton, WI*

PREP: 20 MIN. • **COOK:** 6 HOURS • **MAKES:** 8 SERVINGS

- 3 bacon strips, diced
- 2 lbs. beef stew meat, cut into 1-in. cubes
- ½ tsp. pepper
- ¼ tsp. salt
- 2 Tbsp. canola oil
- 2 cups fresh baby carrots
- 1 medium onion, cut into wedges
- 1 tsp. minced garlic
- 1 bay leaf
- 1 can (12 oz.) beer or nonalcoholic beer
- 1 Tbsp. soy sauce
- 1 Tbsp. Worcestershire sauce
- 1 tsp. dried thyme
- 2 Tbsp. all-purpose flour
- ¼ cup water
  Hot cooked noodles
  Chopped fresh parsley, optional

1. In a large skillet, cook bacon over medium heat until crisp. Remove to paper towels; drain, discarding the drippings. Sprinkle beef with pepper and salt. In the same skillet, brown beef in oil in batches; drain.

2. Transfer to a 5-qt. slow cooker. Add the carrots, bacon, onion, garlic and bay leaf. In a small bowl, combine the beer, soy sauce, Worcestershire sauce and thyme. Pour over beef mixture.

3. Cover and cook on low for 5½-6 hours or until meat and vegetables are tender.

4. In a small bowl, combine flour and water until smooth. Gradually stir into slow cooker. Cover and cook on high for 30 minutes or until thickened. Discard bay leaf. Serve stew with the noodles. If desired, top with chopped parsley.

FREEZE OPTION Freeze cooled stew in freezer containers. To use, partially thaw in refrigerator overnight. Heat through in a saucepan, stirring occasionally; add broth or water if necessary. Serve as directed.

½ CUP 258 cal., 13g fat (4g sat. fat), 74mg chol., 340mg sod., 8g carb. (4g sugars, 1g fiber), 24g pro.

CREAMY CORN CRAB SOUP

This creamy soup is quick, easy and luscious. Corn really shines in this delectable recipe, and crabmeat makes it a little more special. It will get high marks from both busy cooks and lovers of flavorful homemade food.

—Carol Ropchan, Willingdon, AB

TAKES: 30 MIN. • **MAKES:** 6 SERVINGS

1 medium onion, chopped
2 Tbsp. butter
3 cups chicken broth
3 cups frozen corn
3 medium potatoes, peeled and diced
1 can (6 oz.) crabmeat, drained, flaked and cartilage removed
1 cup whole milk
¼ tsp. pepper, plus more for optional topping
   Optional: Minced chives and crushed red pepper flakes

1. In a large saucepan, saute onion in butter until tender. Add broth, corn and potatoes; bring to a boil. Reduce heat; cover and simmer 15 minutes. Remove from heat; cool slightly.

2. In a blender, puree half the corn mixture. Return to pan. Stir in the crab, milk and pepper; cook over low heat until heated through (do not boil). If desired, top with fresh cracked pepper, chives and crushed red pepper flakes.

1¼ CUPS 219 cal., 6g fat (3g sat. fat), 44mg chol., 702mg sod., 33g carb. (6g sugars, 3g fiber), 10g pro. **DIABETIC EXCHANGES** 2 starch, 1 lean meat, 1 fat.

made from scratch
HOMEMADE CHICKEN BROTH

Rich in chicken flavor, this traditional broth is lightly seasoned with herbs. Besides wonderful chicken soups, it can be used in casseroles, rice dishes and other recipes that call for chicken broth.

—Taste of Home *Test Kitchen*

PREP: 10 MIN. • **COOK:** 3¼ HOURS + CHILLING • **MAKES:** ABOUT 6 CUPS

2½ lbs. bony chicken pieces (legs, wings, necks or backbones)
2 celery ribs with leaves, cut into chunks
2 medium carrots, cut into chunks
2 medium onions, quartered
2 bay leaves
½ tsp. dried rosemary, crushed
½ tsp. dried thyme
8 to 10 whole peppercorns
2 qt. cold water

1. Place all ingredients in a soup kettle or Dutch oven. Slowly bring to a boil; reduce heat until mixture is just at a simmer. Simmer, uncovered, 3-4 hours, skimming foam as needed.

2. Set the chicken aside until cool enough to handle. Remove meat from bones. Discard bones; save meat for another use. Strain broth, discarding vegetables and seasonings.

Refrigerate for 8 hours or overnight. Skim fat from surface.

1 CUP 25 cal., 0 fat (0 sat. fat), 0 chol., 130mg sod., 2g carb. (0 sugars, 0 fiber), 4g pro.

GRANDMA'S OXTAIL STEW

This hearty, soul-warming soup is a favorite family heirloom recipe—don't let the name turn you off! Oxtail describes the meaty part of the tail of an ox (now commonly cow). The meat is delicious but requires long and slow cooking.
—Bobbie Keefer, Byers, CO

PREP: 20 MIN. • **COOK:** 10 HOURS • **MAKES:** 8 SERVINGS (3 QT.)

- 2 lbs. oxtails, trimmed
- 2 Tbsp. olive oil
- 4 medium carrots, sliced (about 2 cups)
- 1 medium onion, chopped
- 2 garlic cloves, minced
- 2 cans (14½ oz. each) diced tomatoes, undrained
- 1 can (15 oz.) beef broth
- 3 bay leaves
- 1 tsp. salt
- 1 tsp. dried oregano
- ½ tsp. dried thyme
- ½ tsp. pepper
- 6 cups chopped cabbage

1. In a large skillet, brown oxtails in oil over medium heat. Remove from pan; place in a 5-qt. slow cooker.

2. Add carrots and onion to drippings; cook and stir until just softened, 3-5 minutes. Add the garlic; cook 1 minute longer. Transfer the vegetable mixture to slow cooker. Add tomatoes, broth, bay leaves, salt, oregano, thyme and pepper; stir to combine.

3. Cook, covered, on low 8 hours. Add cabbage; cook until cabbage is tender and meat pulls away easily from bones, about 2 hours longer. Remove oxtails; set aside until cool enough to handle. Remove meat from the bones; discard bones and shred meat. Return meat to soup. Discard bay leaves.

FREEZE OPTION Freeze cooled stew in freezer containers. To use, partially thaw in refrigerator overnight. Heat through in a saucepan, stirring occasionally; add broth or water if necessary.

1½ CUPS 204 cal., 10g fat (3g sat. fat), 34mg chol., 705mg sod., 14g carb. (8g sugars, 5g fiber), 16g pro.

CHILI CON CARNE

At chili suppers, this one always disappears first! It's nice at home too, as the longer it sits in the refrigerator, the better the taste seems to get.
—Janie Turner, Tuttle, OK

PREP: 20 MIN. • **COOK:** 1½ HOURS • **MAKES:** 10 SERVINGS (2½ QT.)

- 2 lbs. ground beef
- 2 Tbsp. olive oil
- 2 medium onions, chopped
- 2 garlic cloves, minced
- 1 medium green pepper, chopped
- 1½ tsp. salt
- 2 Tbsp. chili powder
- 3 tsp. beef bouillon granules
- ⅛ tsp. cayenne pepper
- ¼ tsp. ground cinnamon
- 1 tsp. ground cumin
- 1 tsp. dried oregano
- 2 cans (14½ oz. each) diced tomatoes, undrained
- 1 cup water
- 1 can (16 oz.) kidney beans, rinsed and drained
- Optional: Sour cream and jalapeno slices

1. In a Dutch oven, cook beef over medium heat until no longer pink, 5-7 minutes; crumble beef. Drain and set aside.

2. In the same pot, heat oil; saute onions until tender. Add the garlic; cook 1 minute longer. Stir in the green pepper, salt, chili powder, bouillon, cayenne, cinnamon, cumin and oregano. Cook for 2 minutes, stirring until combined.

3. Add tomatoes and browned beef. Stir in the water. Bring to a boil. Reduce heat; cover and simmer 1 hour. Add the beans and heat through. Top with sour cream and jalapeno if desired.

1 CUP 264 cal., 14g fat (4g sat. fat), 56mg chol., 892mg sod., 15g carb. (5g sugars, 5g fiber), 20g pro.

HOW DO YOU MAKE CHILI CON CARNE EVEN BETTER?

Chili con carne is versatile and easy to adjust to your personal taste. You can choose the type of beef you prefer, swap beef broth for water to enhance the beef flavor, add more cayenne for extra heat and sprinkle with fresh oregano to brighten the dish.

LOUISIANA RED BEANS & RICE

Smoked turkey sausage and red pepper flakes add zip to this slow-cooked
version of the New Orleans classic. For extra heat, add red pepper sauce.
—*Julia Bushree, Menifee, CA*

PREP: 20 MIN. • **COOK:** 3 HOURS • **MAKES:** 8 SERVINGS (2 QT.)

4 cans (16 oz. each) kidney beans, rinsed and drained
1 can (14½ oz.) diced tomatoes, undrained
1 pkg. (14 oz.) smoked turkey sausage, sliced
3 celery ribs, chopped
1 large onion, chopped
1 cup chicken broth
1 medium green pepper, chopped
1 small sweet red pepper, chopped
6 garlic cloves, minced
1 bay leaf
½ tsp. crushed red pepper flakes
2 green onions, chopped
Hot cooked rice

1. In a 4- or 5-qt. slow cooker, combine the first 11 ingredients. Cook, covered, on low until vegetables are tender, 3-4 hours.

2. Stir before serving. Remove bay leaf. Serve with green onion and rice.

FREEZE OPTION Discard bay leaf and freeze cooled bean mixture in freezer containers. To use, partially thaw in refrigerator overnight. Heat through in a saucepan, stirring occasionally; add broth or water if necessary. Serve as directed.

1 CUP 291 cal., 3g fat (1g sat. fat), 32mg chol., 1070mg sod., 44g carb. (8g sugars, 13g fiber), 24g pro.

NOTES

FAVORITE HAMBURGER STEW

I got this recipe from a woman at our church when I needed a way to use up our bounty of home-canned tomatoes. My husband loves it, and I like that it's easy to warm up for a carefree dinner in the winter months.
—*Marcia Clay, Truman, MN*

PREP: 20 MIN. • **COOK:** 65 MIN. • **MAKES:** 16 SERVINGS (4 QT.)

- 2 lbs. ground beef
- 2 medium onions, chopped
- 4 cans (14½ oz. each) stewed tomatoes, undrained
- 8 medium carrots, thinly sliced
- 4 celery ribs, thinly sliced
- 2 medium potatoes, peeled and cubed
- 2 cups water
- ½ cup uncooked long grain rice
- 3 tsp. salt
- 1 tsp. pepper

1. In a Dutch oven, cook beef and onions over medium heat until meat is no longer pink, breaking meat into crumbles; drain. Add tomatoes, carrots, celery, potatoes, water, rice, salt and pepper; bring to a boil. Reduce the heat; cover and simmer 30 minutes or until the vegetables and rice are tender.

2. Uncover; simmer 20-30 minutes longer or until thickened to desired consistency.

FREEZE OPTION Freeze cooled stew in freezer containers. To use, partially thaw in refrigerator overnight. Heat through in a saucepan, stirring occasionally; add a little water if necessary.

1 CUP 191 cal., 7g fat (3g sat. fat), 35mg chol., 689mg sod., 21g carb. (8g sugars, 2g fiber), 12g pro.

QUICK & HEALTHY TURKEY VEGGIE SOUP

I freeze leftover holiday turkey to enjoy comforting meals like this year-round. This soup is especially delicious on a chilly fall or winter day. For a more filling dish, add some cooked pasta.
—*Joan Hallford, North Richland Hills, TX*

TAKES: 30 MIN. • **MAKES:** 9 SERVINGS (3 QT.)

- 2 Tbsp. butter
- 1 medium onion, chopped
- 1 celery rib, chopped
- 2 garlic cloves, minced
- 5 cups reduced-sodium chicken broth
- 3 medium carrots, julienned
- ¼ tsp. pepper
- 1 lb. zucchini or yellow summer squash, julienned (about 6 cups)
- 3 medium tomatoes, chopped
- 1 can (15½ oz.) hominy, rinsed and drained
- 2½ cups frozen lima beans (about 12 oz.), thawed
- 2 cups cubed cooked turkey
- 1½ tsp. minced fresh basil or ½ tsp. dried basil
- Shredded Parmesan cheese

In a Dutch oven, heat the butter over medium-high heat. Add onion, celery and garlic; cook and stir until tender, 5-8 minutes. Add broth, carrots and pepper. Bring to a boil; reduce heat. Simmer, uncovered, 5 minutes. Add the zucchini, tomatoes, hominy, lima beans and turkey. Cook until zucchini is tender, 5-8 minutes. Top with basil; serve with Parmesan cheese.

1⅓ CUPS 187 cal., 4g fat (2g sat. fat), 38mg chol., 614mg sod., 22g carb. (5g sugars, 5g fiber), 16g pro. **DIABETIC EXCHANGES** 2 lean meat, 1½ starch, ½ fat.

SOUPS & STEWS

PICO DE GALLO BLACK BEAN SOUP

Everyone at my table goes for this feel-good soup. It is quick when you're pressed for time and beats fast food, hands down.
—*Darlis Wilfer, West Bend, WI*

TAKES: 20 MIN. • **MAKES:** 6 SERVINGS (ABOUT 2 QT.)

4 cans (15 oz. each) black beans, rinsed and drained
2 cups vegetable broth
2 cups pico de gallo
½ cup water
2 tsp. ground cumin
Optional toppings: Chopped fresh cilantro and additional pico de gallo

Make your own Homemade Vegetable Broth. Recipe on p. 87.

1. In a Dutch oven, combine the first 5 ingredients; bring to a boil over medium heat, stirring occasionally. Reduce heat; simmer, uncovered, until vegetables in pico de gallo are softened, 5-7 minutes, stirring occasionally.

2. Puree the soup using an immersion blender or cool soup slightly and puree in batches in a blender. Return to pan and heat through. Serve with toppings as desired.

FREEZE OPTION Freeze cooled soup in freezer containers. To use, partially thaw in refrigerator overnight. Heat through in a saucepan, stirring occasionally; add a little broth or water if necessary. Top as desired.

1¼ CUPS 241 cal., 0 fat (0 sat. fat), 0 chol., 856mg sod., 44g carb. (4g sugars, 12g fiber), 14g pro.

HEALTH TIP Black beans are naturally low in fat and high in fiber, protein and folate.

made from scratch PICO DE GALLO

This easy pico de gallo recipe is a classic for good reason—it goes with just about everything! For the best flavor, let it chill for an hour or two before serving, and enjoy it the same day you make it.
—*Jeannie Trudell, Del Norte, CO*

PREP: 10 MIN. + CHILLING
MAKES: 2 CUPS

6 plum tomatoes, chopped
1 small onion, finely chopped
½ cup chopped fresh cilantro
1 to 2 jalapeno peppers, seeded and finely chopped
3 Tbsp. lime juice (about 1 lime)
1 Tbsp. cilantro stems, finely chopped
1 garlic clove, minced
¼ tsp. salt

In a medium bowl, combine all ingredients. Cover and refrigerate for 1-2 hours before serving.

¼ CUP 14 cal., 0 fat (0 sat. fat), 0 chol., 40mg sod., 3g carb. (2g sugars, 1g fiber), 1g pro.
DIABETIC EXCHANGES 1 free food.

100 TASTEOFHOME.COM

HUNGARIAN GOULASH

Talk about your heirloom recipes! My grandmother made this for my mother when she was a child, and then my mom made it for us to enjoy. Paprika and caraway add wonderful flavor, and sour cream gives it a creamy richness. It's simply scrumptious!
—*Marcia Doyle, Pompano, FL*

PREP: 20 MIN. • **COOK:** 7 HOURS • **MAKES:** 12 SERVINGS

- 3 medium onions, chopped
- 2 medium carrots, chopped
- 2 medium green peppers, chopped
- 3 lbs. beef stew meat
- ¾ tsp. salt, divided
- ¾ tsp. pepper, divided
- 2 Tbsp. olive oil
- 1½ cups reduced-sodium beef broth
- ¼ cup all-purpose flour
- 3 Tbsp. paprika
- 2 Tbsp. tomato paste
- 1 tsp. caraway seeds
- 1 garlic clove, minced
- Dash sugar
- 12 cups uncooked whole wheat egg noodles
- 1 cup reduced-fat sour cream

1. Place the onions, carrots and green peppers in a 5-qt. slow cooker. Sprinkle meat with ½ tsp. salt and ½ tsp. pepper. In a large skillet, brown the meat in oil in batches. Transfer to slow cooker.

2. Add broth to skillet, stirring to loosen browned bits from pan. Combine the flour, paprika, tomato paste, caraway seeds, garlic, sugar and remaining salt and pepper; stir into skillet. Bring to a boil; cook and stir for 2 minutes or until thickened. Pour over meat. Cover and cook on low 7-9 hours or until the meat is tender.

3. Cook noodles according to package directions. Stir sour cream into slow cooker. Drain noodles; serve with goulash.

⅔ CUP GOULASH WITH 1 CUP NOODLES
388 cal., 13g fat (4g sat. fat), 78mg chol., 285mg sod., 41g carb. (5g sugars, 7g fiber), 31g pro. **DIABETIC EXCHANGES** 3 lean meat, 2 starch, 1 vegetable, 1 fat.

HEARTY PASTA FAJIOLI

Here's a classic Italian favorite. Spaghetti sauce and canned broth form the flavorful base.

—Cindy Garland, Limestone, TN

PREP: 40 MIN. • **COOK:** 40 MIN. • **MAKES:** 24 SERVINGS (7½ QT.)

2 lbs. ground beef
6 cans (14½ oz. each) beef broth
2 cans (28 oz. each) diced tomatoes, undrained
2 jars (26 oz. each) spaghetti sauce
3 large onions, chopped
8 celery ribs, diced
3 medium carrots, sliced
1 can (16 oz.) kidney beans, rinsed and drained
1 can (15 oz.) cannellini beans, rinsed and drained
3 tsp. minced fresh oregano or 1 tsp. dried oregano
2½ tsp. pepper
1½ tsp. hot pepper sauce
8 oz. uncooked medium pasta shells
5 tsp. minced fresh parsley

1. In a large stockpot, cook the beef over medium heat until no longer pink, 5-7 minutes; crumble beef and drain off grease. Add broth, tomatoes, spaghetti sauce, onions, celery, carrots, beans, oregano, pepper and pepper sauce.

2. Bring to a boil. Reduce heat; simmer, covered, 30 minutes. Add pasta and parsley; simmer, covered, until pasta is tender, 10-14 minutes.

1¼ CUPS 212 cal., 6g fat (2g sat. fat), 20mg chol., 958mg sod., 25g carb. (8g sugars, 5g fiber), 14g pro.

made from scratch
HOMEMADE BEEF BROTH

Roasting soup bones in the oven first gives hearty beef flavor to this basic stock. In addition to soups, use the beefy broth to provide extra flavor in stews, gravies, sauces and vegetable dishes.

—Taste of Home *Test Kitchen*

PREP: 25 MIN. • **COOK:** 5½ HOURS • **MAKES:** ABOUT 2½ QT.

4 lbs. meaty beef soup bones (beef shanks or short ribs)
3 medium carrots, cut into chunks
3 celery ribs, cut into chunks
2 medium onions, quartered
½ cup warm water (110° to 115°)
3 bay leaves
3 garlic cloves
8 to 10 whole peppercorns
3 to 4 sprigs fresh parsley
1 tsp. dried thyme
1 tsp. dried marjoram
1 tsp. dried oregano
Cold water

1. Preheat oven to 450°. In a large roasting pan, bake soup bones, uncovered, 30 minutes. Add carrots, celery and onions. Bake 30 minutes; drain fat.

2. Using a slotted spoon, transfer bones and vegetables to a large Dutch oven. Add warm water to roasting pan; stir to loosen browned bits. Transfer pan juices to Dutch oven. Add seasonings and enough cold water just to cover. Slowly bring to a boil, about 30 minutes. Reduce heat; simmer, uncovered, 4-5 hours, skimming foam. If necessary, add water during first 2 hours to keep ingredients covered.

3. Remove the soup bones; cool. If desired, remove meat from bones and save the meat for another use, discarding bones. Strain the broth through a cheesecloth-lined colander, discarding the vegetables and seasonings. If using immediately, skim fat. Or refrigerate 8 hours or overnight; remove fat from surface.

NOTE Broth can be covered and refrigerated up to 3 days or frozen for 4-6 months.

1 CUP 30 cal., 0 fat (0 sat. fat), 0 chol., 75mg sod., 0 carb. (0 sugars, 0 fiber), 6g pro.

SOUPS & STEWS

THE BEST BEEF STEW

This stew recipe has tons of flavor, thanks to its blend of herbs and the addition of red wine and balsamic vinegar. Once you learn how to make this classic, you can customize it to your own tastes.
—*James Schend, Pleasant Prairie, WI*

PREP: 30 MIN. • **COOK:** 2 HOURS • **MAKES:** 6 SERVINGS (2¼ QT.)

- 1½ lbs. beef stew meat, cut into 1-in. cubes
- ½ tsp. salt, divided
- 6 Tbsp. all-purpose flour, divided
- ½ tsp. smoked paprika
- 1 Tbsp. canola oil
- 3 Tbsp. tomato paste
- 2 tsp. herbes de Provence
- 2 garlic cloves, minced
- 2 cups dry red wine
- 2 cups beef broth
- 1½ tsp. minced fresh rosemary, divided
- 2 bay leaves
- 3 cups cubed peeled potatoes
- 3 cups coarsely chopped onions (about 2 large)
- 2 cups sliced carrots
- 2 Tbsp. cold water
- 2 Tbsp. balsamic or red wine vinegar
- 1 cup fresh or frozen peas
- Additional fresh rosemary, optional

1. In a small bowl, toss beef and ¼ tsp. salt. In a large bowl, combine 4 Tbsp. flour and paprika. Add beef, a few pieces at a time, and toss to coat.

2. In a Dutch oven, brown beef in oil over medium heat. Stir in the tomato paste, herbes de Provence and garlic; cook until fragrant and color starts to darken slightly. Add wine; cook until mixture just comes to a boil. Simmer until reduced by half, about 5 minutes. Stir in broth, 1 tsp. rosemary and bay leaves. Bring to a boil. Reduce heat; cover and simmer until the meat is almost tender, about 1½ hours.

3. Add the potatoes, onions and carrots. Cover; simmer until meat and vegetables are tender, about 30 minutes longer.

4. Discard bay leaves. In a small bowl, combine remaining ½ tsp. rosemary, remaining ¼ tsp. salt and remaining 2 Tbsp. flour. Add cold water and vinegar; stir until smooth. Stir into stew. Bring to a boil; add peas. Cook, stirring, until thickened, about 2 minutes. If desired, top with additional fresh rosemary.

1½ CUPS 366 cal., 11g fat (3g sat. fat), 71mg chol., 605mg sod., 40g carb. (9g sugars, 6g fiber), 28g pro. **DIABETIC EXCHANGES** 3 lean meat, 2½ starch, ½ fat.

SOUPS & STEWS

MANGO & COCONUT CHICKEN SOUP

I love preparing dinner in a slow cooker because it's carefree cooking. This chicken dish uses some of my favorite ingredients—coconut milk, edamame and fresh ginger. The Asian-style entree is perfect for a potluck party.
—Roxanne Chan, Albany, CA

PREP: 25 MIN. • **COOK:** 6 HOURS • **MAKES:** 6 SERVINGS

- 1 broiler/fryer chicken (3 to 4 lbs.), skin removed and cut up
- 2 Tbsp. canola oil
- 1 can (15 oz.) whole baby corn, drained
- 1 pkg. (10 oz.) frozen chopped spinach, thawed
- 1 cup frozen shelled edamame, thawed
- 1 small sweet red pepper, chopped
- 1 can (13.66 oz.) light coconut milk
- ½ cup mango salsa
- 1 tsp. minced fresh gingerroot
- 1 medium mango, peeled and chopped
- 2 Tbsp. lime juice
- 2 green onions, chopped

1. In a large skillet, brown the chicken in oil in batches. Transfer the chicken and drippings to a 5-qt. slow cooker. Add the corn, spinach, edamame and pepper. In a small bowl, combine the coconut milk, salsa and ginger; pour over vegetables.

2. Cover and cook on low for 6-8 hours or until the chicken is tender. Remove the chicken; cool slightly. When cool enough to handle, remove meat from bones; cut or shred the meat into bite-sized pieces. Return meat to slow cooker.

3. Just before serving, stir in mango and lime juice. Sprinkle servings with green onions.

1 SERVING 338 cal., 17g fat (6g sat. fat), 73mg chol., 362mg sod., 15g carb. (8g sugars, 4g fiber), 29g pro.

TRADITIONAL NEW ENGLAND CLAM CHOWDER

I left a cruise ship with a wonderful souvenir—the recipe for this splendid chowder! It's a traditional soup that stands the test of time.
—Agnes Ward, Stratford, ON

PREP: 40 MIN. • **COOK:** 15 MIN. • **MAKES:** 7 SERVINGS

- 12 fresh cherrystone clams
- 3 cups cold water
- 2 bacon strips, diced
- 1 small onion, chopped
- 2 medium potatoes, peeled and finely chopped
- ¼ tsp. salt
- ¼ tsp. pepper
- 2 Tbsp. all-purpose flour
- 1 cup whole milk
- ½ cup half-and-half cream

1. Tap clams; discard any that do not close. Place clams and water in a large saucepan. Bring to a boil. Reduce heat; cover and simmer for 5-6 minutes or until clams open.

2. Remove meat from clams; chop meat and set aside. Strain liquid through a cheesecloth-lined colander; set aside.

3. In a large saucepan, cook bacon over medium heat until crisp. Using a slotted spoon, remove to paper towels. Saute onion in drippings until tender.

4. Return bacon to the pan; add clam meat and reserved liquid. Stir in the potatoes, salt and pepper. Bring to a boil. Reduce heat; cover and simmer for 10-12 minutes or until potatoes are tender.

5. Combine flour and milk until smooth; gradually stir into the soup. Bring to a boil; cook and stir for 2 minutes or until thickened. Gradually stir in cream; heat through (do not boil).

1 CUP 138 cal., 6g fat (3g sat. fat), 24mg chol., 175mg sod., 14g carb. (3g sugars, 1g fiber), 6g pro. **DIABETIC EXCHANGES** 1 starch, 1 lean meat, ½ fat.

SOUPS & STEWS 107

from scratch
MAIN COURSES

BEST LASAGNA, PAGE 126

STEAK STIR-FRY

No one would guess this elegant entree comes together in a snap. To save even more prep time, use frozen mixed veggies instead of fresh. Sometimes I substitute chicken, chicken bouillon and curry for beef, beef bouillon and ginger.
—Janis Plourde, Smooth Rock Falls, ON

TAKES: 25 MIN. • **MAKES:** 4 SERVINGS

- 1 tsp. beef bouillon granules
- 1 cup boiling water
- 2 Tbsp. cornstarch
- ⅓ cup soy sauce
- 1 lb. beef top sirloin steak, cut into thin strips
- 1 garlic clove, minced
- 1 tsp. ground ginger
- ¼ tsp. pepper
- 2 Tbsp. canola oil, divided
- 1 large green pepper, julienned
- 1 cup julienned carrots or sliced celery
- 5 green onions, cut into 1-in. pieces
- Toasted sesame seeds, optional
- Hot cooked rice

1. Dissolve bouillon in boiling water. Combine cornstarch and soy sauce until smooth; add to bouillon. Set aside. Toss beef with the garlic, ginger and pepper. In a large skillet or wok over medium-high heat, stir-fry the beef in 1 Tbsp. oil until meat is no longer pink; remove and keep warm.

2. Heat remaining 1 Tbsp. oil; stir-fry vegetables until crisp-tender. Stir soy sauce mixture and add to the skillet; bring to a boil. Cook and stir 2 minutes. Return meat to pan and heat through; if desired, top with sesame seeds. Serve with rice.

1 CUP 266 cal., 13g fat (3g sat. fat), 63mg chol., 1484mg sod., 12g carb. (4g sugars, 2g fiber), 25g pro.

NOTES

QUICK BEAN & RICE BURRITOS

These hearty and zippy burritos can be whipped up in a jiffy.
—*Kimberly Hardison, Maitland, FL*

TAKES: 25 MIN. • **MAKES:** 8 SERVINGS

1½ cups water
1½ cups uncooked instant brown rice
1 Tbsp. olive oil
1 medium green pepper, diced
½ cup chopped onion
1 tsp. minced garlic
1 Tbsp. chili powder
1 tsp. ground cumin
⅛ tsp. crushed red pepper flakes
1 can (15 oz.) black beans, rinsed and drained
1 cup salsa
10 flour tortillas (8 in.), warmed
Optional: Avocado slices, lime wedges, vegan sour cream and salsa

1. In a small saucepan, bring water to a boil. Add rice. Return to a boil. Reduce heat; cover and simmer for 5 minutes. Remove from heat. Let stand until the water is absorbed, about 5 minutes.

2. Meanwhile, in a large skillet, heat oil over medium-high heat. Add green pepper and onion; cook and stir until tender, 3-4 minutes. Add garlic; cook 1 minute longer. Stir in chili powder, cumin and red pepper flakes until combined. Add beans and rice; cook and stir until heated through, 4-6 minutes. Stir in salsa and remove from heat.

3. Spoon about ½ cup filling off-center on each tortilla. Fold sides and ends over the filling and roll up. Serve with optional toppings as desired.

1 BURRITO 345 cal., 7g fat (1g sat. fat), 0 chol., 544mg sod., 61g carb. (2g sugars, 6g fiber), 10g pro.

ALL-AMERICAN TURKEY POTPIE

Ever since my sister-in-law shared this recipe with me, I haven't made any other kind of potpie. The crust is very easy to work with.
—Laureen Naylor, Factoryville, PA

PREP: 30 MIN. + CHILLING • **BAKE:** 45 MIN. • **MAKES:** 6 SERVINGS

- 2½ cups all-purpose flour
- ½ tsp. salt
- ½ cup finely shredded aged sharp cheddar cheese
- 14 Tbsp. cold butter
- 10 to 12 Tbsp. ice water

FILLING
- 1 cup cubed potatoes
- ½ cup thinly sliced carrots
- ⅓ cup chopped celery
- ¼ cup chopped onion
- 1 Tbsp. butter
- 1 garlic clove, minced
- 1 cup chicken broth
- 2 Tbsp. all-purpose flour
- ½ cup 2% milk
- 1½ cups shredded cooked turkey
- ½ cup frozen peas, thawed
- ½ cup frozen corn, thawed
- ½ tsp. salt
- ¼ tsp. dried tarragon
- ¼ tsp. pepper
-   Egg wash, optional

1. In a food processor, combine flour and salt; cover and pulse to blend. Add cheese; pulse until fine crumbs form. Add butter; pulse until coarse crumbs form. While processing, gradually add 10 Tbsp. water; if needed, add remaining water, 1 Tbsp. at a time, until the dough forms a ball.

2. Divide dough in half with 1 ball slightly larger than the other; wrap both halves and refrigerate for 30 minutes.

3. For the filling, in a large saucepan or Dutch oven, saute the potatoes, carrots, celery and onion in butter for 5 minutes. Add garlic; cook 1 minute longer. Stir in broth; cover and cook until vegetables are tender, 10-15 minutes.

4. Combine flour and milk until smooth; gradually add to the vegetable mixture. Bring to a simmer; cook and stir until thickened, 3-5 minutes. Add the next 6 ingredients; cook until heated through, about 5 minutes longer.

5. Preheat the oven to 400°. Roll out the larger dough ball to fit a 9-in. pie plate; transfer to pie plate. Trim crust even with edge. Pour hot turkey filling into crust. Roll out remaining dough to fit top of pie; place over filling. Trim, seal and flute the edge. Cut slits in top or make decorative cutouts in the top crust. If desired, brush with egg wash.

6. Bake for 10 minutes; reduce the oven temperature to 375°. Bake until the crust is golden brown, 35-45 minutes longer, covering edge of crust with foil if needed during the last few minutes of baking to keep from overbrowning.

FREEZE OPTION Cover and freeze unbaked pie. To use, remove from freezer 30 minutes before baking (do not thaw). Preheat oven to 425°. Place pie on baking sheet; cover edge loosely with foil. Bake 30 minutes. Reduce oven setting to 350°; bake 70-80 minutes longer or until crust is golden brown and a thermometer inserted in center reads 165°.

1 PIECE 609 cal., 35g fat (21g sat. fat), 123mg chol., 898mg sod., 54g carb. (3g sugars, 3g fiber), 21g pro.

OVEN-BAKED BRISKET

Texans like brisket cooked on the smoker, but this recipe offers convenient prep in the oven. Sometimes I make extra sauce to serve on the side. Round out the meal with potato salad and slaw.
—Katie Ferrier, Houston, TX

PREP: 15 MIN. + MARINATING • **BAKE:** 4¼ HOURS • **MAKES:** 8 SERVINGS

- 1 fresh beef brisket (4 to 5 lbs.)
- 2 Tbsp. Worcestershire sauce
- 2 Tbsp. soy sauce
- 1 Tbsp. onion salt
- 1 Tbsp. liquid smoke
- 2 tsp. salt
- 2 tsp. pepper
  Dash hot pepper sauce

SAUCE
- ½ cup ketchup
- 3 Tbsp. brown sugar
- 1 Tbsp. lemon juice
- 1 Tbsp. soy sauce
- 1 tsp. ground mustard
- 3 drops hot pepper sauce
  Dash ground nutmeg

1. Place the brisket fat side down in a 13x9-in. baking dish. In a small bowl, mix Worcestershire sauce, soy sauce, onion salt, liquid smoke, salt, pepper and hot pepper sauce; pour over brisket. Turn brisket fat side up; refrigerate, covered, overnight.

2. Remove brisket from refrigerator. Preheat oven to 300°. Bake, covered, 4 hours. In a small bowl, combine sauce ingredients. Spread over brisket. Bake, uncovered, 15-30 minutes longer or until tender. Cut diagonally across the grain into thin slices.

6 OZ. COOKED BEEF 333 cal., 10g fat (4g sat. fat), 97mg chol., 1920mg sod., 11g carb. (10g sugars, 0 fiber), 48g pro.

made from scratch
SPICY KETCHUP

When this zesty ketchup is bubbling on the stove, the aroma takes me back to my childhood. One taste and I'm home again.
—Karen Naihe, Kamuela, HI

PREP: 30 MIN. **COOK:** 1½ HOURS + CHILLING **MAKES:** 1 CUP

- 1 Tbsp. olive oil
- 1 medium onion, chopped
- 3 lbs. tomatoes (about 11 medium), coarsely chopped
- 1 cinnamon stick (3 in.)
- ¾ tsp. celery seed
- ½ tsp. mustard seed
- ¼ tsp. whole allspice
- ⅓ cup sugar
- 1 tsp. salt
- ¾ cup red wine vinegar
- 1½ tsp. smoked paprika
- 1½ tsp. Sriracha chili sauce, optional

1. In a large saucepan, heat oil over medium-high heat. Add onion; cook and stir until tender. Stir in tomatoes; cook, uncovered, over medium heat 25-30 minutes or until tomatoes are softened.

2. Press tomato mixture through a fine-mesh strainer; discard solids. Return mixture to pot; bring to a boil. Cook, uncovered, until the liquid is reduced to 1½ cups, about 10 minutes.

3. Place the cinnamon, celery seed, mustard seed and allspice on a double thickness of cheesecloth. Gather corners of the cloth to enclose spices; tie securely with string. Add to the tomatoes. Stir in sugar and salt; return to a boil. Reduce heat; simmer, uncovered, 20-25 minutes or until thickened.

4. Stir in the vinegar, paprika and, if desired, chili sauce; bring to a boil. Simmer, uncovered, 10-15 minutes longer or until desired consistency is reached, stirring occasionally. Discard spice bag.

5. Transfer to a covered container; cool slightly. Refrigerate until cold. Store in refrigerator for up to 1 week.

1 TBSP. 46 cal., 1g fat (0 sat. fat), 0 chol., 152mg sod., 9g carb. (7g sugars, 1g fiber), 1g pro. **DIABETIC EXCHANGES** ½ starch.

CHICKEN TAMALES

I love making tamales—they take some time to make but are so worth the effort. While I usually make them for Christmas, my family wants them more often, so I freeze a big batch.
—Cindy Pruitt, Grove, OK

PREP: 2½ HOURS + SOAKING • **COOK:** 45 MIN. • **MAKES:** 20 TAMALES

- 24 dried corn husks
- 1 broiler/fryer chicken (3 to 4 lbs.), cut up
- 1 medium onion, quartered
- 2 tsp. salt
- 1 garlic clove, crushed
- 3 qt. water

DOUGH
- 1 cup shortening
- 3 cups masa harina

FILLING
- 6 Tbsp. canola oil
- 6 Tbsp. all-purpose flour
- ¾ cup chili powder
- ½ tsp. salt
- ¼ tsp. garlic powder
- ¼ tsp. pepper
- 2 cans (2¼ oz. each) sliced ripe olives, drained
- Hot water

BEEF IT UP!
For a hearty, beef filling, choose slow-cooked brisket. Let it simmer in a slow cooker until it is melt-in-your-mouth tender and packed with flavor. Use any leftovers to prepare meat pies, sandwiches or other quick meals.

1. Cover corn husks with cold water; soak until softened, at least 2 hours.

2. Place chicken, onion, salt and garlic in a 6-qt. stockpot. Pour in 3 qt. water; bring to a boil. Reduce heat; simmer, covered, until the chicken is tender, 45-60 minutes. Remove chicken from broth. When cool enough to handle, remove the bones and skin; discard. Shred chicken. Strain cooking juices; skim off fat. Reserve 6 cups stock.

3. For dough, beat shortening until light and fluffy, about 1 minute. Beat in small amounts of masa harina alternately with small amounts of reserved stock, using no more than 2 cups stock. Drop a small amount of dough into 1 cup cold water; the dough should float. If not, continue beating, rechecking every 1-2 minutes.

4. For filling, heat oil in a Dutch oven; stir in flour until blended. Cook and stir over medium heat until lightly browned, 7-9 minutes. Stir in seasonings, chicken and remaining stock; bring to a boil. Reduce the heat; simmer, uncovered, stirring occasionally, until thickened, about 45 minutes.

5. Drain corn husks and pat dry; tear 4 husks to make 20 strips for tying tamales. (To prevent husks from drying out, cover with a damp towel until ready to use.) On wide end of each remaining husk, spread 3 Tbsp. dough to within ½ in. of side edges; top each with 2 Tbsp. chicken filling and 2 tsp. olives. Fold long sides of husk over filling, overlapping slightly. Fold over narrow end of husk; tie with a strip of husk to secure.

6. Place a large steamer basket in the stockpot over water; place the tamales upright in steamer. Bring to a boil; steam, covered, adding hot water as needed, until dough peels away from the husk, about 45 minutes.

2 TAMALES 564 cal., 35g fat (7g sat. fat), 44mg chol., 835mg sod., 43g carb. (2g sugars, 7g fiber), 20g pro.

CHICAGO-STYLE DEEP-DISH PIZZA

My husband and I tried to duplicate the pizza from a popular Chicago restaurant, and I think our recipe turned out even better. The secret is baking it in a cast-iron skillet.
—Lynn Hamilton, Naperville, IL

PREP: 35 MIN. + RISING • **BAKE:** 40 MIN. + RESTING • **MAKES:** 2 PIZZAS (8 PIECES EACH)

- 3½ cups all-purpose flour
- ¼ cup cornmeal
- 1 pkg. (¼ oz.) quick-rise yeast
- 1½ tsp. sugar
- ½ tsp. salt
- 1 cup water
- ⅓ cup olive oil

TOPPINGS
- 6 cups shredded part-skim mozzarella cheese, divided
- 1 can (28 oz.) diced tomatoes, well drained
- 1 can (8 oz.) tomato sauce
- 1 can (6 oz.) tomato paste
- ½ tsp. salt
- ¼ tsp. each garlic powder, dried oregano, dried basil and pepper
- 1 lb. bulk Italian sausage
- 48 slices pepperoni
- ½ lb. sliced fresh mushrooms
- ¼ cup grated Parmesan cheese

1. In a large bowl, combine 1½ cups flour, cornmeal, yeast, sugar and salt. In a saucepan, heat the water and oil to 120°-130°. Add to dry ingredients; beat just until moistened. Add the remaining flour to form a stiff dough.

2. Turn onto a floured surface; knead until smooth and elastic, 6-8 minutes. Place in a greased bowl, turning once to grease top. Cover and let rise in a warm place until doubled, about 30 minutes.

3. Punch dough down; divide in half. Roll each portion into an 11-in. circle. Press dough onto the bottoms and up the sides of 2 greased 10-in. cast-iron or other ovenproof skillets. Sprinkle each with 2 cups mozzarella cheese.

4. In a large bowl, combine tomatoes, tomato sauce, tomato paste and seasonings. Spoon 1½ cups over each pizza. Layer each with half each of the sausage, pepperoni and mushrooms, and 1 cup mozzarella. Sprinkle with 2 Tbsp. Parmesan cheese.

5. Cover and bake at 450° for 35 minutes. Uncover; bake until lightly browned, about 5 minutes longer.

1 PIECE 407 cal., 23g fat (9g sat. fat), 49mg chol., 872mg sod., 32g carb. (4g sugars, 2g fiber), 20g pro.

MAIN COURSES

TURKEY IN CREAM SAUCE

I've relied on this recipe for tender turkey since I first moved out on my own years ago. I serve it whenever I have new guests over, and I'm always asked for the recipe.
—Kathy-Jo Winterbottom, Pottstown, PA

PREP: 20 MIN. • **COOK:** 7 HOURS • **MAKES:** 8 SERVINGS

1¼ cups white wine or chicken broth
1 medium onion, chopped
2 garlic cloves, minced
2 bay leaves
2 tsp. dried rosemary, crushed
½ tsp. pepper
3 turkey breast tenderloins (¾ lb. each)
3 Tbsp. cornstarch
½ cup half-and-half cream or whole milk
½ tsp. salt

1. In a 3-qt. slow cooker, combine wine, onion, garlic and bay leaves. Combine rosemary and pepper; rub over turkey. Place in slow cooker. Cover and cook on low for 7-9 hours or until turkey is tender.

2. Remove turkey to a serving platter; keep warm. Strain and skim fat from cooking juices; transfer juices to a small saucepan. Bring liquid to a boil. Combine cornstarch, cream and salt until smooth. Gradually stir into the pan. Bring to a boil; cook and stir until thickened, about 2 minutes. Serve with turkey.

1 SERVING 205 cal., 3g fat (1g sat. fat), 58mg chol., 231mg sod., 6g carb. (1g sugars, 0 fiber), 32g pro. **DIABETIC EXCHANGES** 4 lean meat, ½ starch, ½ fat.

made from scratch
RED WINE CRANBERRY SAUCE

We were feeling festive when we started our holiday cooking, but a bottle of wine was a bit more than we wanted to drink. I added half a cup to the cranberry sauce, in place of juice, and a new recipe was born!
—Helen Nelander, Boulder Creek, CA

PREP: 5 MIN.
COOK: 20 MIN. + CHILLING
MAKES: ABOUT 2⅓ CUPS

1 pkg. (12 oz.) fresh or frozen cranberries
1 cup sugar
1 cup water
½ cup dry red wine or grape juice

1. In a large saucepan, combine all ingredients; bring to a boil, stirring to dissolve sugar. Reduce heat to medium; cook, uncovered, until most of the berries pop, about 15 minutes, stirring occasionally.

2. Transfer to a bowl; cool slightly. Refrigerate, covered, until cold (sauce will thicken upon cooling).

¼ CUP 122 cal., 0 fat (0 sat. fat), 0 chol., 1mg sod., 30g carb. (27g sugars, 2g fiber), 0 pro.

BRAISED SHORT RIBS WITH GRAVY

Hearty and downright delicious is how I describe these ribs. I sometimes finish them in a slow cooker on low for 8-10 hours, instead of baking.
—*Susan Kinsella, East Falmouth, MA*

PREP: 30 MIN. • **BAKE:** 1½ HOURS • **MAKES:** 8 SERVINGS

- 4 lbs. bone-in beef short ribs
- 1 tsp. pepper, divided
- ½ tsp. salt
- 3 Tbsp. canola oil
- 3 celery ribs, chopped
- 2 large carrots, chopped
- 1 large yellow onion, chopped
- 1 medium sweet red pepper, chopped
- 1 garlic clove, minced
- 1 cup dry red wine or reduced-sodium beef broth
- 1 carton (32 oz.) reduced-sodium beef broth
- 1 fresh rosemary sprig
- 1 fresh oregano sprig
- 1 bay leaf

1. Preheat oven to 325°. Sprinkle short ribs with ½ tsp. pepper and salt. In an ovenproof Dutch oven over medium-high heat, brown the ribs in oil in batches. Remove meat and set aside. Add next 5 ingredients to drippings; cook until tender. Add the wine, stirring to loosen browned bits from pan. Bring to a boil; cook until liquid is reduced by half.

2. Return ribs to the pan. Add 4 cups broth, rosemary, oregano, bay leaf and remaining pepper; bring to a boil. Bake, covered, until meat is tender, 1½-2 hours. Remove ribs to a serving platter. Discard herbs. If desired, strain vegetables from the cooking liquid; skim fat and thicken for gravy.

1 SERVING 310 cal., 19g fat (7g sat. fat), 66mg chol., 507mg sod., 8g carb. (3g sugars, 2g fiber), 20g pro.

BAKED TILAPIA

I've decided to cook healthier for my family, and that includes having more fish at home. This is a great recipe, and it's fast too!
—*Hope Stewart, Raleigh, NC*

TAKES: 20 MIN. • **MAKES:** 4 SERVINGS

4 tilapia fillets (6 oz. each)
3 Tbsp. butter, melted
3 Tbsp. lemon juice
1½ tsp. garlic powder
⅛ tsp. salt
2 Tbsp. capers, drained
½ tsp. dried oregano
⅛ tsp. paprika

1. Place tilapia in an ungreased 13x9-in. baking dish. In a small bowl, combine butter, lemon juice, garlic powder and salt; pour over the fillets. Sprinkle with capers, oregano and paprika.

2. Bake, uncovered, at 425° until fish just begins to flake easily with a fork, 10-15 minutes.

1 FILLET 224 cal., 10g fat (6g sat. fat), 106mg chol., 304mg sod., 2g carb. (0 sugars, 0 fiber), 32g pro. **DIABETIC EXCHANGES** 4 lean meat, 2 fat.

MUGHLAI CHICKEN

I enjoy cooking for my family and try to add new healthy foods to our meals. This authentic Indian dish is a favorite.
—*Aruna Kancharla, Bentonville, AR*

TAKES: 30 MIN. • **MAKES:** 6 SERVINGS

4 cardamom pods
10 garlic cloves, peeled
6 whole cloves
4½ tsp. chopped fresh gingerroot
1 Tbsp. unblanched almonds
1 Tbsp. salted cashews
1 tsp. ground cinnamon
6 small red onions, halved and sliced
4 jalapeno peppers, seeded and finely chopped
¼ cup canola oil
3 Tbsp. water
1½ lbs. boneless skinless chicken breasts, cut into ½-in. cubes
1 cup coconut milk
1 cup plain yogurt
1 tsp. ground turmeric
Fresh cilantro leaves
Optional: Naan flatbreads or hot cooked basmati rice

1. Remove seeds from cardamom pods; place in a food processor. Add garlic, cloves, ginger, almonds, cashews and cinnamon; cover and process until blended. Set aside.

2. In a large skillet, saute the onions and jalapenos in oil until tender. Stir in water and the garlic mixture. Add the chicken, milk, yogurt and turmeric. Bring to a boil. Reduce heat; simmer, uncovered, until chicken juices run clear, 8-10 minutes. Sprinkle with cilantro. Serve with naan or rice if desired.

NOTE Wear disposable gloves when cutting hot peppers; the oils can burn skin. Avoid touching your face.

1 CUP 367 cal., 23g fat (10g sat. fat), 68mg chol., 93mg sod., 14g carb. (5g sugars, 3g fiber), 27g pro.

NOTES

MAIN COURSES 121

BEER-BATTERED FISH

Make your own fish fry at home using a classic beer batter. If you're not a drinker, nonalcoholic beer can be used. Serve with fries, coleslaw and rye bread for a traditional restaurant combo.
—Taste of Home *Test Kitchen*

PREP: 10 MIN. • **COOK:** 5 MIN./BATCH • **MAKES:** 4 SERVINGS

Oil for deep-fat frying
1 cup all-purpose flour
1½ tsp. baking powder
¾ tsp. salt
½ tsp. garlic powder
¼ tsp. paprika
¼ tsp. pepper
1 cup very cold beer or nonalcoholic beer
1 large egg, lightly beaten
4 cod fillets (6 oz. each)
Optional: Tartar sauce and lemon wedges

1. In an electric skillet or deep fryer, heat oil to 375°. In a shallow bowl, combine flour, baking powder and seasonings. Stir in beer and egg until smooth. Dip fillets in batter; allow excess to drip off.

2. Fry the fish in hot oil in batches until golden brown, 2-3 minutes on each side. Drain on paper towels. If desired, serve with tartar sauce and lemon wedges.

1 FILLET 338 cal., 20g fat (2g sat. fat), 79mg chol., 285mg sod., 8g carb. (1g sugars, 0 fiber), 28g pro.

READER REVIEW

"Love this recipe! Whether I'm in the mood for fish tacos or crispy battered fish, it's my go-to."

—KAREN9646, TASTEOFHOME.COM

made from scratch
CLASSIC TARTAR SAUCE

You'll never buy the jarred stuff again once you've tried this homemade tartar sauce recipe!
—*Michelle Stromko, Darlington, MD*

TAKES: 10 MIN. • **MAKES:** 1 CUP

⅔ cup chopped dill pickles
½ cup mayonnaise
3 Tbsp. finely chopped onion
Dash pepper

In a small bowl, combine all the ingredients. Cover and refrigerate until serving.

2 TBSP. 93 cal., 10g fat (2g sat. fat), 1mg chol., 167mg sod., 1g carb. (0 sugars, 0 fiber), 0 pro.

PANKO CHICKEN TENDERS

Crispy, savory and simple—what's not to like about chicken tenders? This lightened-up version is baked, not fried.
—*Margaret Knoebel, Milwaukee, WI*

TAKES: 30 MIN. • **MAKES:** 4 SERVINGS

¾ cup panko bread crumbs
2 large eggs
1 Tbsp. prepared mustard
½ tsp. garlic powder
½ tsp. dried oregano
½ tsp. salt
¼ tsp. pepper
1 lb. chicken tenderloins

1. In a small skillet, heat panko over medium heat. Stir consistently, until crumbs are toasted, about 3 minutes. Remove from pan, cool completely.

2. Preheat the oven to 400°. In a shallow bowl, whisk together eggs and mustard. In another shallow bowl, toss toasted panko with seasonings. Dip chicken in egg mixture, then coat with crumb mixture.

3. Place on a baking sheet coated with cooking spray. Bake until the coating is golden brown and chicken is no longer pink, 10-13 minutes.

3 OZ. COOKED CHICKEN 159 cal., 2g fat (0 sat. fat), 83mg chol., 495mg sod., 7g carb. (0 sugars, 0 fiber), 29g pro. **DIABETIC EXCHANGES** 3 lean meat, ½ starch.

---

made from scratch
COPYCAT MCDONALD'S SWEET & SOUR SAUCE

Re-create your favorite dipping sauce at home with this McDonald's copycat recipe. It's sweet and tangy, just like the real deal.
—Taste of Home *Test Kitchen*

TAKES: 15 MIN. • **MAKES:** 1¾ CUPS

1¼ cups apricot preserves
3 to 4 Tbsp. water
3 Tbsp. white vinegar
2 Tbsp. light corn syrup
1 Tbsp. cornstarch
1 tsp. yellow mustard
1 tsp. soy sauce
¼ tsp. garlic powder

Place all the ingredients in a blender; cover and blend until smooth. Transfer mixture to a small saucepan. Bring to a boil; cook and stir until thickened, 1-2 minutes. Refrigerate leftovers.

2 TBSP. 81 cal., 0 fat (0 sat. fat), 0 chol., 39mg sod., 21g carb. (15g sugars, 0 fiber), 0 pro.

SUNDAY PORK ROAST

Mom would prepare pork roast for our family, friends and customers at the three restaurants she and Dad owned. The herb rub and vegetables give it a remarkable flavor. It's one of my favorite pork roast recipes.
—Sandi Pichon, Memphis, TN

PREP: 20 MIN. • **BAKE:** 1¾ HOURS + STANDING • **MAKES:** 12 SERVINGS

- 2 medium onions, chopped
- 2 medium carrots, chopped
- 1 celery rib, chopped
- 4 Tbsp. all-purpose flour, divided
- 1 bay leaf, finely crushed
- ½ tsp. dried thyme
- 1¼ tsp. salt, divided
- 1¼ tsp. pepper, divided
- 1 boneless pork loin roast (3 to 4 lbs.)
- ⅓ cup packed brown sugar

ROAST TO YOUR HEALTH
Roasting is one of the healthiest ways to cook vegetables, as it typically uses less fat than sauteing and helps retain more nutrients than boiling would. The high heat caramelizes the outside, leaving the inside tender and delicious.

1. Preheat oven to 325°. Place vegetables on bottom of a shallow roasting pan. Mix 2 Tbsp. flour, bay leaf, thyme and 1 tsp. each salt and pepper; rub over roast. Place roast fat side up on top of the vegetables. Add 2 cups water to pan.

2. Roast, uncovered, 1½ hours. Sprinkle brown sugar over roast. Roast 15-20 minutes longer or until a thermometer reads 140°. (Temperature of roast will continue to rise another 5°-10° upon standing.)

3. Remove roast to a platter. Tent with foil; let stand 15 minutes before slicing.

4. Strain drippings from roasting pan into a measuring cup; skim fat. Add enough water to the drippings to measure 1½ cups.

5. In a small saucepan over medium heat, whisk remaining 2 Tbsp. flour and ⅓ cup water until smooth. Gradually whisk in the drippings mixture and remaining salt and pepper. Bring to a boil over medium-high heat, stirring constantly; cook and stir 2 minutes or until thickened. Serve roast with gravy.

FREEZE OPTION Freeze cooled sliced pork and gravy in freezer containers. To use, partially thaw in refrigerator overnight. Heat through in a covered saucepan, gently stirring; add broth or water if necessary.

3 OZ. COOKED PORK WITH ABOUT 2 TBSP. GRAVY 174 cal., 5g fat (2g sat. fat), 57mg chol., 280mg sod., 8g carb. (6g sugars, 0 fiber), 22g pro. **DIABETIC EXCHANGES** 3 lean meat, ½ starch.

MAIN COURSES 125

BEST LASAGNA

Want to make lasagna for a casual holiday meal? You can't go wrong with this deliciously rich and meaty lasagna. My grown sons and daughter-in-law request it for their birthdays too.
—Pam Thompson, Girard, IL

PREP: 1 HOUR • **BAKE:** 50 MIN. + STANDING • **MAKES:** 12 SERVINGS

- 9 lasagna noodles
- 1¼ lbs. bulk Italian sausage
- ¾ lb. ground beef
- 1 medium onion, diced
- 3 garlic cloves, minced
- 2 cans (one 28 oz., one 15 oz.) crushed tomatoes
- 2 cans (6 oz. each) tomato paste
- ⅔ cup water
- 2 to 3 Tbsp. sugar
- 3 Tbsp. plus ¼ cup minced fresh parsley, divided
- 2 tsp. dried basil
- ¾ tsp. fennel seed
- ¾ tsp. salt, divided
- ¼ tsp. coarsely ground pepper
- 1 large egg, lightly beaten
- 1 carton (15 oz.) ricotta cheese
- 4 cups shredded part-skim mozzarella cheese
- ¾ cup grated Parmesan cheese

1. Cook noodles according to package directions; drain. Meanwhile, in a Dutch oven, cook sausage, beef and onion over medium heat for 8-10 minutes or until meat is no longer pink, breaking up meat into crumbles. Add garlic; cook 1 minute. Drain.

2. Stir in tomatoes, tomato paste, water, sugar, 3 Tbsp. parsley, basil, fennel, ½ tsp. salt and pepper; bring to a boil. Reduce heat; simmer, uncovered, 30 minutes, stirring occasionally.

3. In a small bowl, mix the egg, ricotta cheese, remaining ¼ cup parsley and ¼ tsp. salt.

4. Preheat oven to 375°. Spread 2 cups meat sauce into an ungreased 13x9-in. baking dish. Layer with 3 noodles and a third of the ricotta mixture. Sprinkle with 1 cup mozzarella cheese and 2 Tbsp. Parmesan cheese. Repeat layers twice. Top with the remaining meat sauce and cheeses (dish will be full).

5. Bake, covered, 25 minutes. Bake, uncovered, 25 minutes longer or until bubbly. Let stand 15 minutes before serving. If desired, top with additional parsley and Parmesan cheese.

1 SERVING 519 cal., 27g fat (13g sat. fat), 109mg chol., 1013mg sod., 35g carb. (10g sugars, 4g fiber), 35g pro.

BAKED TERIYAKI SALMON

Need a quick, healthy weeknight meal? This easy, gluten-free, teriyaki flavored salmon is a must for your weeknight rotation. The glaze is sticky sweet and a perfect topper to this mild roasted salmon.
—*Karen Kelly, Germantown, MD*

PREP: 10 MIN. + MARINATING • **BAKE:** 10 MIN. • **MAKES:** 4 SERVINGS

- ¼ cup soy sauce
- 2 Tbsp. brown sugar or honey
- 3 garlic cloves, minced
- 1 Tbsp. sesame oil
- 4 salmon fillets (6 oz. each)

1. In a small bowl, combine soy sauce, brown sugar, garlic and oil until blended. Pour ¼ cup marinade into a large shallow dish. Add salmon; turn to coat. Refrigerate for up to 30 minutes. Cover and refrigerate remaining marinade.

2. Preheat oven to 400°. Drain salmon, discarding marinade in dish. Place the salmon skin side down on a greased baking sheet. Bake until the fish flakes easily with a fork, 10-12 minutes. Brush with reserved marinade.

1 FILLET 317 cal., 18g fat (4g sat. fat), 85mg chol., 775mg sod., 6g carb. (5g sugars, 0 fiber), 30g pro.

BISTRO MAC & CHEESE

I like mac and cheese with a salad and crusty bread. It's a satisfying meal that feels upscale but will fit just about any budget. And because the Gorgonzola is so mild in this dish, even the kiddos will go for it.
—Charlotte Giltner, Mesa, AZ

TAKES: 25 MIN. • **MAKES:** 8 SERVINGS

- 1 pkg. (16 oz.) uncooked elbow macaroni
- 5 Tbsp. butter, divided
- 3 Tbsp. all-purpose flour
- 2½ cups 2% milk
- 1 tsp. salt
- ½ tsp. onion powder
- ½ tsp. pepper
- ¼ tsp. garlic powder
- 1 cup shredded part-skim mozzarella cheese
- 1 cup shredded cheddar cheese
- ½ cup crumbled Gorgonzola cheese
- 3 oz. cream cheese, softened
- ½ cup sour cream
- ½ cup seasoned panko bread crumbs
  Minced fresh parsley, optional

1. Cook macaroni according to package directions; drain. Meanwhile, in a Dutch oven, melt 3 Tbsp. butter over low heat. Stir in the flour until smooth; gradually whisk in the milk and seasonings. Bring to a boil, stirring constantly; cook and stir for 2 minutes or until thickened.

2. Reduce heat; stir in the cheeses until melted. Stir in the sour cream. Add macaroni; toss to coat. In a small skillet, heat remaining butter over medium heat. Add the bread crumbs; cook and stir until golden brown. Sprinkle over top. If desired, sprinkle with parsley.

1 CUP 468 cal., 22g fat (14g sat. fat), 68mg chol., 649mg sod., 49g carb. (7g sugars, 2g fiber), 20g pro.

BAKED BISTRO MAC Place prepared macaroni in a greased 3-qt. baking dish. Combine ⅓ cup seasoned bread crumbs and 2 Tbsp. melted butter; sprinkle over macaroni. Bake, uncovered, at 350° for 20-25 minutes or until bubbly.

EASY & ELEGANT TENDERLOIN ROAST

I love the simplicity of the rub in this recipe—olive oil, garlic, salt and pepper. Just add the tenderloin, pop it in the oven and in about an hour, you'll have an impressive main dish to feed a crowd. This leaves you with more time to visit with family and less time fussing in the kitchen.
—Mary Kandell, Huron, OH

PREP: 10 MIN. • **BAKE:** 45 MIN. + STANDING • **MAKES:** 12 SERVINGS

- 1 beef tenderloin (5 lbs.)
- 2 Tbsp. olive oil
- 4 garlic cloves, minced
- 2 tsp. sea salt
- 1½ tsp. coarsely ground pepper

1. Preheat oven to 425°. Place roast on a rack in a shallow roasting pan. In a small bowl, mix oil, garlic, salt and pepper; rub over roast.

2. Roast until meat reaches desired doneness (for medium-rare, a thermometer should read 135°; medium, 140°; medium-well, 145°), 45-65 minutes. Remove from the oven; tent with foil. Let stand 15 minutes before slicing.

5 OZ. COOKED BEEF 294 cal., 13g fat (5g sat. fat), 82mg chol., 394mg sod., 1g carb. (0 sugars, 0 fiber), 40g pro.
DIABETIC EXCHANGES 5 lean meat, ½ fat.

MEDITERRANEAN RACK OF LAMB

It's elegant. It's special. And it'll have your guests thinking you went all out. They don't have to know how simple it really is!
—*Susan Nilsson, Sterling, VA*

PREP: 10 MIN. • **BAKE:** 30 MIN. • **MAKES:** 4 SERVINGS

2 racks of lamb (1½ lbs. each)
¼ cup grated lemon zest
¼ cup minced fresh oregano or 4 tsp. dried oregano
6 garlic cloves, minced
1 Tbsp. olive oil
¼ tsp. salt
¼ tsp. pepper
Optional: Fresh oregano and lemon wedges

1. Preheat oven to 375°. Place lamb in a shallow roasting pan. In a small bowl, combine lemon zest, oregano, garlic, oil, salt and pepper. Rub over the lamb.

2. Bake 30-40 minutes or until meat reaches the desired doneness (for medium-rare, a thermometer should read 135°; medium, 140°; medium-well, 145°). Let stand 5 minutes before cutting. If desired, serve with fresh oregano and lemon wedges.

½ RACK 307 cal., 19g fat (6g sat. fat), 100mg chol., 241mg sod., 3g carb. (0 sugars, 1g fiber), 30g pro.

made from scratch
MINT SAUCE FOR LAMB

This mint sauce recipe has been in our family for nearly 80 years. Our backyard mint patch provided the main ingredient. We won't eat lamb without it.
—*Ruth Bogdanski, Grants Pass, OR*

PREP: 10 MIN. + STANDING
MAKES: 6 SERVINGS

¼ cup loosely packed mint leaves, finely chopped
¼ cup boiling water
2 Tbsp. cider vinegar
2 Tbsp. sugar
¼ tsp. salt
⅛ tsp. pepper

Place mint leaves in a small bowl. Stir in the water, vinegar, sugar, salt and pepper until the sugar is dissolved. Cover and let steep for 20 minutes, then serve immediately with lamb.

1 TBSP. 19 cal., 0 fat (0 sat. fat), 0 chol., 100mg sod., 5g carb. (4g sugars, 0 fiber), 0 pro. **DIABETIC EXCHANGES** 1 free food.

MAIN COURSES   131

POTLUCK FRIED CHICKEN

This Sunday dinner staple is first fried and then baked to a crispy golden brown. Well-seasoned with oregano and sage, this classic is sure to satisfy diners at church potlucks or late-summer picnics. I love fixing it for family and friends.
—Donna Kuhaupt, Slinger, WI

PREP: 40 MIN. • **BAKE:** 25 MIN. • **MAKES:** 12 SERVINGS

- 1½ cups all-purpose flour
- ½ cup cornmeal
- ¼ cup cornstarch
- 3 tsp. salt
- 2 tsp. paprika
- 1 tsp. dried oregano
- 1 tsp. rubbed sage
- 1 tsp. pepper
- 2 large eggs
- ¼ cup water
- 2 broiler/fryer chickens (3 to 4 lbs. each), cut up
-   Oil for frying

1. In a large shallow dish, combine flour, cornmeal, cornstarch, salt, paprika, oregano, sage and pepper. In a shallow bowl, beat eggs and water. Dip chicken into egg mixture; place in flour mixture, a few pieces at a time, and turn to coat.

2. In an electric skillet, heat 1 in. oil to 375°. Fry chicken, a few pieces at a time, until golden and crispy, 3-5 minutes on each side.

3. Place in 2 ungreased 15x10x1-in. baking pans. Bake, uncovered, at 350° until juices run clear, 25-30 minutes.

5 OZ. COOKED CHICKEN 497 cal., 29g fat (6g sat. fat), 135mg chol., 693mg sod., 20g carb. (0 sugars, 1g fiber), 36g pro.

NOTES

THE BEST MARINARA SAUCE

A friend and I created this recipe to use up a bumper crop of tomatoes. Now, we make huge batches and gift jars with a pound of pasta around the holidays. Sharing this sauce, made with the best ingredients, with my family and friends brings me so much joy.
—Shannon Norris, Cudahy, WI

PREP: 1 HOUR + SIMMERING • **PROCESS:** 40 MIN. • **MAKES:** 9 CUPS

- 3 Tbsp. olive oil
- 1 cup chopped onion
- ⅓ cup minced garlic, divided
- 12 lbs. plum tomatoes, quartered
- 2 cups water
- 1¼ cups minced fresh basil, divided
- ¼ cup minced fresh oregano
- ¼ cup tomato paste
- 2 tsp. kosher salt
- 1 tsp. coarsely ground pepper
- ¼ cup plus 1½ tsp. bottled lemon juice

1. In a stockpot, heat oil over medium heat. Add onion; cook and stir until softened, 3-4 minutes. Add 2 Tbsp. garlic; cook 1 minute longer. Add the tomatoes, water and ½ cup basil; bring to a boil. Reduce heat; simmer, covered, until tomatoes are completely broken down and soft, about 1 hour, stirring occasionally.

2. Press tomato mixture through a food mill into a large bowl; discard skins and seeds. Return the tomato mixture to the stockpot; add ½ cup of remaining basil, oregano and remaining garlic. Bring to a boil. Reduce heat; simmer, uncovered, until thickened, 3½-4 hours, stirring occasionally. Add tomato paste and remaining ¼ cup of basil; season with salt and pepper.

3. Add 1 Tbsp. plus 1½ tsp. lemon juice to each of 3 hot 1½-pint jars. Ladle the hot mixture into the jars, leaving ½-in. headspace. Remove air bubbles and adjust headspace, if necessary, by adding hot mixture. Wipe the rims. Center lids on jars; screw on bands until fingertip tight.

4. Place jars into canner with simmering water, ensuring that they are completely covered with the water. Bring to a boil; process for 40 minutes. Remove jars and let them cool.

¾ CUP 131 cal., 4g fat (1g sat. fat), 0 chol., 348mg sod., 22g carb. (13g sugars, 6g fiber), 5g pro.

PLUM PICKINGS
Plum tomatoes really are the best variety for marinara sauce because they are meaty, have minimal seeds and create a rich red sauce that isn't too acidic. Start off with fresh whole tomatoes—seeds, skin and all. Skipping the peeling and deseeding not only saves time but also amps up the flavor of the sauce.

MAIN COURSES

HOMEMADE PASTA DOUGH

Once you try homemade pasta, you're hooked. Go for it!
—Kathryn Conrad, Milwaukee, WI

PREP: 15 MIN. + STANDING • **MAKES:** 6 SERVINGS

- 2 large eggs
- 1 large egg yolk
- ¼ cup water
- 1 Tbsp. olive oil
- ¼ tsp. salt
- ½ tsp. coarsely ground pepper, optional
- 1½ cups all-purpose flour
- ½ cup semolina flour

MAKE HOMEMADE PASTA WITH A STAND MIXER
Replace the pasta roller with the noodle-cutting attachment on your stand mixer. Feed the dough through to cut it into individual noodles. Once cut, toss the noodles with flour, so they don't stick together.

1. In a small bowl, whisk the first 5 ingredients and, if desired, pepper. On a clean work surface, mix flours, forming a mound. Make a large well in center. Pour egg mixture into well. Using a fork or your fingers, gradually mix flour mixture into egg mixture, forming a soft dough (dough will be slightly sticky).

2. Lightly dust the work surface with all-purpose flour; knead dough gently 5 times. Divide into 6 portions; cover and let rest 30 minutes.

3. To make fettuccine, roll each ball into a 10x8-in. rectangle, dusting lightly with the flour. Roll up jelly-roll style. Cut into ¼-in.-wide strips. Cook in boiling water 1-3 minutes.

1 SERVING 217 cal., 5g fat (1g sat. fat), 93mg chol., 124mg sod., 34g carb. (0 sugars, 1g fiber), 8g pro.

ROASTED CHICKEN WITH ROSEMARY

Herbs, garlic and butter give this hearty meal-in-one a classic flavor. It's a lot like pot roast, only it uses chicken instead of beef.
—Isabel Zienkosky, Salt Lake City, UT

PREP: 20 MIN. • **BAKE:** 2 HOURS + STANDING • **MAKES:** 9 SERVINGS

½ cup butter, cubed
4 Tbsp. minced fresh rosemary or
   2 Tbsp. dried rosemary, crushed
2 Tbsp. minced fresh parsley
1 tsp. salt
½ tsp. pepper
3 garlic cloves, minced
1 whole roasting chicken (5 to 6 lbs.)
6 small red potatoes, halved
6 medium carrots, halved lengthwise
   and cut into 2-in. pieces
2 medium onions, quartered

1. In a small saucepan, melt the butter; stir in the seasonings and garlic. Place the chicken breast side up on a rack in a shallow roasting pan; tie drumsticks together with kitchen string. Spoon half the butter mixture over chicken. Place the potatoes, carrots and onions around chicken. Drizzle the remaining butter mixture over vegetables.

2. Bake at 350° for 1½ hours. Baste with cooking juices; bake 30-60 minutes longer, basting occasionally, until a thermometer inserted in thickest part of thigh reads 170°-175°. (Cover loosely with foil if chicken browns too quickly.)

3. Let stand 10-15 minutes, tented with foil if necessary, before carving. Serve with vegetables.

1 SERVING 449 cal., 28g fat (11g sat. fat), 126mg chol., 479mg sod., 16g carb. (5g sugars, 3g fiber), 33g pro.

SHRIMP ALFREDO

Instead of buying a jar of Alfredo sauce, make it from scratch with this simple recipe. The garlic aroma will call your family to the table.
—Taste of Home *Test Kitchen*

TAKES: 30 MIN. • **MAKES:** 4 SERVINGS

8 oz. uncooked fettuccine
¼ cup butter, cubed
1½ cups heavy whipping cream
1 lb. cooked medium shrimp, peeled
   and deveined
¾ cup grated Parmesan cheese
1 garlic clove, minced
¼ tsp. pepper
1 tsp. minced fresh parsley
   Lemon wedges, optional

1. Cook fettuccine according to package directions. Meanwhile, in a large saucepan or skillet, melt the butter over medium heat. Stir in the cream. Bring to a gentle boil. Reduce heat; simmer, uncovered, 3 minutes, stirring constantly.

2. Add shrimp, cheese, garlic and pepper; cook and stir until heated through. Drain fettuccine; toss with shrimp mixture. Sprinkle with parsley; if desired, top with additional Parmesan cheese and serve with lemon wedges.

1 CUP 788 cal., 51g fat (31g sat. fat), 317mg chol., 573mg sod., 45g carb. (4g sugars, 2g fiber), 38g pro.

HAVE IT YOUR WAY
Try folding in fresh spinach for color and nutrition or fresh chopped basil for flavor. Drained chopped tomatoes or sauteed mushrooms work well, too. If pressed for time, you may use thawed shrimp.

PORK CHOPS & MUSHROOMS

My mother-in-law gave me this recipe years ago, and I've used it ever since. Tarragon is such a special flavor—my family loves it.
—*Hilary Rigo, Wickenburg, AZ*

TAKES: 25 MIN. • **MAKES:** 4 SERVINGS

- 4 boneless pork loin chops (6 oz. each)
- ¾ tsp. salt, divided
- ⅛ tsp. white pepper
- 3 tsp. butter, divided
- ¾ lb. sliced fresh mushrooms
- ½ cup dry white wine or reduced-sodium chicken broth
- ½ tsp. dried tarragon

1. Sprinkle the pork with ½ tsp. salt and white pepper. In a large nonstick skillet, heat 2 tsp. butter over medium heat. Add pork chops; cook 5-6 minutes on each side or until a thermometer reads 145°. Remove from pan.

2. In same skillet, heat the remaining butter over medium-high heat. Add mushrooms; cook and stir 6-8 minutes or until tender. Add the wine, tarragon and remaining salt, stirring to loosen browned bits from pan. Bring to a boil; cook until liquid is reduced by half. Return chops to pan; heat through.

1 PORK CHOP WITH ⅓ CUP MUSHROOMS 299 cal., 13g fat (5g sat. fat), 89mg chol., 515mg sod., 4g carb. (1g sugars, 1g fiber), 35g pro. **DIABETIC EXCHANGES** 5 lean meat, 1 vegetable, ½ fat.

COPYCAT HONEY BAKED HAM

For holidays and special occasions, my family loves a good old-fashioned baked ham. This one is really easy.
—*Donna Gribbins, Shelbyville, KY*

PREP: 10 MIN. • **COOK:** 4 HOURS 5 MIN. + STANDING • **MAKES:** 16 SERVINGS

- 1 spiral-sliced fully cooked bone-in ham (8 to 10 lbs.)
- 1 cup water
- ¾ cup honey, divided

GLAZE
- 1 cup sugar
- ½ tsp. ground cinnamon
- ½ tsp. ground allspice
- ½ tsp. pepper
- ½ tsp. paprika
- ¼ tsp. ground ginger
- ¼ tsp. ground nutmeg
- ¼ tsp. ground mustard
- ¼ tsp. Chinese five-spice powder
- ⅛ tsp. ground cloves

READER REVIEW

"I prepared this delicious ham today to test it out for upcoming holiday dinners, and it was a hit with everyone! It was perfectly moist, and the texture was spot-on."

—JELLYBUG, TASTEOFHOME.COM

1. In a 7-qt. slow cooker, place the ham and water. Brush the ham with ½ cup honey. Cook, covered, on low until a thermometer reads 140°, 4-5 hours.

2. Preheat broiler. Combine the glaze ingredients. Transfer ham to a rack in a shallow roasting pan, cut side down. Brush with the remaining ¼ cup honey; sprinkle with glaze mixture, pressing to adhere. Broil 6-8 in. from heat until lightly browned and sugar is melted, 3-5 minutes, rotating as needed. Cover with foil; let stand until glaze hardens, about 30 minutes.

5 OZ. COOKED HAM 288 cal., 6g fat (2g sat. fat), 100mg chol., 1192mg sod., 26g carb. (26g sugars, 0 fiber), 33g pro.

MAIN COURSES

HEARTY RAGU BOLOGNESE

My robust ragu combines ground beef, sausage and chicken. Enjoy it over pasta or polenta, or simply with hot buttered garlic bread.
—Caroline Brody, Forest Hills, NY

PREP: 20 MIN. • **COOK:** 3¾ HOURS • **MAKES:** 12 SERVINGS (2¼ QT.)

- 2 medium onions, coarsely chopped
- 2 celery ribs, coarsely chopped
- 1 medium carrot, coarsely chopped
- 4 garlic cloves, peeled
- 2 Tbsp. olive oil
- 1 Tbsp. butter
- ¼ tsp. ground nutmeg
- 1 lb. ground beef
- ¾ tsp. salt
- ½ tsp. pepper
- 1½ lbs. bulk Italian sausage
- 1 cup dry white wine
- 1 can (14½ oz.) beef broth
- ½ lb. boneless skinless chicken breasts
- 2 cups heavy whipping cream
- 3 cans (6 oz. each) tomato paste
- Hot cooked pasta
- Grated Parmesan cheese, optional

1. Place onions, celery, carrot and garlic in a food processor; pulse until finely chopped. In a Dutch oven, heat oil and butter over medium heat. Add vegetable mixture and nutmeg; cook and stir for 6-8 minutes or until the vegetables are softened.

2. Add beef; cook 6-8 minutes longer or until beef is no longer pink, breaking up beef into crumbles. Stir in the salt and pepper. Remove with a slotted spoon; discard drippings from pot.

3. In same pot, cook sausage over medium heat 6-8 minutes or until no longer pink, breaking into crumbles; drain. Return beef mixture to pan. Stir in the wine. Bring to a boil; cook and stir until wine is evaporated. Add broth and chicken breasts; return to a boil. Reduce heat; simmer, covered, 12-15 minutes or until a thermometer inserted in chicken reads 165°. Remove chicken; cool slightly. Finely chop chicken.

4. Add cream and tomato paste to pot; bring to a boil, stirring occasionally. Return chicken to the pot; reduce heat and simmer, covered, 3-4 hours or until flavors are blended, stirring occasionally. Serve with the pasta. If desired, sprinkle with Parmesan cheese.

FREEZE OPTION Freeze cooled sauce in freezer containers for up to 3 months. To use, partially thaw in the refrigerator overnight. Heat through in a saucepan, stirring occasionally; add broth if necessary.

¾ CUP 461 cal., 35g fat (16g sat. fat), 112mg chol., 712mg sod., 13g carb. (6g sugars, 2g fiber), 21g pro.

PORTOBELLO PIZZAS

Portobello mushroom caps are the creative crust in this upscale spin on pizza.
I also cut the caps into wedges and serve them as an appetizer.

—*Lisa Scheevel, LeRoy, MN*

TAKES: 30 MIN. • **MAKES:** 6 SERVINGS

6 large portobello mushrooms (4 to 4½ in.), stems removed
1 Tbsp. olive oil
1 lb. bulk Italian sausage
1 can (15 oz.) pizza sauce
1 medium green pepper, chopped
1 medium onion, chopped
½ cup chopped fresh mushrooms
¼ cup grated Parmesan cheese
2 garlic cloves, minced
1 cup shredded part-skim mozzarella cheese
  Thinly sliced fresh basil leaves, optional

1. Place mushrooms stem side down on a greased baking sheet; drizzle with oil. Bake at 350° for 20-25 minutes or until tender, turning once.

2. Meanwhile, cook the sausage over medium heat until no longer pink; drain. Stir in the pizza sauce, pepper, onion, mushrooms, Parmesan cheese and garlic. Divide among the mushrooms; sprinkle with mozzarella cheese. Broil 2-3 in. from heat for 1-2 minutes or until cheese is melted. Sprinkle with basil if desired.

1 PIZZA 353 cal., 24g fat (8g sat. fat), 56mg chol., 899mg sod., 16g carb. (6g sugars, 3g fiber), 18g pro.

made from scratch
HOMEMADE PIZZA SAUCE

For years, I had trouble finding a pizza sauce my family likes, so I started making my own. The evening I served it to company and they asked for my recipe, I knew I'd finally gotten it right! I usually fix enough for three to four pizzas and freeze it. Feel free to spice it up to suit your family's tastes.

—*Cheryl Kravik, Spanaway, WA*

PREP: 10 MIN. • **COOK:** 70 MIN.
MAKES: ABOUT 4 CUPS

2 cans (15 oz. each) tomato sauce
1 can (12 oz.) tomato paste
1 Tbsp. Italian seasoning
1 Tbsp. dried oregano
1 to 2 tsp. fennel seed, crushed
1 tsp. onion powder
1 tsp. garlic powder
½ tsp. salt

In a large saucepan over medium heat, combine tomato sauce and paste. Add remaining ingredients; mix well. Bring to a boil, stirring constantly. Reduce heat; cover and simmer for 1 hour, stirring occasionally.

¼ CUP 26 cal., 0 fat (0 sat. fat), 0 chol., 189mg sod., 6g carb. (3g sugars, 2g fiber), 1g pro.

MAIN COURSES

CLASSIC COTTAGE PIE

A combination of ground lamb and mashed potatoes topped with a bubbling layer of cheese is the perfect comfort food. It's a good remedy for the winter chills.
—*Shannon Copley, Upper Arlington, OH*

PREP: 45 MIN. • **BAKE:** 20 MIN. • **MAKES:** 6 SERVINGS

- 1 lb. ground beef or lamb
- 2 medium carrots, finely chopped
- 1 medium onion, finely chopped
- 2 Tbsp. all-purpose flour
- 2 Tbsp. minced fresh parsley
- 1 Tbsp. Italian seasoning
- ¾ tsp. salt
- ¼ tsp. pepper
- 1 Tbsp. tomato paste
- 1 tsp. brown sugar
- 1½ cups reduced-sodium beef broth
- 2 Tbsp. dry red wine or additional reduced-sodium beef broth
- ½ cup frozen peas

TOPPING
- 4 medium potatoes, peeled and cubed
- ½ cup 2% milk
- ¼ cup butter, cubed
- ¾ cup shredded cheddar cheese, divided
- ¼ tsp. salt
- ⅛ tsp. pepper

Make your own Homemade Beef Broth. Recipe on p. 103.

1. In a large skillet, cook beef, carrots and onion over medium heat until meat is no longer pink and vegetables are tender; drain. Stir in flour, parsley, Italian seasoning, salt and pepper until blended. Add the tomato paste and brown sugar; gradually add broth and wine, stirring to combine. Bring to a boil. Reduce the heat; simmer, uncovered, 10-15 minutes or until thickened, stirring occasionally. Stir in peas.

2. Meanwhile, place potatoes in a large saucepan and cover with water. Bring to a boil. Reduce heat; cover and cook 10-15 minutes or until tender.

3. Preheat oven to 400°. Transfer meat mixture into a greased 9-in. deep-dish pie plate. Drain potatoes; mash with milk and butter. Stir in ½ cup cheese, salt and pepper. Spread over meat mixture; sprinkle with remaining ¼ cup cheese.

4. Place the pie plate on a foil-lined baking sheet (plate will be full). Bake it for 20-25 minutes or until the top is golden brown.

1 SERVING 403 cal., 22g fat (11g sat. fat), 84mg chol., 740mg sod., 30g carb. (6g sugars, 3g fiber), 21g pro.

from scratch
SIDES & SALADS

DAD'S GREEK SALAD, PAGE 154

HOMEMADE TATER TOTS

If you love using Tater Tots as a crunchy topping for Tater Tot hot dish and casseroles, the next step is making them from scratch. It's surprisingly simple, and once you master the basic technique, you can make them your own!
—Taste of Home *Test Kitchen*

PREP: 20 MIN. • **COOK:** 5 MIN./BATCH • **MAKES:** 6 SERVINGS

Oil for deep-fat frying
2 lbs. russet potatoes, peeled and cut into 1-in. pieces
2 Tbsp. minced fresh parsley or 2 tsp. dried parsley flakes
1 Tbsp. cornstarch
1 tsp. kosher salt
½ tsp. onion powder
¼ tsp. pepper
Optional: Sriracha mayonnaise or ranch dressing

1. In an electric skillet or deep fryer, heat oil to 350°. Place potatoes in a bowl of cold water and stir for 15 seconds. Drain potatoes; pat dry with paper towels. Fry potatoes in batches in oil until lightly browned, 6-8 minutes. Remove with a slotted spoon; drain on paper towels.

2. Increase the heat to 375°. In batches, place the potatoes in a food processor. Pulse until the potatoes are ⅛-to-¼-in. pieces. Transfer to a large bowl. Stir in the remaining ingredients. Shape 1 Tbsp. potato mixture into 1-in. long cylinder. Repeat with remaining mixture.

3. Fry the Tots in oil in batches until crisp and golden brown, 4-5 minutes, turning frequently. Drain Tots on paper towels; serve immediately. If desired, sprinkle with additional salt and minced parsley and serve with Sriracha mayonnaise or ranch dressing.

FREEZE OPTION Freeze unfried, shaped Tots on a baking sheet; freeze until firm, at least 1 hour. Transfer frozen Tater Tots to a freezer container and store for up to 3 months. Fry frozen Tots in 375° oil until golden brown, 6-8 minutes.

6 TOTS 173 cal., 9g fat (1g sat. fat), 0 chol., 324mg sod., 22g carb. (2g sugars, 2g fiber), 2g pro.

made from scratch RANCH DRESSING

Why buy bottled ranch dressing when the from-scratch version is so easy to make (and tastes so much better)? Fresh chives are a colorful addition if you have them on hand.
—Taste of Home *Test Kitchen*

TAKES: 10 MIN. • **MAKES:** 1 CUP

⅔ cup buttermilk
½ cup mayonnaise
½ cup sour cream
2 Tbsp. minced fresh parsley
2 garlic cloves, minced
½ tsp. sugar
1 tsp. dill weed
½ tsp. salt
½ tsp. onion powder
½ tsp. ground mustard
¼ tsp. pepper

In a bowl, combine all ingredients. Whisk until smooth. Cover and refrigerate until serving.

2 TBSP. 66 cal., 7g fat (2g sat. fat), 3mg chol., 131mg sod., 1g carb. (1g sugars, 0 fiber), 1g pro.

AIR-FRYER SWEET POTATO FRIES

I can never get enough of these sweet potato fries! Even though my grocery store sells them in the frozen foods section, I still love to pull sweet potatoes out of my garden and slice them up fresh!
—Amber Massey, Argyle, TX

TAKES: 20 MIN. • **MAKES:** 4 SERVINGS

- 2 large sweet potatoes, cut into thin strips
- 2 Tbsp. canola oil
- 1 tsp. garlic powder
- 1 tsp. paprika
- 1 tsp. kosher salt
- ¼ tsp. cayenne pepper

Preheat air fryer to 400°. Combine all the ingredients; toss to coat. Place on a greased tray in air-fryer basket. Cook until lightly browned, 10-12 minutes, stirring once. Serve immediately.

1 SERVING 243 cal., 7g fat (1g sat. fat), 0 chol., 498mg sod., 43g carb. (17g sugars, 5g fiber), 3g pro.

WHAT GOES WELL WITH SWEET POTATO FRIES?

Burgers and sweet potato fries are a classic duo, but don't stop there. They are perfect with pub fare such as fried fish, chicken tenders or hearty sandwiches. For a lighter, healthier meal, pair them with grilled chicken, seafood, sheet-pan suppers and other quick entrees.

EDDIE'S FAVORITE FIESTA CORN

When sweet corn is available, I love making this splurge of a side dish.
Frozen corn works, but taste as you go and add sugar if needed.
—*Anthony Bolton, Bellevue, NE*

PREP: 15 MIN. • **COOK:** 25 MIN. • **MAKES:** 8 SERVINGS

½ lb. bacon strips, chopped
5 cups fresh or frozen super sweet corn
1 medium sweet red pepper, finely chopped
1 medium sweet yellow pepper, finely chopped
1 pkg. (8 oz.) reduced-fat cream cheese
½ cup half-and-half cream
1 can (4 oz.) chopped green chiles, optional
2 tsp. sugar
1 tsp. pepper
¼ tsp. salt

1. In a 6-qt. stockpot, cook the bacon over medium heat until crisp, stirring occasionally. Remove with a slotted spoon; drain on paper towels. Discard drippings, reserving 1 Tbsp. in pan.

2. Add the corn, red pepper and yellow pepper to the drippings; cook and stir over medium-high heat until tender, 5-6 minutes. Stir in the cream cheese, half-and-half, chiles if desired, sugar, pepper and salt until blended; bring to a boil. Reduce heat; simmer, covered, until thickened, 8-10 minutes.

⅔ CUP 249 cal., 14g fat (7g sat. fat), 39mg chol., 399mg sod., 22g carb. (9g sugars, 2g fiber), 10g pro.

READER REVIEW

"I've made this fabulous recipe at least a dozen times! Perfect to pair with enchiladas or grilled steak. It tastes even better when made ahead and reheated to let the flavors meld."

—HUGOFLA, TASTEOFHOME.COM

JEN'S BAKED BEANS

My daughters wanted baked beans, so I gave homemade ones a shot. With mustard,
molasses and a dash of heat, I made these beans absolutely irresistible.
—*Jennifer Heasley, York, PA*

PREP: 20 MIN. • **BAKE:** 50 MIN. • **MAKES:** 8 SERVINGS

6 bacon strips, chopped
4 cans (15½ oz. each) great northern beans, rinsed and drained
1⅓ cups ketchup
⅔ cup packed brown sugar
⅓ cup molasses
3 Tbsp. yellow mustard
2½ tsp. garlic powder
1½ tsp. hot pepper sauce
¼ tsp. crushed red pepper flakes

1. Preheat oven to 325°. In an ovenproof Dutch oven, cook bacon over medium heat until crisp, stirring occasionally. Remove with a slotted spoon; drain on paper towels. Discard drippings.

2. Return bacon to pan. Stir in remaining ingredients; bring to a boil. Place in oven; bake, covered, 50-60 minutes to allow flavors to blend.

FREEZE OPTION Freeze cooled baked beans in freezer containers. To use, partially thaw in refrigerator overnight. Heat through in a saucepan, stirring occasionally. Add broth or water if necessary.

¾ CUP 362 cal., 3g fat (1g sat. fat), 6mg chol., 1000mg sod., 71g carb. (39g sugars, 11g fiber), 13g pro.

SIDES & SALADS

KENTUCKY SPOON BREAD

This is a traditional Kentucky recipe. Softer and creamier than cornbread, it's a popular side dish served all year long. If you've never tried spoon bread before, I think you'll enjoy it!
—Caroline Brown, Lexington, KY

PREP: 20 MIN. • **BAKE:** 40 MIN. • **MAKES:** 8 SERVINGS

- 4 cups 2% milk, divided
- 1 cup cornmeal
- 3 tsp. sugar
- 1 tsp. salt
- ½ tsp. baking powder
- 2 Tbsp. butter
- 3 large eggs, separated

NOTES

1. In a large saucepan, heat 3 cups milk over medium heat until bubbles form around side of pan.

2. Meanwhile, in a small bowl, combine cornmeal, sugar, salt and remaining 1 cup milk until smooth. Slowly whisk cornmeal mixture into hot milk. Cook and stir until mixture comes to a boil. Reduce heat; simmer for 5 minutes, stirring constantly.

3. Remove from heat. Sprinkle baking powder over cornmeal mixture, then stir it in with the butter. In a small bowl, beat egg yolks; stir in a small amount of hot cornmeal mixture. Return all to the pan and mix well.

4. In a small bowl, beat egg whites until stiff peaks form. Fold a fourth of the egg whites into the cornmeal mixture. Fold in the remaining egg whites until blended.

5. Transfer to a greased 2½-qt. baking dish. Bake, uncovered, at 350° for 40-45 minutes or until puffed and golden brown. Serve immediately.

1 SERVING 192 cal., 7g fat (4g sat. fat), 87mg chol., 433mg sod., 23g carb. (8g sugars, 1g fiber), 8g pro.

SIDES & SALADS

HONEY CHIPOTLE VINAIGRETTE

We've all been there. It's 7 p.m., and you're at home with a sudden craving for Chipotle. You don't feel like going all the way to Chipotle, they don't have a drive-thru and delivery is kind of slow. What's a hungry person to do? You make an at-home Chipotle salad complete with a copycat version of their Honey Chipotle Vinaigrette! It's one of our favorite homemade salad dressings.
—*Lauren Habermehl, Pewaukee, WI*

TAKES: 15 MIN. • **MAKES:** 1 CUP

- ⅓ cup red wine vinegar
- 3 Tbsp. honey
- 1 chipotle pepper in adobo sauce
- 1½ tsp. adobo sauce
- 1 tsp. garlic powder
- 1 tsp. ground cumin
- ¾ tsp. salt
- ½ tsp. dried oregano
- ¼ tsp. pepper
- ½ cup extra virgin olive oil

In a blender or food processor, combine first 9 ingredients; puree until smooth. With the motor running, slowly drizzle in olive oil.

2 TBSP. 152 cal., 14g fat (2g sat. fat), 0 chol., 253mg sod., 8g carb. (7g sugars, 0 fiber), 0 pro.

NO PROCESSOR? NO PROBLEM!

You can make the chipotle vinaigrette using a Mason jar or any small container with a tight lid. Finely mince the whole chipotle pepper, mix everything in the jar, seal it up and shake until well mixed.

TANGY MACARONI SALAD

Classic macaroni salad is a potluck staple. It's not only easy to make ahead and transport but also a perfect side for grilled meats or sandwiches.

—Taste of Home *Test Kitchen*

PREP: 20 MIN. + CHILLING • **COOK:** 15 MIN. • **MAKES:** 11 SERVINGS

- 1 pkg. (16 oz.) elbow macaroni
- 1 cup mayonnaise
- 2 Tbsp. cider vinegar
- 1 Tbsp. sugar
- 2 tsp. yellow mustard
- 1½ tsp. salt
- ¼ tsp. pepper
- 1 medium sweet red pepper, chopped
- ½ cup finely chopped red onion
- 1 celery rib, finely chopped
- 2 hard-boiled large eggs, chopped

1. Cook macaroni according to package directions. Drain; rinse with cold water and drain again.

2. In a small bowl, mix the mayonnaise, vinegar, sugar, mustard, salt and pepper until blended. In a large bowl, combine the macaroni, sweet red pepper, onion, celery and eggs. Add the dressing; toss gently to coat. Cover and refrigerate at least 1 hour before serving.

1 CUP 305 cal., 17g fat (3g sat. fat), 41mg chol., 451mg sod., 33g carb. (3g sugars, 2g fiber), 7g pro.

ORZO WITH PARMESAN & BASIL

Basil adds its rich flavor to this creamy and delicious skillet side dish that's table-ready in just minutes!

—*Anna Chaney, Antigo, WI*

TAKES: 20 MIN. • **MAKES:** 4 SERVINGS

- 1 cup uncooked orzo pasta or pearl couscous
- 2 Tbsp. butter
- 1 can (14½ oz.) chicken broth
- ½ cup grated Parmesan cheese
- 2 tsp. dried basil
- ⅛ tsp. pepper
  Thinly sliced fresh basil, optional

Make your own Homemade Chicken Broth. Recipe on p. 92.

1. In a large cast-iron or other heavy skillet, saute orzo in butter until lightly browned, 3-5 minutes.

2. Stir in the broth and bring to a boil. Reduce heat; cover and simmer until liquid is absorbed and orzo is tender, 10-15 minutes. Stir in cheese, basil and pepper. If desired, top with fresh basil.

½ CUP 285 cal., 10g fat (5g sat. fat), 26mg chol., 641mg sod., 38g carb. (2g sugars, 1g fiber), 11g pro.

CORN & PEPPER ORZO Omit Parmesan cheese, basil and pepper. Prepare orzo as directed in recipe. In a large skillet coated with cooking spray, saute 1 chopped large red sweet pepper and 1 chopped medium onion in 1 Tbsp. olive oil. Stir in 2 cups thawed frozen corn, 2 tsp. Italian seasoning and ⅛ tsp. each salt and pepper. Stir into cooked orzo. Yield: 6 servings.

SIDES & SALADS   153

DAD'S GREEK SALAD

The heart of a Greek salad is in the olives, feta and fresh veggies. Dress it with oil and vinegar, then add more olives and cheese.
—*Arge Salvatori, Waldwick, NJ*

TAKES: 20 MIN. • **MAKES:** 8 SERVINGS

- 4 large tomatoes, seeded and coarsely chopped
- 2½ cups thinly sliced English cucumbers
- 1 small red onion, halved and thinly sliced
- ¼ cup olive oil
- 3 Tbsp. red wine vinegar
- ¼ tsp. salt
- ⅛ tsp. pepper
- ¼ tsp. dried oregano, optional
- ¾ cup pitted Greek olives
- ¾ cup crumbled feta cheese

Place tomatoes, cucumbers and onion in a large bowl. In a small bowl, whisk the oil, vinegar, salt and pepper and, if desired, oregano until blended. Drizzle over salad; toss to coat. Top with olives and cheese.

¾ CUP 148 cal., 12g fat (2g sat. fat), 6mg chol., 389mg sod., 7g carb. (3g sugars, 2g fiber), 3g pro. **DIABETIC EXCHANGES** 2 vegetable, 2 fat.

NOTES

HERBED ONION SALAD DRESSING

My dad is an excellent cook, and this is one of his favorites.
The slightly sweet dressing has plenty of onion flavor and a tasty blend of herbs.
—*Nancy Fettig, Billings, MT*

TAKES: 10 MIN. • **MAKES:** 4 CUPS

½ cup cider vinegar
1½ cups sugar
1 large onion, cut into wedges
2 tsp. salt
1 tsp. celery seed
1 tsp. ground mustard
¼ tsp. each dried basil, marjoram, oregano and thyme
¼ tsp. dried rosemary, crushed
¼ tsp. pepper
2 cups canola oil

In a blender, combine vinegar, sugar and onion; cover and process until smooth. Add the seasonings; cover and blend well. While processing, gradually add oil in a steady stream until dressing is thickened. Store in the refrigerator.

2 TBSP. 160 cal., 14g fat (2g sat. fat), 0 chol., 148mg sod., 10g carb. (10g sugars, 0 fiber), 0 pro.

READER REVIEW

"I love this salad dressing recipe! It's easy and makes a quart, perfect for how much everyone enjoys it."

—KATHARINELHIDDINK, TASTEOFHOME.COM

CRANBERRY WILD RICE

Cranberries and red onion make this wild rice recipe colorful and perfect for fall.
Don't skip toasting the pine nuts—the flavor boost is well worth the effort.
—*Dawn E. Bryant, Thedford, NE*

PREP: 15 MIN. • **COOK:** 50 MIN. • **MAKES:** 4 SERVINGS

4 cups water
¾ cup uncooked wild rice
1 small red onion, chopped
½ cup chopped dried cranberries
1 tsp. dried thyme
1 Tbsp. olive oil
3 garlic cloves, minced
2 Tbsp. pine nuts, toasted

1. In a large saucepan, bring the water and rice to a boil. Reduce heat; simmer, uncovered, for 50-60 minutes or until rice is tender.

2. In a large skillet, saute the onion, cranberries and thyme in oil until onion is tender. Add the garlic; cook 1 minute longer. Drain rice if needed; stir in onion mixture and pine nuts.

NOTE Also known as pignolia or pinon, pine nuts are edible seeds of pine trees. These small, ivory-colored seeds are about ⅜ in. long, with a soft texture and buttery flavor. Common in Italian dishes and sauces such as pesto, they are often toasted to enhance their flavor.

¾ CUP 238 cal., 6g fat (1g sat. fat), 0 chol., 1mg sod., 42g carb. (11g sugars, 3g fiber), 6g pro.

HOMEMADE POTATO GNOCCHI

My Italian mother remembers her mother making these dumplings for special occasions. She still has the bowl Grandma mixed the dough in, which will be passed down to me some day.
—Tina Mirilovich, Johnstown, PA

PREP: 30 MIN. • **COOK:** 10 MIN./BATCH • **MAKES:** 8 SERVINGS

- 4 medium potatoes, peeled and quartered
- 1 egg, lightly beaten
- 1½ tsp. salt, divided
- 1¾ to 2 cups all-purpose flour
- Spaghetti sauce, warmed
- Optional: Grated Parmesan cheese, crushed red pepper flakes and fresh herbs, such as basil, oregano or parsley

1. Place the potatoes in a saucepan and cover with water. Bring to a boil. Reduce heat; cover and cook for 15-20 minutes or until tender. Drain and mash.

2. Place 2 cups mashed potatoes in a large bowl (save any remaining mashed potatoes for another use). Stir in egg and 1 tsp. salt. Gradually beat in flour until blended (dough will be firm and elastic).

3. Turn onto a lightly floured surface; knead 15 times. Roll into ½-in.-wide ropes. Cut ropes into 1-in. pieces. Press down on each piece with a lightly floured fork.

4. In a Dutch oven, bring 3 qt. water and remaining salt to a boil. Add gnocchi in small batches; cook for 8-10 minutes or until gnocchi float to top and are cooked through. Remove with a slotted spoon. Serve immediately with spaghetti sauce. Add toppings as desired.

1 SERVING 159 cal., 1g fat (0 sat. fat), 27mg chol., 674mg sod., 33g carb. (1g sugars, 2g fiber), 5g pro.

SIDES & SALADS

CAESAR SALAD

Make the ultimate Caesar salad with fresh and flavorful ingredients. The secret is in the dressing, where lemon juice, red wine vinegar, anchovy paste, garlic and more come together to create that creamy, tangy taste.
—*JoLynn Unruh, Dumas, AR*

TAKES: 20 MIN. • **MAKES:** 4 SERVINGS

3 large pasteurized egg yolks
2 garlic cloves
2 Tbsp. lemon juice
2 Tbsp. red wine vinegar
1 Tbsp. anchovy paste
2 tsp. Dijon mustard
1 tsp. Worcestershire sauce
¼ tsp. salt
¼ tsp. coarsely ground pepper
Dash hot pepper sauce, optional
½ cup olive oil
¼ cup grated Parmesan cheese

SALAD
2 large bunches romaine chopped
1 cup salad croutons
¼ cup shaved Parmesan cheese

1. Place first 9 ingredients in a blender; cover and process until smooth. Add hot sauce if desired. While processing, gradually add oil in a steady stream. Stir in Parmesan cheese. Chill until serving.

2. Place romaine into a large salad bowl. Drizzle with the dressing; toss to coat. Sprinkle with croutons and Parmesan.

1 SERVING 411 cal., 36g fat (7g sat. fat), 161mg chol., 763mg sod., 14g carb. (2g sugars, 4g fiber), 10g pro.

made from scratch
SALAD CROUTONS

Homemade croutons are a delight to serve with your favorite mixed green salad or as a crunchy snack. These well-seasoned salad toppers will set you back a mere 4 cents per serving!
—*Fayne Lutz, Taos, NM*

TAKES: 25 MIN.
MAKES: 6 SERVINGS

1 Tbsp. olive oil
1 garlic clove, minced
1 cup cubed day-old bread
Pinch onion salt

Pour the oil into an 8-in. square baking pan; add garlic. Bake at 325° until garlic is lightly browned, 3-4 minutes. Add bread and onion salt; stir to coat. Bake until bread is lightly browned, 10-12 minutes longer, stirring frequently. Store in an airtight container.

2 TBSP. 36 cal., 2g fat (0 sat. fat), 0 chol., 50mg sod., 3g carb. (0 sugars, 0 fiber), 1g pro.

STRAWBERRY SALAD WITH POPPY SEED DRESSING

My family is always happy to see this fruit and veggie salad. If strawberries aren't available, substitute mandarin oranges and dried cranberries.
—Irene Keller, Kalamazoo, MI

TAKES: 30 MIN. • **MAKES:** 10 SERVINGS

- ¼ cup sugar
- ⅓ cup slivered almonds
- 1 bunch romaine, torn (about 8 cups)
- 1 small onion, halved and thinly sliced
- 2 cups halved fresh strawberries

DRESSING
- ¼ cup mayonnaise
- 2 Tbsp. sugar
- 1 Tbsp. sour cream
- 1 Tbsp. 2% milk
- 2¼ tsp. cider vinegar
- 1½ tsp. poppy seeds

1. Place sugar in a small heavy skillet; cook and stir over medium-low heat until melted and caramel-colored, about 10 minutes. Stir in almonds until coated. Spread on foil to cool.

2. Place romaine, onion and strawberries in a large bowl. Whisk together dressing ingredients; toss with salad. Break the candied almonds into pieces; sprinkle over salad. Serve immediately.

¾ CUP 110 cal., 6g fat (1g sat. fat), 1mg chol., 33mg sod., 13g carb. (10g sugars, 2g fiber), 2g pro. **DIABETIC EXCHANGES** 1 vegetable, 1 fat, ½ starch.

HEALTH TIP Turn this potluck salad into something heartier. Grill 2 lbs. boneless skinless chicken breasts, slice and add to the salad for 10 main-dish servings.

SOUTHERN VINEGAR SLAW

This tangy coleslaw has been a favorite from my recipe box for years! Before I retired, it was always a hit at office potlucks. My family loves it too.
—Fern Hammock, Garland, TX

PREP: 20 MIN. + CHILLING • **MAKES:** 16 SERVINGS

- 12 cups shredded cabbage (1 medium head)
- 1 green pepper, chopped
- 1 large sweet onion, chopped
- 2 carrots, shredded

DRESSING
- 1 cup sugar
- 1 cup white vinegar
- ¾ cup canola oil
- 1 tsp. salt
- 1 tsp. celery seed
- 1 tsp. ground mustard

In a large bowl, combine the first 4 ingredients. In a small saucepan, combine dressing ingredients; bring to a boil. Cook and stir until sugar is dissolved. Pour over cabbage mixture; toss to coat. Cover and refrigerate until chilled, 2-3 hours. Stir well before serving. Serve with a slotted spoon.

1 CUP 167 cal., 11g fat (1g sat. fat), 0 chol., 164mg sod., 18g carb. (14g sugars, 2g fiber), 1g pro.

SOUTHERN VINEGAR SLAW WITH COLESLAW MIX?

Absolutely! Shredding cabbage is quick, but coleslaw mix saves even more time. Many slaw mixes already contain carrots and red cabbage, so you can leave out the carrots in the recipe, unless you'd like a little extra in every bite.

SIDES & SALADS 161

BAKED MAC & CHEESE

Even people who have had their own homemade macaroni and cheese recipe for years ask for mine when they taste this crumb-topped version. Bake it with extra-sharp white cheddar for more flavor.
—*Shelby Thompson, Dover, DE*

PREP: 15 MIN. • **BAKE:** 30 MIN. • **MAKES:** 8 SERVINGS

- 1 pkg. (16 oz.) uncooked elbow macaroni
- ⅓ cup plus ¼ cup butter, divided
- ¾ cup finely chopped onion
- 6 Tbsp. all-purpose flour
- 1 tsp. ground mustard
- ¾ tsp. salt
- ¼ tsp. pepper
- 4½ cups 2% milk
- 4 cups shredded sharp cheddar cheese
- ¾ cup dry bread crumbs

1. Preheat oven to 350°. Cook macaroni according to the package directions for al dente; drain.

2. In a Dutch oven, heat ⅓ cup butter over medium heat; saute the onion until tender. Stir in flour and seasonings until blended; gradually stir in milk. Bring to a boil, stirring constantly; cook and stir until thickened. Stir in the cheese until melted. Stir in macaroni. Transfer to a greased 13x9-in. baking dish.

3. In a microwave, melt remaining butter; toss with bread crumbs. Sprinkle over casserole. Bake, uncovered, until heated through, 30-35 minutes.

1 CUP 688 cal., 37g fat (21g sat. fat), 103mg chol., 839mg sod., 63g carb. (10g sugars, 3g fiber), 27g pro.

GINGER DRESSING

I love this flavorful dressing because it's quick to make with pantry staples—perfect with salad greens or veggies on a weeknight.
—Rashanda Cobbins, Aurora, CO

TAKES: 10 MIN. • **MAKES:** 1½ CUPS

- ⅓ cup rice vinegar
- 3 Tbsp. finely chopped onion
- 2 Tbsp. minced fresh gingerroot
- 2 Tbsp. soy sauce
- 1 Tbsp. honey
- ¼ tsp. pepper
- ¾ cup olive oil or peanut oil

In a blender, combine first 6 ingredients; cover and process until blended. While processing, gradually add oil in a steady stream. Chill until serving.

2 TBSP. 137 cal., 14g fat (2g sat. fat), 0 chol., 260mg sod., 4g carb. (4g sugars, 0 fiber), 0 pro.

MISSING THE ZING?

Ginger dressing lasts for up to a week in the refrigerator. Homemade salad dressings typically don't last as long as store-bought ones, so keep them in an airtight jar and check for freshness before use.

HOMEMADE PIEROGI

Pierogi are dumplings or tiny pies stuffed with a filling. These are a family favorite.
—Diane Gawrys, Manchester, TN

PREP: 1 HOUR • **COOK:** 5 MIN./BATCH • **MAKES:** 6 DOZEN

- 5 cups all-purpose flour
- 1 tsp. salt
- 1 cup water
- 3 large eggs, room temperature
- ½ cup butter, softened

FILLING
- 4 medium potatoes, peeled and cubed
- 2 medium onions, chopped
- 2 Tbsp. butter
- 5 oz. cream cheese, softened
- ½ tsp. salt
- ½ tsp. pepper

ADDITIONAL INGREDIENTS (FOR EACH SERVING)
- ¼ cup chopped onion
- 1 Tbsp. butter
- Minced fresh parsley

1. In a food processor, combine flour and salt; cover and pulse to blend. Add water, eggs and butter; cover and pulse until dough forms a ball, adding an additional 1-2 Tbsp. water or flour if needed. Let rest, covered, 15-30 minutes.

2. Place potatoes in a large saucepan and cover with water. Bring to a boil over high heat. Reduce the heat; cover and simmer until tender, 10-15 minutes. Meanwhile, in a large skillet over medium-high heat, saute onions in butter until tender.

3. Drain the potatoes. Over very low heat, stir potatoes until steam has evaporated, 1-2 minutes. Press through a potato ricer or strainer into a large bowl. Stir in the cream cheese, salt, pepper and onion mixture.

4. Divide dough into 4 parts. On a lightly floured surface, roll 1 portion of dough to ⅛-in. thickness; cut with a floured 3-in. biscuit cutter. Place 2 tsp. filling in center of each circle. Moisten edges with water; fold in half and press the edges to seal. Repeat with remaining dough and filling.

5. Fill a Dutch oven half full with water. Bring to a boil over high heat; add pierogi in batches. Reduce the heat to a gentle simmer; cook until pierogi float to the top and are tender, 1-2 minutes. Remove with a slotted spoon. In a large skillet, saute 4 pierogi and onion in butter until pierogi are lightly browned and heated through; sprinkle with parsley. Repeat with the remaining pierogi.

FREEZE OPTION Place cooled pierogi on waxed paper-lined 15x10x1-in. baking pans; freeze until firm. Transfer to an airtight freezer container; freeze up to 3 months. To use, for each serving, in a large skillet, saute 4 pierogi and ¼ cup chopped onion in 1 Tbsp. butter until pierogi are lightly browned and heated through; sprinkle with minced fresh parsley.

4 PIEROGI 373 cal., 22g fat (13g sat. fat), 86mg chol., 379mg sod., 38g carb. (3g sugars, 2g fiber), 6g pro.

SIDES & SALADS

MAMA'S POTATO SALAD

This old-fashioned potato salad may not be as colorful as many modern ones, but Mama made it the way her mother did, and that's the way I still make it today. Give it a try—it might just be the best-tasting potato salad you've ever had!
—*Sandra Anderson, New York, NY*

TAKES: 30 MIN. • **MAKES:** 12 SERVINGS

- 3 to 3½ lbs. potatoes (about 10 medium)
- 6 hard-boiled large eggs
- 1 medium onion, finely chopped
- ½ cup mayonnaise
- ½ cup evaporated milk
- 3 Tbsp. white vinegar
- 2 Tbsp. prepared mustard
- ¼ cup sugar
- 1 tsp. salt
- ¼ tsp. pepper
- Additional hard-boiled large eggs, sliced
- Paprika

1. In a large kettle, cook potatoes in boiling salted water until tender. Drain and cool. Peel potatoes; cut into chunks. Separate egg yolks from whites. Set yolks aside. Chop whites and add to potatoes with onion.

2. In a small bowl, mash yolks. Stir in mayonnaise, milk, vinegar, mustard, sugar, salt and pepper. Pour over the potatoes; toss well. Adjust seasonings if necessary. Spoon into a serving bowl. Garnish with the egg slices and paprika. Chill until serving.

1 CUP 231 cal., 11g fat (2g sat. fat), 113mg chol., 323mg sod., 27g carb. (8g sugars, 2g fiber), 6g pro.

NOTES

SIDES & SALADS

SPANISH RICE

You'll find that my Spanish rice is so much better than any boxed variety in grocery stores. Best of all, it can be prepared in about the same time as those so-called convenience foods, using items in your pantry.
—Anne Yaeger, Washington DC

TAKES: 25 MIN. • **MAKES:** 6 SERVINGS

¼ cup butter, cubed
2 cups uncooked instant rice
1 can (14½ oz.) diced tomatoes, undrained
1 cup boiling water
2 beef bouillon cubes
1 medium onion, chopped
1 garlic clove, minced
1 bay leaf
1 tsp. sugar
1 tsp. salt
¼ tsp. pepper

In a saucepan, melt butter over medium heat. Add rice; cook and stir until lightly browned. Add the remaining ingredients; bring to a boil. Reduce heat; cover and simmer until the liquid is absorbed and rice is tender, 10-15 minutes. Remove bay leaf before serving.

¾ CUP 217 cal., 8g fat (5g sat. fat), 20mg chol., 886mg sod., 33g carb. (4g sugars, 2g fiber), 4g pro.

GARLIC MASHED RED POTATOES

These creamy garlic mashed potatoes are so good, you can serve them without butter or gravy. This is the only way I make my mashed potatoes.
—Valerie Mitchell, Olathe, KS

TAKES: 30 MIN. • **MAKES:** 6 SERVINGS

8 medium red potatoes, quartered
3 garlic cloves, peeled
2 Tbsp. butter
½ cup fat-free milk, warmed
½ tsp. salt
¼ cup grated Parmesan cheese

1. Place potatoes and garlic in a large saucepan; cover with water. Bring to a boil. Reduce heat; cover and simmer for 15-20 minutes or until potatoes are very tender.

2. Drain well. Add the butter, milk and salt; mash. Stir in cheese.

1 CUP 190 cal., 5g fat (3g sat. fat), 14mg chol., 275mg sod., 36g carb. (0 sugars, 4g fiber), 8g pro. **DIABETIC EXCHANGES** 2 starch, ½ fat.

GET YOUR MASH ON!

For fluffy mashed potatoes, warm the milk and butter before adding them to the potatoes. Mash gently, just until combined—overworking the potatoes will make them gummy. This little trick gives them a light, creamy texture.

RUSTIC TOMATO PIE

Perk up your plate with this humble tomato pie. We like to use fresh-from-the-garden tomatoes and herbs, but store-bought produce will work in a pinch.
—Taste of Home *Test Kitchen*

PREP: 15 MIN. **BAKE:** 30 MIN. + STANDING • **MAKES:** 8 SERVINGS

- Dough for single-crust pie
- 1¾ lbs. mixed tomatoes, seeded and cut into ½-in. slices
- ¼ cup thinly sliced green onions
- ½ cup mayonnaise
- ½ cup shredded cheddar cheese
- 2 Tbsp. minced fresh basil
- ¼ tsp. salt
- ¼ tsp. pepper
- 2 bacon strips, cooked and crumbled
- 2 Tbsp. grated Parmesan cheese

1. Preheat oven to 400°. On a lightly floured surface, roll the dough to a ⅛-in.-thick circle; transfer to a 9-in. pie plate. Trim crust to ½ in. beyond the rim of plate.

2. Place half the tomatoes and half the green onion in crust. Combine mayonnaise, cheddar cheese, basil, salt and pepper; spread over tomatoes. Top with the remaining green onion and tomatoes. Fold crust edge over filling, pleating as you go and leaving an 8-in. opening in center. Sprinkle with bacon and Parmesan cheese. Bake on a lower oven rack until crust is golden and filling is bubbly, 30-35 minutes. Let stand for 10 minutes before cutting. If desired, sprinkle with additional basil.

1 PIECE 325 cal., 25g fat (11g sat. fat), 41mg chol., 409mg sod., 19g carb. (3g sugars, 2g fiber), 6g pro.

made from scratch DOUGH FOR SINGLE-CRUST PIE

Combine 1¼ cups all-purpose flour and ¼ tsp. salt; cut in ½ cup cold butter until crumbly. Gradually add 3-5 Tbsp. ice water, tossing with a fork until dough holds together when pressed. Shape into a disk; wrap and refrigerate 1 hour.

SIDES & SALADS   169

from scratch
BREADS, BISCUITS & MORE

CHALLAH, PAGE 188

FOCACCIA

Focaccia is one of my favorite breads, not just for its flavor but also for being the least labor-intensive—no heavy kneading required. After years of adjusting the quantities, I'm happy where this recipe is at. The dough is very wet, perfect for a tender yet chewy bread with a distinct salty bite.
—James Schend, Pleasant Prairie, WI

PREP: 30 MIN. + RISING • **BAKE:** 20 MIN. • **MAKES:** 1 LOAF (24 PIECES)

- 1 pkg. (¼ oz.) active dry yeast
- 1¼ cups warm water (110° to 115°)
- 1 Tbsp. honey
- 3 cups all-purpose flour
- ¼ cup plus 3 Tbsp. olive oil, divided
- ¾ tsp. kosher salt
- 1 tsp. flaky sea salt, optional

1. In a large bowl, dissolve yeast in ½ cup warm water and honey; let stand 5 minutes. Add flour, ¼ cup oil, kosher salt and remaining ¾ cup warm water; mix until smooth (dough will be wet). Scrape the side of the bowl clean; cover and let rise in a warm place until doubled, about 45 minutes.

2. Preheat oven to 425°. Brush a 13x9-in. baking dish or 12-in. cast-iron skillet with 1 Tbsp. oil. Gently scrape dough directly into the pan. With oiled hands, gently spread dough. If dough springs back, wait 10 minutes and stretch again. Make indentations in the dough with your fingers. Drizzle with remaining 2 Tbsp. oil; let rise until doubled in size, 30-40 minutes.

3. If desired, sprinkle with sea salt. Bake until golden brown, 20-25 minutes. Cut into squares; serve warm.

1 PIECE 95 cal., 4g fat (1g sat. fat), 0 chol., 61mg sod., 13g carb. (1g sugars, 1g fiber), 2g pro.

BUTTERY CORNBREAD

A friend gave me this recipe several years ago, and it's my favorite. I love to serve the melt-in-your-mouth cornbread hot from the oven with butter and syrup. It gets rave reviews on holidays and at potluck dinners.
—Nicole Callen, Auburn, CA

PREP: 15 MIN. • **BAKE:** 25 MIN. • **MAKES:** 15 SERVINGS

- 2/3 cup butter, softened
- 1 cup sugar
- 3 large eggs, room temperature
- 1 2/3 cups 2% milk
- 2 1/3 cups all-purpose flour
- 1 cup cornmeal
- 4 1/2 tsp. baking powder
- 1 tsp. salt

1. Preheat oven to 400°. In a large bowl, cream butter and sugar until light and fluffy, 5-7 minutes. Combine the eggs and milk. Combine the flour, cornmeal, baking powder and salt; add to creamed mixture alternately with egg mixture.

2. Pour into a greased 13x9-in. baking pan. Bake for 22-27 minutes or until a toothpick inserted in center comes out clean. Cut into squares; serve warm.

1 PIECE 262 cal., 10g fat (6g sat. fat), 61mg chol., 395mg sod., 38g carb. (15g sugars, 1g fiber), 5g pro.

READER REVIEW

"This has been my go-to recipe for years, always a hit at family meals and potlucks. I love its sweetness and moistness—it's perfect crumbled over chili or served with butter and honey."
—SHARON3089, TASTEOFHOME.COM

JOSH'S MARBLED RYE BREAD

This impressive marble rye bread may look complex but is surprisingly easy to make! With mild yet satisfying flavors, the bread is perfect with a simple spread of butter or for a hearty sandwich loaded with your favorite fixings.
—*Josh Rink, Milwaukee, WI*

PREP: 50 MIN. + RISING • **BAKE:** 45 MIN. + COOLING • **MAKES:** 1 LOAF (16 PIECES)

- 5 cups bread flour, divided
- 2 cups plus 1 Tbsp. rye flour, divided
- ½ cup potato flour
- ⅓ cup nonfat dry milk powder
- 2 Tbsp. sugar
- 2 Tbsp. caraway seeds
- 3 tsp. instant or quick-rise yeast
- 2½ tsp. onion powder
- 2 tsp. salt
- 2¾ cups warm water (110° to 115°)
- ¼ cup canola oil
- 2 Tbsp. dark baking cocoa
- 1 large egg, lightly beaten with 1 Tbsp. water

1. In a large bowl, whisk together 4 cups bread flour, 2 cups rye flour, potato flour, milk powder, sugar, caraway seeds, yeast, onion powder and salt. In another bowl, whisk warm water and oil; pour over the flour mixture and stir until combined (dough will be sticky). Turn dough onto a lightly floured surface; with floured hands, knead the dough, incorporating remaining 1 cup bread flour as needed until dough becomes smooth and elastic, 8-10 minutes. Divide dough in half. Mix dark cocoa powder with remaining 1 Tbsp. rye flour; knead cocoa mixture into 1 portion of dough until fully incorporated.

2. Lightly coat 2 large bowls with oil. Place 1 portion of dough into each bowl and turn to coat. Cover and allow dough to rise until doubled in size, 1-1½ hours. Working with 1 portion of dough at a time, turn onto a lightly floured surface; roll each into a 14x12-in. rectangle. Place dough with cocoa on top of remaining dough; starting with a long side, roll jelly-roll style to form a spiral, pinching seam together to seal. Place seam side down in a greased 13x4-in. Pullman loaf pan, tucking ends under to form smooth loaf. Loosely cover pan with damp cloth and allow to rise until doubled in size, 1-1½ hours; dough should rise about ½ in. above edge of loaf pan.

3. Brush loaf with egg wash; using a sharp knife, cut 3-4 deep diagonal slashes on top of the loaf. Cover with nonstick foil and place in a preheated 400° oven; bake 15 minutes. Reduce heat to 375°; bake 20 minutes. Remove foil; bake until the loaf is deep golden brown and a thermometer reads 200°, about 10 minutes longer. Remove from oven; allow to cool 10 minutes. Remove loaf from pan. Cool completely on wire rack.

1 PIECE 273 cal., 5g fat (1g sat. fat), 12mg chol., 312mg sod., 49g carb. (3g sugars, 4g fiber), 8g pro.

BREADS, BISCUITS & MORE

SWEET POTATO BISCUITS WITH HONEY BUTTER

Why not give sweet potatoes a starring role at your dining table? Served with cinnamon-honey butter, these biscuits are downright surprising and delicious.
—*Cathy Bell, Joplin, MO*

TAKES: 30 MIN. • **MAKES:** 15 BISCUITS (ABOUT ½ CUP HONEY BUTTER)

- 2 cups all-purpose flour
- 4 tsp. sugar
- 3 tsp. baking powder
- 1 tsp. salt
- 1 tsp. ground cinnamon
- ½ tsp. ground nutmeg
- ¼ cup shortening
- 1 cup mashed sweet potatoes
- ½ cup half-and-half cream

HONEY BUTTER
- ½ cup butter, softened
- 2 Tbsp. honey
- 1 tsp. ground cinnamon

1. In a small bowl, combine the first 6 ingredients. Cut in shortening until mixture resembles coarse crumbs. Combine sweet potatoes and cream; stir into the crumb mixture just until moistened. Turn onto a lightly floured surface; gently knead 8-10 times.

2. Pat or roll out to ½-in. thickness; cut with a floured 2½-in. biscuit cutter. Reroll and repeat once. Place 1 in. apart on a greased baking sheet.

3. Bake at 400° for 9-11 minutes or until golden brown. Meanwhile, in a small bowl, beat butter, honey and cinnamon until blended. Serve with warm biscuits.

1 BISCUIT WITH 1½ TSP. BUTTER 186 cal., 10g fat (5g sat. fat), 20mg chol., 312mg sod., 21g carb. (5g sugars, 1g fiber), 2g pro.

BREADS, BISCUITS & MORE

HONEY-KISSED SAVORY SHORTBREAD CRACKERS

Homemade crackers may seem like a lot of effort, but these honey-kissed shortbread crackers are worth it. Crispy, cheesy, salty with a sweet honey finish, they're basically cracker perfection.
—Colleen Delawder, Herndon, VA

PREP: 45 MIN. • **BAKE:** 15 MIN./BATCH + COOLING • **MAKES:** 7 DOZEN

- 1 cup unsalted butter, softened
- ⅓ cup minced fresh parsley
- 2 cups all-purpose flour
- 1 Tbsp. sugar
- 1 tsp. paprika
- ½ tsp. kosher salt
- ½ tsp. garlic powder
- ½ tsp. pepper
- 1 cup grated shredded cheddar cheese
- ¼ cup heavy whipping cream

HONEY-KISSED TOPPING
- 1 Tbsp. unsalted butter
- 1 Tbsp. honey
- ⅔ cup confectioners' sugar
- ⅓ cup minced fresh parsley
- Flaky sea salt, such as Maldon, optional

1. Preheat oven to 350°. In a large bowl, beat butter for 2 minutes. Mix in parsley. In another bowl, whisk the flour, sugar, paprika, kosher salt, garlic powder and pepper. Add cheese; toss to coat. Add to butter mixture alternately with cream, beating until mixture comes together. Divide dough into 3 portions.

2. On a lightly floured surface, roll each portion of dough to ¼-in. thickness. Cut with a floured 1½-in. round cookie cutter. Place 1 in. apart on parchment-lined baking sheets. Reroll and refrigerate scraps as needed. Bake until crisp, 15-20 minutes. Cool completely on wire racks.

3. In a microwave, melt butter and honey; stir until smooth. Stir in confectioners' sugar until smooth; fold in parsley. Top crackers with honey mixture; if desired, sprinkle with flaky sea salt. Let stand until set. Store between layers of waxed paper in an airtight container at room temperature.

1 CRACKER 45 cal., 3g fat (2g sat. fat), 8mg chol., 21mg sod., 4g carb. (1g sugars, 0 fiber), 1g pro.

RHUBARB ROSEMARY FLATBREAD

I love the simple ingredients and flavor combination in this recipe. Using rhubarb in a savory bread is unexpected, but it never fails to impress!
—*Maryalice Wood, Langley, BC*

PREP: 35 MIN. + RISING • **BAKE:** 15 MIN. • **MAKES:** 8 SERVINGS

- 1 Tbsp. quick-rise yeast
- 1 tsp. sugar
- 1 cup warm water (110° to 115°)
- 3 to 4 rhubarb ribs, trimmed
- 3 to 3½ cups all-purpose flour
- 4 Tbsp. olive oil, divided
- 1½ tsp. sea salt, divided
- 3 fresh rosemary sprigs, divided
- 1 large egg
- ⅛ tsp. freshly ground pepper
- Honey, optional

1. In a small bowl, dissolve yeast and sugar in the warm water. Meanwhile, finely chop enough rhubarb to measure ½ cup; set aside. Slice each remaining rhubarb rib lengthwise into 4 thin strips; cut strips into 4-in. pieces; reserve for topping.

2. In a large bowl, combine 2 cups flour, 2 Tbsp. oil, 1 tsp. salt, reserved chopped rhubarb and the yeast mixture. Remove and finely chop rosemary leaves from 2 sprigs (discard stems); add to flour mixture. Beat on medium speed until smooth. Stir in enough remaining flour to form a soft dough (dough will be sticky).

3. Turn dough onto a floured surface; knead until smooth and elastic, 6-8 minutes. Place in a greased bowl, turning once to grease top. Cover and let rise in a warm place until doubled, about 25 minutes.

4. Preheat oven to 450°. Punch down the dough. Turn onto a lightly floured surface; divide into 4 portions. Roll each portion to a 7x5-in. rectangle. Place on a parchment-lined baking sheet. In a small bowl, whisk egg with remaining 2 Tbsp. oil; roll reserved rhubarb strips in the egg wash. Gently press 3-5 strips into the top of each piece of dough. Brush remaining egg wash over tops. Remove leaves from the remaining rosemary sprig; sprinkle leaves over tops (discard stem). Sprinkle with remaining ½ tsp. salt and pepper.

5. Bake until golden brown and rhubarb is tender, 13-15 minutes. If desired, drizzle with honey before serving.

½ FLATBREAD 251 cal., 8g fat (1g sat. fat), 23mg chol., 372mg sod., 38g carb. (1g sugars, 2g fiber), 6g pro.

BREADS, BISCUITS & MORE 179

QUICK JALAPENO HUSH PUPPIES

The crunchy exterior of this southern-style snack is a nice contrast to the moist cornbread. Jalapeno peppers and hot sauce add a hint of heat.
—Taste of Home *Test Kitchen*

PREP: 15 MIN. • **COOK:** 5 MIN./BATCH • **MAKES:** 2½ DOZEN

1½ cups yellow cornmeal
½ cup all-purpose flour
1 tsp. baking powder
1 tsp. salt
2 large eggs, room temperature, lightly beaten
¾ cup 2% milk
2 jalapeno peppers, seeded and minced
¼ cup finely chopped onion
1 tsp. Louisiana-style hot sauce
Oil for deep-fat frying

1. In a large bowl, combine cornmeal, flour, baking powder and salt. In another bowl, beat eggs, milk, jalapenos, onion and hot sauce. Stir into dry ingredients just until combined.

2. In a cast-iron or other heavy skillet, heat the oil to 375°. Drop the batter by tablespoonfuls, a few at a time, into the hot oil. Fry until golden brown, about 5 minutes on each side. Drain on paper towels. Serve warm.

NOTE Wear disposable gloves when cutting hot peppers; the oils can burn skin. Avoid touching your face.

1 HUSH PUPPY 56 cal., 3g fat (0 sat. fat), 14mg chol., 94mg sod., 7g carb. (0 sugars, 1g fiber), 1g pro.

made from scratch HOMEMADE SPICY HOT SAUCE

I created this spicy recipe using fresh picks from my garden—hot peppers, carrots, onions and garlic. The carrots make it stand out.
—Carolyn Wheel, Venice, FL

PREP: 45 MIN. • **PROCESS:** 10 MIN. • **MAKES:** 5 HALF-PINTS

20 habanero peppers (4½ oz.)
5 serrano peppers (2½ oz.)
15 dried arbol chiles
2 large carrots (5½ oz.), peeled, halved lengthwise and quartered
1 large sweet onion (15 oz.), cut into 8 wedges
8 garlic cloves, halved
1 cup water
¾ cup white vinegar (minimum 5% acetic acid)
½ cup fresh lime juice
3 tsp. salt
1 tsp. coarsely ground pepper

1. Cut habanero and serrano peppers in half; discard the stems and seeds. In a bowl, combine arbol chiles and enough boiling water to cover. Let stand, covered, 10 minutes; drain.

2. Meanwhile, in a well-ventilated area, fill a 6-qt. stockpot three-quarters with water; bring to a boil. Add the carrots, onion and garlic. Return to a boil; cook until soft, 20-22 minutes. Remove with a slotted spoon to a bowl. Add peppers to the stockpot; return to a boil. Boil for 1 minute; drain. Place the water, vinegar, lime juice, salt and pepper in a blender. Add vegetables; cover and process until smooth. Return to the stockpot; bring to a boil.

3. Carefully ladle the mixture into 5 hot half-pint jars, leaving ½-in. headspace. Remove air bubbles, and adjust headspace by adding hot mixture if necessary. Wipe rims. Center lids on jars; screw on bands until fingertip tight.

4. Place the jars into a canner with simmering water, ensuring that they are completely covered with water. Bring to a boil; process 10 minutes. Remove jars and cool.

1 TSP. 3 cal., 0 fat (0 sat. fat), 0 chol., 30mg sod., 1g carb. (0 sugars, 0 fiber), 0 pro.

THIN CRUST PIZZA DOUGH

My family loves pizza, and this crust is our go-to recipe.
It is healthier and less expensive than delivery and tastes so much better.
—*Theresa Rohde, Scottville, MI*

PREP: 10 MIN. + RESTING • **MAKES:** 2 LBS. (ENOUGH FOR FOUR 12-IN. PIZZAS)

3½ cups bread flour
1 cup whole wheat flour
5 tsp. quick-rise yeast
1 tsp. salt
1 tsp. honey
1½ to 1⅔ cups warm water (120° to 130°)

1. Place flours, yeast and salt in a food processor; pulse until blended. Add the honey. While processing, gradually add the water until a ball forms. Continue processing 60 seconds to knead dough.

2. Turn dough onto a floured surface; shape into a ball. Cover; let rest for 10 minutes. Divide dough into quarters. Use immediately or freeze for later use.

FREEZE OPTION Place each portion of dough in an airtight container; freeze up to 1 month. To use, thaw in the refrigerator overnight. Proceed as directed.

¼ OF 1 PIZZA CRUST 139 cal., 1g fat (0 sat. fat), 0 chol., 149mg sod., 28g carb. (0 sugars, 2g fiber), 5g pro.

BEST-EVER BANANA BREAD

Whenever I pass a display of bananas in the grocery store, I can almost smell the wonderful aroma of this bread. It really is good!
—*Gert Kaiser, Kenosha, WI*

PREP: 15 MIN. • **BAKE:** 1¼ HOURS + COOLING • **MAKES:** 1 LOAF (16 PIECES)

1¾ cups all-purpose flour
1½ cups sugar
1 tsp. baking soda
½ tsp. salt
2 large eggs, room temperature
2 medium ripe bananas, mashed (1 cup)
½ cup canola oil
¼ cup plus 1 Tbsp. buttermilk
1 tsp. vanilla extract
1 cup chopped walnuts, optional

1. Preheat oven to 350°. In a large bowl, stir together flour, sugar, baking soda and salt. In another bowl, combine eggs, bananas, oil, buttermilk and vanilla; add to the flour mixture, stirring just until combined. If desired, fold in the nuts.

2. Pour the batter into a greased or parchment-lined 9x5-in. loaf pan. Bake until a toothpick comes out clean, 1¼-1½ hours. Cool in pan for 15 minutes before removing to a wire rack.

1 PIECE 257 cal., 13g fat (1g sat. fat), 23mg chol., 171mg sod., 34g carb. (21g sugars, 1g fiber), 4g pro.

READER REVIEW

"This recipe is superb; easy to mix and prepare! I sometimes add about ½ cup of mini semisweet chocolate chips along with the nuts for chocolate lovers."

—LVARNER, TASTEOFHOME.COM

BASIC HOMEMADE BREAD

If you'd like to learn how to make bread, here's a wonderful place to start. This easy recipe bakes up deliciously golden brown. There's nothing like the homemade aroma wafting through my kitchen as it bakes.
—Sandra Anderson, New York, NY

PREP: 20 MIN. + RISING • **BAKE:** 30 MIN. • **MAKES:** 2 LOAVES (16 PIECES EACH)

- 1 pkg. (¼ oz.) active dry yeast
- 3 Tbsp. plus ½ tsp. sugar
- 2¼ cups warm water (110° to 115°)
- 1 Tbsp. salt
- 6¼ to 6¾ cups bread flour
- 2 Tbsp. canola oil

1. In a large bowl, dissolve yeast and ½ tsp. sugar in warm water; let stand until bubbles form on surface. Whisk salt, 3 cups flour and remaining 3 Tbsp. sugar. Stir oil into yeast mixture; pour into flour mixture and beat until smooth. Stir in enough remaining flour, ½ cup at a time, to form a soft dough.

2. Turn out onto a floured surface; knead until smooth and elastic, 8-10 minutes. Place in a greased bowl, turning once to grease the top. Cover and let rise in a warm place until doubled, 1½-2 hours.

3. Punch dough down. Turn onto a lightly floured surface; divide the dough in half. Shape each into a loaf. Place in 2 greased 9x5-in. loaf pans. Cover and let rise until doubled, 1-1½ hours.

4. Bake at 375° for 30-35 minutes or until loaf is golden brown and sounds hollow when tapped or a thermometer reads 200°. Remove from pans to wire racks to cool.

1 PIECE 102 cal., 1g fat (0 sat. fat), 0 chol., 222mg sod., 20g carb. (1g sugars, 1g fiber), 3g pro.

IT'S THE YEAST YOU CAN DO!

Yeast can be tricky to work with at first, but once you master proofing it, you should be all set. The trick is to get the water temperature just right—never go above 110°. Excessive heat can kill the yeast.

CINNAMON SWIRL BREAKFAST BREAD

My aunt gave me the recipe for these rich, flavorful loaves many years ago.
I use my bread machine for the first step in the recipe.
—*Peggy Burdick, Burlington, MI*

PREP: 20 MIN. + RISING • **BAKE:** 30 MIN. • **MAKES:** 2 LOAVES (16 PIECES EACH)

- 1 cup warm 2% milk (70° to 80°)
- ¼ cup water (70° to 80°)
- 2 large eggs, room temperature
- ¼ cup butter, softened
- 1 tsp. salt
- ¼ cup sugar
- 5 cups bread flour
- 2¼ tsp. active dry yeast

FILLING
- 2 Tbsp. butter, melted
- ⅓ cup sugar
- 1 Tbsp. ground cinnamon

GLAZE
- 1 cup confectioners' sugar
- ½ tsp. vanilla extract
- 4 to 5 tsp. milk

1. In the bread machine pan, place the first 8 ingredients in order suggested by manufacturer. Select dough setting (check dough after 5 minutes of mixing; add 1-2 Tbsp. water or flour if needed).

2. When cycle is completed, turn dough onto a lightly floured surface; divide in half. Roll each portion into a 10x8-in. rectangle. Brush with butter. Combine sugar and cinnamon; sprinkle over the dough.

3. Roll up tightly jelly-roll style, starting with a short side. Pinch the seams and ends to seal. Place seam side down in 2 greased 9x5-in. loaf pans. Cover and let rise in a warm place until doubled, about 1 hour. Preheat oven to 350°.

4. Bake for 25 minutes. Cover with foil; bake until golden brown, 5-10 minutes longer. Remove from pans to wire racks to cool completely.

5. In a large bowl, mix the confectioners' sugar, vanilla and enough milk to achieve desired consistency; drizzle over warm loaves.

1 PIECE 121 cal., 3g fat (2g sat. fat), 20mg chol., 104mg sod., 22g carb. (7g sugars, 1g fiber), 3g pro.

BREADS, BISCUITS & MORE

BUTTERY CROISSANTS

A traditional roll like this is always a welcome addition to dinner. The recipe makes a big batch, so it's great for entertaining.
—Loraine Meyer, Bend, OR

PREP: 1 HOUR + CHILLING • **BAKE:** 15 MIN./BATCH • **MAKES:** ABOUT 3 DOZEN

1½ cups butter, softened
⅓ cup all-purpose flour

DOUGH
1 pkg. (¼ oz.) active dry yeast
¼ cup warm water (110° to 115°)
1 cup warm 2% milk (110° to 115°)
¼ cup sugar
1 large egg, room temperature
1 tsp. salt
3½ to 3¾ cups all-purpose flour

1. In a small bowl, beat butter and flour until combined; spread into a 12x6-in. rectangle on a piece of waxed paper. Cover with another piece of waxed paper; refrigerate for at least 1 hour.

2. In a large bowl, dissolve the yeast in warm water. Add the milk, sugar, egg, salt and 2 cups flour; beat until smooth. Stir in enough remaining flour to form a soft dough. Turn onto a floured surface; knead until smooth and elastic, about 6-8 minutes.

3. Roll the dough into a 14-in. square. Remove top sheet of waxed paper from butter; invert onto half of dough. Remove waxed paper. Fold dough over the butter; seal edges.

4. Roll into a 20x12-in. rectangle. Fold into thirds. Repeat rolling and folding twice. (If the butter softens, chill after folding.) Cover and refrigerate overnight.

5. Unwrap dough. On a lightly floured surface, roll into a 25x20-in. rectangle. Cut into 5-in. squares. Cut each square diagonally in half, forming 2 triangles.

6. Roll up triangles from the wide end; place 2 in. apart with point down on ungreased baking sheets. Curve ends down to form crescent shape. Cover and let rise until doubled, about 45 minutes.

7. Bake at 375° until golden brown, 12-14 minutes. Remove to wire racks. Serve warm.

1 CROISSANT 115 cal., 7g fat (4g sat. fat), 25mg chol., 133mg sod., 11g carb. (2g sugars, 0 fiber), 2g pro.

ARE CROISSANTS YOUR JAM?

Add your own flavorful twist on homemade croissants! For something sweet, fill them with chocolate ganache, strawberry jam, Nutella or almond paste. If you're craving savory, try combinations such as ham and Gruyere cheese, egg and cheddar cheese, tuna and mayonnaise or mozzarella and fresh basil.

HOMEMADE TORTILLAS

I usually have to double this recipe because we go through these so quickly.
The tortillas are so tender, chewy and simple, you'll never use store-bought again.

—*Kristin Van Dyken, Kennewick, WA*

TAKES: 30 MIN. • **MAKES:** 8 TORTILLAS

2 cups all-purpose flour
½ tsp. salt
¾ cup water
3 Tbsp. olive oil

1. In a large bowl, combine the flour and salt. Stir in water and oil. Turn out onto a floured surface; knead 10-12 times, adding flour or water if needed to achieve a smooth dough. Let rest 10 minutes.

2. Divide the dough into 8 portions. On a lightly floured surface, roll each portion into a 7-in. circle.

3. In a greased cast-iron or other heavy skillet, cook tortillas over medium heat until lightly browned, about 1 minute on each side. Serve warm.

1 TORTILLA 159 cal., 5g fat (1g sat. fat), 0 chol., 148mg sod., 24g carb. (0 sugars, 1g fiber), 3g pro. **DIABETIC EXCHANGES** 1½ starch, 1 fat.

NAAN BREAD

Naan is a leavened flatbread from India, made with all-purpose flour (*maida*) and traditionally cooked in a *tandoor*, a dome-topped clay oven reaching over 500°. The dough is pressed onto the oven's side, where it cooks until puffed and slightly charred before being pulled out with a stake.

—*Anvita Bhatnagar Mistry, Erlangen, Germany*

PREP: 15 MIN. + RISING • **COOK:** 25 MIN. • **MAKES:** 8 SERVINGS

2 cups maida or all-purpose flour
½ tsp. salt
2 tsp. sugar
1 pkg. (¼ oz.) quick-rise yeast
¾ cup warm whole milk (110° to 115°)
3 Tbsp. canola oil
2 Tbsp. butter, melted
1 Tbsp. nigella seeds or black sesame seeds
¼ cup coarsely chopped fresh cilantro

1. In the bowl of a stand mixer, mix the first 4 ingredients. Add milk and oil; mix until combined. Using the dough hook attachment, knead on low until dough is smooth and elastic, about 6 minutes. Place in a greased bowl, turning once to grease the top. Cover and let rise in a warm place until doubled, about 2 hours or up to 8 hours.

2. Punch down dough. Turn onto a lightly floured surface; divide into 8 portions. Roll each portion into a 10x6-in. oval, stretching the dough as needed. Brush 1 side with half the butter and sprinkle with nigella seeds and cilantro; gently roll to adhere to dough.

3. In a large cast-iron skillet, cook naan, seed side up, over medium heat until air bubbles form and dough starts to brown in spots. Turn and cook until bubbles form, 1-2 minutes longer. Remove and brush with remaining melted butter. Keep warm until serving.

1 SERVING 223 cal., 10g fat (3g sat. fat), 10mg chol., 182mg sod., 30g carb. (2g sugars, 1g fiber), 4g pro.

BREADS, BISCUITS & MORE

CHALLAH

Eggs lend to the richness of this traditional challah bread recipe.
The attractive golden color and delicious flavor make it hard to resist.
—Taste of Home *Test Kitchen*

PREP: 30 MIN. + RISING • **BAKE:** 30 MIN. • **MAKES:** 2 LOAVES (16 PIECES EACH)

- 2 pkg. (¼ oz. each) active dry yeast
- 1 cup warm water (110° to 115°)
- ½ cup canola oil
- ⅓ cup sugar
- 1 Tbsp. salt
- 4 large eggs, room temperature
- 6 to 6½ cups all-purpose flour

TOPPING
- 1 large egg
- 1 tsp. cold water
- 1 Tbsp. sesame or poppy seeds, optional

NOTES

1. In a large bowl, dissolve yeast in warm water. Add oil, sugar, salt, eggs and 4 cups flour. Beat until smooth. Stir in enough remaining flour to form a firm dough. Turn out onto a floured surface; knead until smooth and elastic, 6-8 minutes. Place in a greased bowl, turning once to grease top. Cover and let rise in a warm place until doubled, about 1 hour.

2. Punch dough down. Turn out onto a lightly floured surface; divide in half. Divide each portion into thirds. Shape each piece into a 15-in. rope.

3. Place 3 ropes on a greased baking sheet and braid; pinch ends to seal and tuck under. Repeat with the remaining dough. Cover and let rise until doubled, about 1 hour.

4. Preheat oven to 350°. Beat egg and cold water; brush over braids. Sprinkle with sesame or poppy seeds if desired. Bake until golden brown, 30-40 minutes. Remove to wire racks to cool.

1 PIECE 139 cal., 5g fat (1g sat. fat), 29mg chol., 233mg sod., 20g carb. (2g sugars, 1g fiber), 4g pro.

TUSCAN CORNBREAD WITH ASIAGO BUTTER

With fresh basil on hand and a bag of cornmeal in the pantry, I decided to give cornbread a Tuscan twist. Canned tomatoes make it easy year-round, but in peak tomato season, I use fresh instead—peeled, seeded and finely diced.
—Michelle Anderson, Eagle, ID

PREP: 25 MIN. • **BAKE:** 20 MIN. • **MAKES:** 8 SERVINGS (1¼ CUPS BUTTER)

- 2 oz. sliced pancetta or bacon strips, finely chopped
- 1 to 2 Tbsp. olive oil, as needed
- 1½ cups white cornmeal
- ½ cup all-purpose flour
- 2 tsp. baking powder
- ½ tsp. salt
- 2 large eggs, room temperature
- 1 cup buttermilk
- ¼ cup minced fresh basil
- 1 garlic clove, minced
- 1 can (14½ oz.) diced tomatoes, drained
- 1 can (2¼ oz.) sliced ripe olives, drained

BUTTER
- 1 cup butter, softened
- 2 Tbsp. olive oil
- ⅓ cup shredded Asiago cheese
- 2 Tbsp. thinly sliced green onion
- 1½ tsp. minced fresh basil
- ½ tsp. minced fresh oregano
- 1 garlic clove, minced, optional

1. Preheat the oven to 400°. In a 10-in. cast-iron or other ovenproof skillet, cook pancetta over medium heat until crisp, stirring occasionally. Remove with a slotted spoon; drain on paper towels. Reserve drippings in skillet. If necessary, add enough oil to drippings to measure 2 Tbsp.

2. In a large bowl, whisk cornmeal, flour, baking powder and salt. In another bowl, whisk eggs, buttermilk, basil and garlic until blended; stir in tomatoes. Add to flour mixture; stir just until moistened. Fold in olives and pancetta.

3. Place skillet with drippings in oven; heat 2 minutes. Tilt pan to coat bottom and side with drippings. Add batter to hot pan. Bake until a toothpick inserted in the center comes out clean, 20-25 minutes. Cool in pan on a wire rack.

4. Meanwhile, in a small bowl, beat butter until light and fluffy. Beat in oil until blended; stir in cheese, green onion, basil, oregano and, if desired, garlic. Serve ½ cup butter mixture with warm cornbread (save remaining butter for another use).

NOTE If desired, remaining butter may be shaped into a log. Cover and refrigerate for a week or freeze for several months. To use, slice and serve with bread, pasta, vegetables, seafood or poultry.

1 WEDGE WITH 1 TBSP. BUTTER 329 cal., 18g fat (8g sat. fat), 79mg chol., 695mg sod., 34g carb. (4g sugars, 2g fiber), 8g pro.

MOM'S ITALIAN BREAD

I think Mom used to bake at least four of these tender loaves at once, and they never lasted long. She served the bread with every Italian meal. I love it toasted too.
—Linda Harrington, Windham, NH

PREP: 30 MIN. + RISING • **BAKE:** 20 MIN. • **MAKES:** 2 LOAVES (12 PIECES EACH)

- 1 pkg. (¼ oz.) active dry yeast
- 2 cups warm water (110° to 115°)
- 1 tsp. sugar
- 2 tsp. salt
- 5½ cups all-purpose flour

1. In a large bowl, dissolve yeast in warm water. Add sugar, salt and 3 cups flour. Beat on medium speed for 3 minutes. Stir in the remaining flour to form a soft dough.

2. Turn onto a floured surface; knead until smooth and elastic, 6-8 minutes. Place in a greased bowl, turning once to grease top. Cover and let rise in a warm place until doubled, about 1 hour.

3. Punch the dough down. Turn onto a floured surface; divide in half. Shape each portion into a loaf. Place each loaf seam side down on a greased baking sheet. Cover and let rise until doubled, about 30 minutes.

4. Meanwhile, preheat oven to 400°. With a sharp knife, make 4 shallow slashes across top of each loaf. Bake 20-25 minutes or until golden brown. Remove from pans to wire racks to cool.

1 PIECE 106 cal., 0 fat (0 sat. fat), 0 chol., 197mg sod., 22g carb. (1g sugars, 1g fiber), 3g pro.

BREADS, BISCUITS & MORE

HONEY BAGELS

Who has time to make from-scratch bagels? You do, with this easy recipe! The chewy golden bagels offer a hint of honey and are sure to impress the pickiest of palates.
—Taste of Home *Test Kitchen*

PREP: 1 HOUR + STANDING • **BAKE:** 20 MIN. • **MAKES:** 1 DOZEN

- 1 Tbsp. active dry yeast
- 1¼ cups warm water (110° to 115°)
- 3 Tbsp. canola oil
- 3 Tbsp. sugar
- 3 Tbsp. plus ¼ cup honey, divided
- 1 tsp. brown sugar
- 1½ tsp. salt
- 1 large egg, room temperature
- 4 to 5 cups bread flour
- 1 Tbsp. dried minced onion
- 1 Tbsp. sesame seeds
- 1 Tbsp. poppy seeds

READER REVIEW

"I was always afraid to make bagels, but this recipe changed that. Now I mix fresh fruit in the dough, and they come out great. Thanks for the inspiration!"
—PAUL3303, TASTEOFHOME.COM

1. In a large bowl, dissolve yeast in warm water. Add the oil, sugar, 3 Tbsp. honey, brown sugar, salt and egg; mix well. Stir in enough flour to form a soft dough.

2. Turn onto a floured surface; knead until a smooth, firm dough forms, 8-10 minutes. Cover and let rest 10 minutes.

3. Punch dough the down. Shape into 12 balls. Push thumb through each center to form a 1½-in. hole. Stretch and shape the dough to form even rings. Place on a floured surface. Cover and let rest for 10 minutes; flatten bagels slightly.

4. In a large saucepan or Dutch oven, bring 8 cups water and remaining ¼ cup honey to a boil. Drop bagels, 1 at a time, into boiling water. Cook the bagels for 45 seconds; turn and cook 45 seconds longer. Remove bagels with a slotted spoon; drain and sprinkle with minced onion, sesame seeds and poppy seeds.

5. Place bagels 2 in. apart on baking sheets lined with parchment. Bake at 425° for 12 minutes. Turn and bake until golden brown, about 5 minutes longer.

1 BAGEL 265 cal., 5g fat (1g sat. fat), 16mg chol., 303mg sod., 48g carb. (14g sugars, 2g fiber), 7g pro.

BREADS, BISCUITS & MORE

SOUR CREAM ROLLS WITH WALNUT FILLING

When I was a little girl, my grandmother taught me how to make these rolls. I remember feeling so special when we served them. If you have never worked with yeast, this is the recipe for you.
—Nadine Mesch, Mount Healthy, OH

PREP: 1 HOUR + RISING • **BAKE:** 20 MIN. • **MAKES:** 8 LOAVES (6 PIECES EACH)

- 4 cups ground walnuts (about 14 oz.)
- 1 cup sugar
- ¾ cup butter, melted
- ½ cup 2% milk
- ⅓ cup honey

DOUGH
- 2 pkg. (¼ oz. each) active dry yeast
- 1 tsp. plus ⅓ cup sugar, divided
- ½ cup warm 2% milk (110° to 115°)
- 1 cup butter, melted
- 1 cup sour cream
- 4 large eggs, room temperature, divided use
- 1 tsp. salt
- 5¼ to 5¾ cups all-purpose flour

1. In a large bowl, mix first 5 ingredients until blended. In a small bowl, dissolve yeast and 1 tsp. sugar in warm milk; let stand 5 minutes. In a large bowl, combine butter, sour cream, 3 eggs, salt, remaining sugar, yeast mixture and 2 cups flour; beat on medium speed for 3 minutes. Stir in enough remaining flour to form a soft dough (dough will be sticky).

2. Turn dough onto a floured surface; knead until smooth and elastic, 6-8 minutes. Place in a greased bowl, turning once to grease top. Cover and let rise in a warm place until doubled, about 1 hour.

3. Punch down the dough. Turn onto a lightly floured surface; divide and shape into 8 portions. Roll each into a 12x8-in. rectangle (dough will be very thin). Spread each with ½ cup walnut mixture to within ¾ in. of edges. Carefully roll up jelly-roll style, starting with a long side; pinch seam and ends to seal.

4. Place rolls 2 in. apart on baking sheets lined with parchment, seam side down. Prick tops with a fork. Cover; let rise in a warm place until almost doubled, about 1 hour. Preheat oven to 350°.

5. Lightly beat remaining egg; brush over rolls. Bake until golden brown, 20-25 minutes, switching position of the pans halfway through baking (filling may leak during baking). Remove loaves to wire racks to cool. To serve, cut into slices.

1 PIECE 201 cal., 13g fat (5g sat. fat), 37mg chol., 113mg sod., 20g carb. (8g sugars, 1g fiber), 3g pro.

SEA SALT STICKS

When my daughter was in school, her class had a recipe exchange—she came home raving about these breadsticks and wanted to make them for the family. They pair well with spaghetti, and you can even add 2 Tbsp. poppy seeds to the flour before mixing.
—Marina Castle Kelley, Canyon Country, CA

PREP: 45 MIN. + RISING • **BAKE:** 20 MIN. • **MAKES:** 20 SERVINGS

1 Tbsp. sugar
1 pkg. (¼ oz.) quick-rise yeast
1 tsp. sea salt
3¼ to 3¾ cups all-purpose flour
1¼ cups water
¼ cup olive oil

TOPPING
1 large egg white
1 Tbsp. water
 Coarse sea salt

1. Preheat oven to 325°. In a large bowl, mix sugar, yeast, salt and 2 cups flour. In a small saucepan, heat water and oil to 120°-130°; stir into dry ingredients. Stir in enough remaining flour to form a soft dough (dough will be sticky). Turn out the dough onto a floured surface; knead until smooth and elastic, 6-8 minutes. Place in a greased bowl, turning once to grease the top. Cover and let rest 10 minutes.

2. Divide dough into 20 portions. On a lightly floured surface, roll each portion into a 14-in. rope. Place the ropes 1 in. apart on greased baking sheets. Cover and let rise in a warm place until almost doubled, 15-20 minutes.

3. In a small bowl, whisk egg white with water; brush over tops of dough. Sprinkle with the coarse sea salt. Bake until light brown, 20-25 minutes. Remove from the pans to wire racks. Serve warm.

1 BREADSTICK 102 cal., 3g fat (0 sat. fat), 0 chol., 97mg sod., 16g carb. (1g sugars, 1g fiber), 2g pro.

ROLLED BUTTERMILK BISCUITS

I scribbled down this recipe when our family visited the Cooperstown Farm Museum more than 25 years ago. I must have gotten it right because these biscuits turn out great every time.
—Patricia Kile, Elizabethtown, PA

PREP: 20 MIN. • **BAKE:** 15 MIN. • **MAKES:** 8 BISCUITS

2 cups all-purpose flour
3 tsp. baking powder
½ tsp. baking soda
¼ tsp. salt
3 Tbsp. cold butter
¾ to 1 cup buttermilk
1 Tbsp. fat-free milk

1. Preheat oven to 450°. In a large bowl, combine flour, baking powder, baking soda and salt; cut in butter until mixture resembles coarse crumbs. Stir in enough buttermilk just to moisten dough.

2. Turn onto a lightly floured surface; knead 3-4 times. Pat or roll to ¾-in. thickness. Cut with a floured 2½-in. biscuit cutter. Place in a large ungreased cast-iron or other ovenproof skillet.

3. Brush with milk. Bake until golden brown, 12-15 minutes.

1 BISCUIT 162 cal., 5g fat (3g sat. fat), 12mg chol., 412mg sod., 25g carb. (1g sugars, 1g fiber), 4g pro. **DIABETIC EXCHANGES** 1½ starch, 1 fat.

BREADS, BISCUITS & MORE 195

WONDERFUL ENGLISH MUFFINS

When I was growing up on a farm, my mom always seemed to be baking homemade bread—nothing tasted so good! Now I like to make these simple, delicious muffins for my own family.
—Linda Rasmussen, Twin Falls, ID

PREP: 30 MIN. + RISING • **COOK:** 25 MIN. • **MAKES:** 12 MUFFINS

- 1 cup whole milk
- ¼ cup butter, cubed
- 2 Tbsp. sugar
- 1 tsp. salt
- 2 pkg. (¼ oz. each) active dry yeast
- 1 cup warm water (110° to 115°)
- 2 cups all-purpose flour
- 3 to 3½ cups whole wheat flour
- 1 Tbsp. sesame seeds
- 1 Tbsp. poppy seeds
- Cornmeal

1. Scald milk in a saucepan; add butter, sugar and salt. Stir until butter melts; cool to lukewarm. In a small bowl, dissolve yeast in warm water; add to milk mixture. Stir in all-purpose flour and 1 cup whole wheat flour until smooth. Add sesame seeds, poppy seeds and enough remaining whole wheat flour to make a soft dough.

2. Turn onto a floured surface; knead until smooth and elastic, 8-10 minutes. Place in a greased bowl, turning once to grease top. Cover and let rise until doubled, about 1 hour.

3. Punch dough down. Roll to ⅓-in. thickness on a cornmeal-covered surface. Cut into circles with a 3½-in. or 4-in. cutter; cover with a towel and let rise until nearly doubled, about 30 minutes.

4. Place muffins, cornmeal side down, in a greased skillet; cook over medium-low heat until the bottoms are browned, 12-14 minutes. Turn and cook until other side is browned, 12-14 minutes. Cool on wire racks; split and toast to serve.

1 MUFFIN 240 cal., 6g fat (3g sat. fat), 13mg chol., 248mg sod., 41g carb. (4g sugars, 4g fiber), 7g pro.

GARLIC ROSEMARY PULL-APART BREAD

This recipe is a different type of pull-apart bread. Eat it by itself, dipped in marinara or as part of a meal. For a different flavor, add sun-dried tomatoes, pesto or an onion soup mix instead of the rosemary-garlic combo.
—Christina Trikoris, Clarksville, TN

PREP: 25 MIN. + RISING • **BAKE:** 55 MIN. + COOLING • **MAKES:** 16 SERVINGS

- 3 tsp. active dry yeast
- 1 tsp. salt
- 5¼ to 6 cups all-purpose flour
- 1 cup water
- 1 cup butter, cubed
- ½ cup 2% milk
- 2 large eggs, room temperature

FLAVORING
- ½ cup butter, melted
- 6 garlic cloves, minced
- 2 Tbsp. minced fresh rosemary or 2 tsp. dried rosemary, crushed
- 1 tsp. salt
- 1 cup grated Parmesan cheese

1. In a large bowl, mix the yeast, salt and 2 cups flour. In a small saucepan, heat water, cubed butter and milk to 120°-130°. Add to dry ingredients; beat on medium speed for 2 minutes. Add eggs; beat on high speed for 2 minutes. Stir in enough remaining flour to form a soft dough (dough will be sticky).

2. Turn dough onto a floured surface; knead dough until smooth and elastic, 6-8 minutes. Place in a greased bowl, turning once to grease top. Cover and let rise in a warm place until doubled, about 1 hour.

3. Punch dough down. Turn onto a lightly floured surface; shape into 1½-in. balls. Combine melted butter, garlic, rosemary and salt. Dip 10 dough balls into butter mixture. Place balls in a greased 10-in. fluted tube pan; sprinkle with a scant ¼ cup Parmesan cheese. Repeat with the remaining balls and Parmesan cheese. Drizzle with any remaining butter mixture. Cover and let rise until doubled, about 45 minutes. Preheat oven to 350°.

4. Bake for 55-70 minutes or until golden brown and a thermometer reads 200°. Cool 10 minutes before inverting onto a serving plate. Serve warm.

1 SERVING 341 cal., 20g fat (12g sat. fat), 74mg chol., 536mg sod., 33g carb. (1g sugars, 1g fiber), 7g pro.

APPLESAUCE BREAD

I make this applesauce bread recipe with plump raisins and crunchy nuts. My kids love a slice in their lunch box or as a snack after school.
—*Tracey Jo Schley, Sherburn, MN*

PREP: 15 MIN. • **BAKE:** 50 MIN. + COOLING • **MAKES:** 1 LOAF

⅓ cup butter, softened
1 cup sugar
1 large egg, room temperature
1¼ cups applesauce
1½ cups all-purpose flour
¾ tsp. baking soda
¾ tsp. ground cinnamon
½ tsp. baking powder
½ tsp. salt
½ tsp. ground nutmeg
⅛ tsp. ground cloves
½ cup raisins
½ cup chopped walnuts

1. In a large bowl, cream butter and sugar. Add the egg and applesauce; mix well. Combine flour, baking soda, cinnamon, baking powder, salt, nutmeg and cloves. Stir into creamed mixture just until moistened. Fold in the raisins and nuts.

2. Pour into a greased 8x4-in. loaf pan. Bake at 350° for 60-65 minutes or until a toothpick inserted in center comes out clean. Cool for 10 minutes before removing from pan to a wire rack to cool completely.

1 PIECE 175 cal., 6g fat (3g sat. fat), 23mg chol., 189mg sod., 28g carb. (17g sugars, 1g fiber), 3g pro.

READER REVIEW

"This is a great recipe! I added mini caramel chips, and it turned out amazing! A perfect treat for the fall season."

—ERINSHEA1982, TASTEOFHOME.COM

---

made from scratch
OLD-FASHIONED APPLESAUCE

Growing up, we had all kinds of apple trees in our yard, so I'm not sure which ones Mother preferred for applesauce. (I use Cortlands now.) What I do know is that her applesauce was very white—her secret was to soak the apples in salt water while peeling to keep them from browning.
—*Doris Natvig, Jesup, IA*

TAKES: 30 MIN. • **MAKES:** 6 CUPS

4 lbs. tart apples
1 cup water
1 cinnamon stick or ½ tsp. cinnamon extract
½ to 1 cup sugar

Peel, core and quarter the apples. In a Dutch oven, bring apples, water and cinnamon to a boil. Reduce heat; cover and simmer 10-15 minutes or until apples are tender. Remove from the heat. Add sugar to taste and stir until dissolved. If you used a cinnamon stick, remove and discard. Mash apples with a potato masher until desired texture is reached. Serve warm or chilled.

½ CUP 122 cal., 1g fat (0 sat. fat), 0 chol., 0 sod., 31g carb. (26g sugars, 4g fiber), 0 pro.

BREADS, BISCUITS & MORE

TRADITIONAL SCONES

Making scones is surprisingly simple, as I learned when my wife and I hosted an English tea. These are light and delicious!
—*Chuck Hinz, Parma, OH*

PREP: 20 MIN. • **BAKE:** 25 MIN. • **MAKES:** 1 DOZEN

- 2 cups all-purpose flour
- 2 Tbsp. sugar
- 3 tsp. baking powder
- ⅛ tsp. baking soda
- 6 Tbsp. cold butter, cubed
- 1 large egg
- ½ cup buttermilk
  Jam of your choice, optional

1. Preheat oven to 350°. In a large bowl, combine flour, sugar, baking powder and baking soda. Cut in butter until mixture resembles coarse crumbs. In a small bowl, whisk the egg and buttermilk until blended; add to crumb mixture just until moistened.

2. Turn dough onto a lightly floured surface; gently knead 10 times. Divide dough in half; pat each portion into a 5-in. circle. Cut each circle into 6 wedges.

3. Separate wedges and place 1 in. apart on an ungreased baking sheet. Bake until golden brown, 25-30 minutes. Serve warm, with jam if desired.

NOTE To substitute for each cup of buttermilk, use 1 Tbsp. white vinegar or lemon juice plus enough milk to measure 1 cup. Stir, then let stand 5 minutes. Or use 1 cup plain yogurt or 1¾ tsp. cream of tartar plus 1 cup milk.

1 SCONE 144 cal., 6g fat (4g sat. fat), 33mg chol., 170mg sod., 19g carb. (3g sugars, 1g fiber), 3g pro.

BREADS, BISCUITS & MORE

ZUCCHINI NUT BREAD

Lighter and fluffier than most zucchini breads, this recipe is a great way to put that vegetable to good use!
—Kevin Bruckerhoff, Columbia, MO

PREP: 15 MIN. • **BAKE:** 55 MIN. + COOLING • **MAKES:** 2 LOAVES (12 PIECES EACH)

- 2 cups sugar
- 1 cup canola oil
- 3 large eggs, room temperature
- 2 tsp. vanilla extract
- 3 cups all-purpose flour
- 1 tsp. salt
- 1 tsp. baking soda
- 1 tsp. grated lemon zest
- 1 tsp. ground cinnamon
- ¼ tsp. baking powder
- 2 cups shredded zucchini (about 2 medium)
- ½ cup chopped walnuts or pecans

1. Preheat oven to 350°. Grease two 8x4-in. loaf pans. In a large bowl, beat sugar, oil, eggs and vanilla until well blended. In another bowl, whisk flour, salt, baking soda, lemon zest, cinnamon and baking powder; gradually beat into sugar mixture, mixing just until moistened. Stir in zucchini and walnuts.

2. Transfer to prepared pans. Bake 55-65 minutes or until a toothpick inserted in center comes out clean. Cool 10 minutes before removing from pans to wire racks to cool.

1 PIECE 229 cal., 11g fat (1g sat. fat), 26mg chol., 165mg sod., 29g carb. (17g sugars, 1g fiber), 3g pro.

DUTCH APPLE LOAF

Being of Dutch descent, I knew I had to try this recipe for a moist, fruity quick bread.
It freezes well, so I often have a loaf on hand for church bazaars.
—Gladys Meyer, Ottumwa, IA

PREP: 15 MIN. • **BAKE:** 55 MIN. + COOLING • **MAKES:** 1 LOAF (16 PIECES)

- ½ cup butter, softened
- 1 cup sugar
- 2 large eggs, room temperature
- ¼ cup buttermilk
- 1 tsp. vanilla extract
- 2 cups all-purpose flour
- 1½ tsp. baking powder
- ½ tsp. salt
- ¼ tsp. baking soda
- 2 cups diced peeled tart apples
- ½ cup chopped walnuts

TOPPING
- ¼ cup sugar
- ¼ cup all-purpose flour
- 2 tsp. ground cinnamon
- ¼ cup cold butter, cubed

1. In a large bowl, cream the butter and sugar until light and fluffy, 5-7 minutes. Add eggs, 1 at a time, beating well after each addition. Beat in buttermilk and vanilla. Combine flour, baking powder, salt and baking soda; gradually add to creamed mixture. Fold in apples and walnuts. Pour into a greased 9x5-in. loaf pan.

2. For the topping, combine sugar, flour and cinnamon. Cut in butter until mixture resembles coarse crumbs. Sprinkle over batter.

3. Bake at 350° for 55-60 minutes or until a toothpick inserted in center comes out clean. Cool 10 minutes before removing from pan to a wire rack.

1 PIECE 243 cal., 12g fat (6g sat. fat), 50mg chol., 252mg sod., 32g carb. (17g sugars, 1g fiber), 4g pro.

EASY CHEESY BISCUITS

I'm a big fan of homemade biscuits but not of the rolling and cutting that goes into making them. The drop biscuit method solves everything!
—Christy Addison, Clarksville, OH

TAKES: 30 MIN. • **MAKES:** 1 DOZEN

- 3 cups all-purpose flour
- 3 tsp. baking powder
- 1 Tbsp. sugar
- 1 tsp. salt
- ¾ tsp. cream of tartar
- ½ cup cold butter
- 1 cup shredded sharp cheddar cheese
- 1 garlic clove, minced
- ¼ to ½ tsp. crushed red pepper flakes
- 1¼ cups 2% milk

1. Preheat oven to 450°. In a large bowl, whisk flour, baking powder, sugar, salt and cream of tartar. Cut in butter until the mixture resembles coarse crumbs. Stir in cheese, garlic and pepper flakes. Add milk; stir just until moistened.

2. Drop dough by heaping ¼ cupfuls 2 in. apart onto a greased baking sheet. Bake for 18-20 minutes or until golden brown. Serve warm.

1 BISCUIT 237 cal., 12g fat (7g sat. fat), 32mg chol., 429mg sod., 26g carb. (2g sugars, 1g fiber), 7g pro.

READER REVIEW

"These drop biscuits are so easy to make, I made them while preparing dinner! I loved the garlic and red pepper flakes—they complement the cheese perfectly. Goes great with pork dishes!"

—NH-RESCUE, TASTEOFHOME.COM

BREADS, BISCUITS & MORE

CLASSIC IRISH SODA BREAD

This traditional Irish soda bread can be made with an assortment of mix-ins such as dried fruit and nuts, but I like it with a handful of raisins. It's the perfect change-of-pace item to bring to a get-together.
—*Gloria Warczak, Cedarburg, WI*

PREP: 15 MIN. • **BAKE:** 30 MIN. • **MAKES:** 1 LOAF (8 PIECES)

- 2 cups all-purpose flour
- 2 Tbsp. brown sugar
- 1 tsp. baking powder
- 1 tsp. baking soda
- ½ tsp. salt
- 3 Tbsp. cold butter, cubed
- 2 large eggs, room temperature, divided use
- ¾ cup buttermilk
- ⅓ cup raisins

1. Preheat oven to 375°. Whisk together the first 5 ingredients. Cut in butter until mixture resembles coarse crumbs. In another bowl, whisk together 1 egg and buttermilk. Add to flour mixture; stir just until moistened. Stir in raisins.

2. Turn onto a lightly floured surface; gently knead 6-8 times. Shape into a 6½-in. round loaf; place on a greased baking sheet. Using a sharp knife, make a shallow cross on top of loaf. Whisk the remaining egg; brush over top.

3. Bake until loaf is golden brown, 30-35 minutes. Remove from pan to a wire rack. Serve warm.

NOTE To substitute for each cup of buttermilk, use 1 Tbsp. white vinegar or lemon juice plus enough milk to measure 1 cup. Stir, then let stand for 5 minutes. Or use 1 cup plain yogurt or 1¾ tsp. cream of tartar plus 1 cup milk.

1 PIECE 210 cal., 6g fat (3g sat. fat), 59mg chol., 463mg sod., 33g carb. (8g sugars, 1g fiber), 6g pro.

COPYCAT STARBUCKS PUMPKIN BREAD

Skip the line and bake Starbucks's pumpkin bread in your own kitchen. This copycat recipe is better than the original!
—Taste of Home *Test Kitchen*

PREP: 25 MIN. • **BAKE:** 1 HOUR + COOLING • **MAKES:** 2 LOAVES (16 PIECES EACH)

- 1 can (15 oz.) solid-pack pumpkin
- 4 large eggs, room temperature
- ¾ cup canola oil
- ⅔ cup water
- 2 cups sugar
- 1 cup honey
- 1½ tsp. vanilla extract
- 3½ cups all-purpose flour
- 2 tsp. baking soda
- 1½ tsp. salt
- 1½ tsp. ground cinnamon
- 1 tsp. ground nutmeg
- ½ tsp. ground cloves
- ½ tsp. ground ginger
- ½ cup salted pumpkin seeds or pepitas

1. Preheat oven to 350°. In a large bowl, beat the pumpkin, eggs, oil, water, sugar, honey and vanilla until well blended. In another bowl, whisk flour, baking soda, salt and spices; gradually beat into pumpkin mixture.

2. Transfer to 2 greased 9x5-in. loaf pans. Sprinkle tops with pumpkin seeds.

3. Bake 60-70 minutes or until a toothpick inserted in center comes out clean. Cool in pan for 10 minutes before removing to a wire rack to cool.

1 PIECE 202 cal., 7g fat (1g sat. fat), 23mg chol., 205mg sod., 33g carb. (22g sugars, 1g fiber), 3g pro.

NOTES

FETA & CHIVE MUFFINS

This is a spring variation on a savory muffin my husband has made for years.
It has a light texture, almost like a popover, and tastes best when eaten hot, straight from the oven.
—Angela Buchanan, Boulder, CO

PREP: 15 MIN. • **BAKE:** 20 MIN. • **MAKES:** 1 DOZEN

1½ cups all-purpose flour
3 tsp. baking powder
¼ tsp. salt
2 large eggs, room temperature
1 cup fat-free milk
2 Tbsp. butter, melted
½ cup crumbled feta cheese
3 Tbsp. minced chives

1. In a large bowl, combine the flour, baking powder and salt. In another bowl, combine eggs, milk and butter; stir into the dry ingredients just until moistened. Fold in feta cheese and chives.

2. Fill 12 greased or paper-lined muffin cups two-thirds full. Bake at 400° for 18-22 minutes or until a toothpick inserted in the center comes out clean. Cool for 5 minutes before removing from pan to a wire rack. Serve warm. Refrigerate leftovers.

1 MUFFIN 105 cal., 4g fat (2g sat. fat), 39mg chol., 250mg sod., 13g carb. (1g sugars, 1g fiber), 4g pro. **DIABETIC EXCHANGES** 1 starch, ½ fat.

made from scratch
GARLIC BASIL BUTTER

Instead of serving plain butter alongside an assortment of fresh breads, prepare this herb laden whipped butter.
—Taste of Home *Test Kitchen*

TAKES: 10 MIN. • **MAKES:** ½ CUP

½ cup butter, softened
4 tsp. minced fresh basil
1½ tsp. minced fresh parsley
½ tsp. garlic powder
Fresh sage and thyme

In a small bowl, combine butter, basil, parsley and garlic powder. Beat on medium-low speed until mixture is combined. Garnish with sage and thyme.

1 TSP. 101 cal., 11g fat (7g sat. fat), 31mg chol., 116mg sod., 0 carb. (0 sugars, 0 fiber), 0 pro.

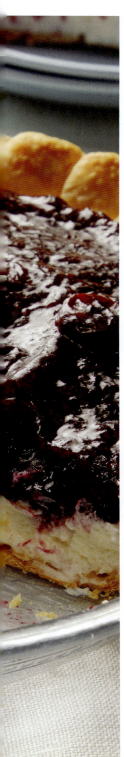

from scratch CAKES & PIES

CREAM CHEESE BLUEBERRY PIE, PAGE 234

FLOURLESS CHOCOLATE CAKE

One bite of this and you'll agree it's pure pleasure for confirmed chocoholics! A small slice of this rich, dense dessert goes a long way. Chocolate ganache on top takes it to the next level.
—Taste of Home *Test Kitchen*

PREP: 20 MIN. • **BAKE:** 30 MIN. + COOLING • **MAKES:** 16 SERVINGS

- 4 large eggs, separated
- 10 Tbsp. butter, cubed
- ½ cup sugar, divided
- 6 oz. semisweet chocolate, chopped
- 3 oz. unsweetened chocolate, chopped
- 2 tsp. vanilla extract
  Chocolate ganache, optional

READER REVIEW

"I've made this cake many times with rave reviews, and it's a great choice for those with wheat allergies. Topped with chocolate ganache, homemade whipped cream and a fan-cut strawberry, it has a gourmet look and taste."

—RLIBERTY, TASTEOFHOME.COM

1. Let the egg whites stand at room temperature for 30 minutes. Preheat oven to 350°. In a heavy saucepan, melt butter, ¼ cup sugar and chocolates over low heat, stirring constantly. Cool until mixture is lukewarm.

2. In a large bowl, beat the egg yolks until thick and lemon-colored, about 3 minutes. Beat in vanilla. Gradually beat in chocolate mixture.

3. In a small bowl and with clean beaters, beat the egg whites on medium speed until soft peaks form. Gradually add the remaining sugar, 1 Tbsp. at a time, beating on high speed until stiff peaks form. Stir a small amount of the whites into the chocolate mixture. Fold in the remaining whites.

4. Pour into a greased 9-in. springform pan. Place on a baking sheet. Bake until cake is just set and jiggles slightly when tapped or until a toothpick inserted in the center comes out with a few moist crumbs, 28-30 minutes. Cool on a wire rack for 20 minutes.

5. Carefully run a knife around edge of pan to loosen; remove side of the pan. Drizzle with chocolate ganache if desired.

1 PIECE 202 cal., 15g fat (9g sat. fat), 66mg chol., 76mg sod., 14g carb. (11g sugars, 2g fiber), 3g pro.

---

made from scratch
CHOCOLATE GANACHE

This satiny, smooth chocolate treat brings elegance to even the simplest dessert. It's so versatile!
—Taste of Home *Test Kitchen*

PREP: 15 MIN. + CHILLING
MAKES: 1¼ CUPS

- 1 cup semisweet chocolate chips
- ⅔ cup heavy whipping cream

1. Place chocolate chips in a small bowl. In a small saucepan, bring cream just to a boil. Pour over chocolate; whisk until smooth.

2. For a pourable ganache, cool, stirring occasionally, until mixture reaches 85°-90° and is slightly thickened, about 40 minutes. Pour over cake, allowing some to drape down the side. Spread ganache with a spatula if necessary to evenly coat, working quickly before it thickens. Let stand until set.

3. For spreadable ganache, refrigerate, stirring occasionally, until mixture reaches a spreading consistency. Spread over cake.

2 TBSP. 135 cal., 11g fat (7g sat. fat), 22mg chol., 8mg sod., 11g carb. (10g sugars, 1g fiber), 1g pro.

SHORTBREAD LEMON TART

For a change from ordinary lemon bars, we added orange zest to both crust and filling and turned the recipe into a tart.
—Taste of Home *Test Kitchen*

PREP: 20 MIN. • **BAKE:** 25 MIN. + COOLING • **MAKES:** 10 SERVINGS

- 3 large eggs
- 1¼ cups sugar
- ¼ cup lemon juice
- 1 Tbsp. grated orange zest
- ¼ cup butter, melted

CRUST
- 1 cup all-purpose flour
- ⅓ cup confectioners' sugar
- ½ cup ground almonds
- 1 tsp. grated lemon zest
- 1 tsp. grated orange zest
- ½ cup cold butter, cubed
- Additional confectioners' sugar
- Fresh raspberries, optional

1. Let eggs stand at room temperature for 30 minutes.

2. Preheat oven to 350°. Whisk together eggs, sugar, lemon juice and orange zest. Whisk in butter until smooth.

3. For crust, pulse the first 6 ingredients in a food processor until mixture forms a ball. Press dough onto the bottom and up the side of an ungreased 9-in. fluted tart pan with removable bottom.

4. Pour lemon mixture into crust. Bake until center is almost set, 25-30 minutes. Cool on a wire rack. Just before serving, sprinkle with confectioners' sugar and, if desired, fresh raspberries.

1 PIECE 332 cal., 18g fat (9g sat. fat), 92mg chol., 132mg sod., 41g carb. (30g sugars, 1g fiber), 4g pro.

MOTHER'S WALNUT CAKE

Even though Mother baked this tall, beautiful cake often when I was growing up, it was a real treat every time. I like the walnuts in the cake and the frosting. Mother frequently used black walnuts from our trees.
—*Helen Vail, Glenside, PA*

PREP: 20 MIN. • **BAKE:** 20 MIN. + COOLING • **MAKES:** 16 SERVINGS

½ cup butter, softened
½ cup shortening
2 cups sugar
4 large eggs, room temperature
3½ cups all-purpose flour
2 tsp. baking soda
½ tsp. salt
1½ cups buttermilk
2 tsp. vanilla extract
1½ cups ground walnuts

FROSTING
11 oz. cream cheese, softened
¾ cup butter, softened
5 to 5½ cups confectioners' sugar
1½ tsp. vanilla extract
⅓ cup finely chopped walnuts

1. Preheat oven to 350°. Cream butter, shortening and sugar. Add eggs, 1 at a time, beating well after each addition. Combine flour, baking soda and salt; gradually add to the creamed mixture alternately with buttermilk and vanilla. Beat on low speed just until combined. Stir in the ground walnuts.

2. Pour batter into 3 greased and floured 9-in. round pans. Bake until a toothpick inserted in center comes out clean, 20-25 minutes. Cool 5 minutes; remove from pans to wire racks to cool completely.

3. For frosting, beat the cream cheese and butter. Add the confectioners' sugar; mix well. Beat in the vanilla until smooth. Spread frosting between layers and over the top and side of cake. Sprinkle with walnuts. Refrigerate.

1 PIECE 685 cal., 35g fat (16g sat. fat), 114mg chol., 475mg sod., 86g carb. (61g sugars, 1g fiber), 9g pro.

NOTES

CAKES & PIES

APPLE PIE

I remember coming home sullen one day because we'd lost a softball game. Grandma, in her wisdom, suggested, "Maybe a slice of hot apple pie will make you feel better." She was right.
—*Maggie Greene, Granite Falls, WA*

PREP: 20 MIN. • **BAKE:** 1 HOUR • **MAKES:** 8 SERVINGS

Dough for double-crust pie
- ⅓ cup sugar
- ⅓ cup packed brown sugar
- ¼ cup all-purpose flour
- 1 tsp. ground cinnamon
- ¼ tsp. ground ginger
- ¼ tsp. ground nutmeg
- 6 to 7 cups thinly sliced peeled tart apples
- 1 Tbsp. lemon juice
- 1 Tbsp. butter
- 1 large egg white

Optional: Turbinado or coarse sugar, ground cinnamon, vanilla bean ice cream and caramel sauce

Make your own Dough for Double-Crust Pie. Recipe on p. 218.

Make your own Salted Caramel Sauce. Recipe on p. 282.

1. Preheat the oven to 375°. On a lightly floured surface, roll out half the dough to a ⅛-in.-thick circle; transfer to a 9-in. pie plate. Chill while preparing filling. In a small bowl, combine sugars, flour and spices. In a large bowl, toss apples with lemon juice. Add sugar mixture; toss to coat. Add filling to crust; dot with butter.

2. Roll out the remaining dough to a ⅛-in.-thick circle; cut into 1-in.-wide strips. Arrange over filling in a lattice pattern. Trim and seal strips to edge of bottom crust; flute edge. Beat egg white until foamy; brush over crust. If desired, sprinkle with turbinado sugar and cinnamon.

3. Bake the pie on the lowest rack, 60-70 minutes, until crust is golden brown and filling is bubbly, covering with foil halfway through if the crust begins to get too dark. Cool on a wire rack. If desired, serve with ice cream and caramel sauce.

1 PIECE 467 cal., 25g fat (15g sat. fat), 64mg chol., 331mg sod., 58g carb. (26g sugars, 2g fiber), 5g pro.

CAKES & PIES

REFRESHING KEY LIME PIE

Everyone who tries this pie says it's the best Key lime pie they've ever had.
It's so easy that you can make it last minute for a wonderful dessert!
—Denise Gursky, Miami, FL

PREP: 20 MIN. • **BAKE:** 15 MIN. + CHILLING • **MAKES:** 8 SERVINGS

1½ cups graham cracker crumbs
¼ cup sugar
⅓ cup butter, melted
2 cans (14 oz. each) sweetened condensed milk
4 large egg yolks
1 cup Key lime juice
Optional: Sweetened whipped cream and lime slices

Make your own Sweetened Whipped Cream. Recipe on p. 300.

1. Preheat oven to 375°. In a small bowl, combine the cracker crumbs, sugar and butter until crumbly. Press onto bottom and up the side of an ungreased 9-in. pie plate. Bake until crust is lightly browned, 8-10 minutes. Cool on a wire rack while making the filling.

2. In a large bowl, beat milk, egg yolks and lime juice on low for 2 minutes or until smooth and slightly thickened.

3. Pour into prepared crust. Bake until a knife inserted in the center comes out clean, 15-20 minutes. Cool on a wire rack for 1 hour. Refrigerate until chilled, about 3 hours. If desired, serve with whipped cream and lime slices.

1 PIECE 637 cal., 24g fat (13g sat. fat), 158mg chol., 321mg sod., 96g carb. (84g sugars, 1g fiber), 13g pro.

SOUR CREAM PEACH KUCHEN

For an old-fashioned sweet, there's nothing that beats my mom's peach kuchen.
With a melt-in-your-mouth crust and a lightly sweet filling, this treat is perfect after a big meal.
—Cathy Eland, Hightstown, NJ

PREP: 15 MIN. • **BAKE:** 45 MIN. • **MAKES:** 12 SERVINGS

3 cups all-purpose flour
1¼ cups sugar, divided
½ tsp. baking powder
¼ tsp. salt
1 cup cold butter, cubed
2 cans (29 oz. each) sliced peaches, drained or 13 small peaches, peeled and sliced
1 tsp. ground cinnamon

TOPPING
4 large egg yolks
2 cups sour cream
2 to 3 Tbsp. sugar
¼ tsp. ground cinnamon

1. In a large bowl, combine the flour, ¼ cup sugar, baking powder and salt; cut in butter until mixture resembles coarse crumbs. Press onto the bottom and 1 in. up the sides of a greased 13x9-in. baking dish.

2. Arrange peaches over the crust. Combine cinnamon and remaining sugar; sprinkle over the peaches. Bake at 400° for 15 minutes.

3. Meanwhile, for topping, in a small bowl, combine the egg yolks and sour cream. Spread evenly over peaches. Combine the sugar and cinnamon; sprinkle over top.

4. Bake 30-35 minutes longer or until set. Serve warm or cold. Store leftovers in the refrigerator.

1 PIECE 507 cal., 24g fat (15g sat. fat), 135mg chol., 197mg sod., 66g carb. (41g sugars, 2g fiber), 6g pro.

GERMAN CHOCOLATE CAKE

This cake is my husband's favorite! Every bite has a light crunch from the pecans, a sweet taste of coconut and a drizzle of chocolate.
—Joyce Platfoot, Wapakoneta, OH

PREP: 30 MIN. • **BAKE:** 25 MIN. + COOLING • **MAKES:** 16 SERVINGS

- 4 oz. German sweet chocolate, chopped
- ½ cup water
- 1 cup butter, softened
- 2 cups sugar
- 4 large eggs, separated, room temperature
- 1 tsp. vanilla extract
- 2½ cups cake flour
- 1 tsp. baking soda
- ½ tsp. salt
- 1 cup buttermilk

FROSTING
- 1½ cups sugar
- 1½ cups evaporated milk
- ¾ cup butter
- 5 large egg yolks, room temperature, beaten
- 2 cups sweetened shredded coconut
- 1½ cups chopped pecans
- 1½ tsp. vanilla extract

GLAZE
- 2 oz. semisweet chocolate
- 1 tsp. shortening

1. Line 3 greased 9-in. round baking pans with waxed paper. Grease waxed paper and set aside. In a small saucepan, melt chocolate with water over low heat; cool.

2. Preheat oven to 350°. In a large bowl, cream butter and sugar until light and fluffy, 5-7 minutes. Beat in egg yolks, 1 at a time, beating well after each addition. Blend in melted chocolate and vanilla. Combine the flour, baking soda and salt; add to the creamed mixture alternately with buttermilk, beating well after each addition.

3. In a small bowl and with clean beaters, beat the 4 egg whites until stiff peaks form. Fold a fourth of the egg whites into the creamed mixture; fold in the remaining whites.

4. Pour the batter into prepared pans. Bake 24-28 minutes or until a toothpick inserted in the center comes out clean. Cool 10 minutes before removing from pans to wire racks to cool completely.

5. For the frosting, in a small saucepan, heat sugar, milk, butter and egg yolks over medium-low heat until mixture is thickened and golden brown, stirring constantly. Remove from heat. Stir in coconut, pecans and vanilla. Cool until thick enough to spread. Spread a third of the frosting over each cake layer and stack the layers.

6. For the glaze, in a microwave, melt the chocolate and shortening; stir until smooth. Drizzle over cake.

NOTE To substitute for each cup of buttermilk, use 1 Tbsp. white vinegar or lemon juice plus enough milk to measure 1 cup. Stir, then let stand for 5 minutes. Or use 1 cup plain yogurt or 1¾ tsp. cream of tartar plus 1 cup milk.

1 PIECE 691 cal., 40g fat (21g sat. fat), 166mg chol., 415mg sod., 78g carb. (58g sugars, 3g fiber), 8g pro.

CAKES & PIES

SHAKER LEMON PIE

Also known as Ohio lemon pie, this dessert is a Midwestern favorite. Its thrifty use of whole lemons is unique and gives the pie a lovely combination of sweet, tart and slightly bitter flavors. Lemon lovers won't be able to stop at a single piece.
—*Deb Perry, Traverse City, MI*

PREP: 20 MIN. + STANDING • **BAKE:** 35 MIN. • **MAKES:** 8 SERVINGS

- 2 medium lemons, seeded and very thinly sliced
- 2 cups sugar
- ⅛ tsp. salt
  Dough for double-crust pie
- 4 large eggs, room temperature
- 2 Tbsp. all-purpose flour
- 1 tsp. vanilla extract

1. In a large glass bowl, combine the lemons, sugar and salt. Cover and let stand overnight at room temperature.

2. Preheat oven to 450°. On a lightly floured surface, roll half the dough to a ⅛-in.-thick circle; transfer to a 9-in. cast-iron or other ovenproof skillet. Trim even with rim. In a large bowl, whisk the eggs until frothy; lightly brush over crust. Add lemon mixture, flour and vanilla to eggs; mix well. Pour into crust. Roll the remaining dough to a ⅛-in.-thick circle; place over filling. Trim, seal and flute edge. Cut slits on top.

3. Bake 15 minutes. Reduce oven setting to 400°. Bake until the crust is golden brown and the filling is bubbly, 20-25 minutes longer. Cover edge loosely with foil during the last 10 minutes if needed to prevent overbrowning. Remove foil. Cool on a wire rack; serve warm.

1 PIECE 587 cal., 26g fat (15g sat. fat), 153mg chol., 383mg sod., 83g carb. (52g sugars, 2g fiber), 8g pro.

---

made from scratch
DOUGH FOR DOUBLE-CRUST PIE

Use this recipe from our Test Kitchen when you need pastry for a double-crust or lattice-topped pie.
—Taste of Home *Test Kitchen*

TAKES: 30 MIN. • **MAKES:** DOUGH FOR 1 DOUBLE-CRUST OR LATTICE-TOPPED PIE (9 OR 10 IN.)

- 2 cups all-purpose flour
- ¾ tsp. salt
- ⅔ cup shortening
- 6 to 7 Tbsp. cold water

1. In a bowl, mix flour and salt; cut in shortening until crumbly. Gradually add cold water, tossing with a fork until dough holds together when pressed. Divide dough in half. Shape each into a disk; wrap and refrigerate 1 hour or overnight.

2. On a lightly floured surface, roll out half the dough to a ⅛-in.-thick circle; transfer to a 9-in. or 10-in. pie plate. Trim even with rim. Add desired filling.

3. Roll remaining dough to a ⅛-in.-thick circle. Place over filling. Trim, seal and flute edge. Cut slits on top. Bake according to recipe directions.

1 PIECE 260 cal., 16g fat (4g sat. fat), 0 chol., 222mg sod., 24g carb. (0 sugars, 1g fiber), 3g pro.

GRANDMA'S RED VELVET CAKE

No one believes it's Christmas at our house until this jolly cake appears.
It's different from other red velvets I've tasted; the icing is as light as snow.
—Kathryn Davison, Charlotte, NC

PREP: 30 MIN. • **BAKE:** 20 MIN. + COOLING • **MAKES:** 14 SERVINGS

- ½ cup butter, softened
- 1½ cups sugar
- 2 large eggs, room temperature
- 2 bottles (1 oz. each) red food coloring
- 1 Tbsp. white vinegar
- 1 tsp. vanilla extract
- 2¼ cups cake flour
- 2 Tbsp. baking cocoa
- 1 tsp. baking soda
- 1 tsp. salt
- 1 cup buttermilk

FROSTING
- ½ cup cold water
- 1 Tbsp. cornstarch
- 2 cups butter, softened
- 2 tsp. vanilla extract
- 3½ cups confectioners' sugar

1. Preheat oven to 350°. Cream butter and sugar until light and fluffy, 5-7 minutes. Add eggs, 1 at a time, beating well after each addition. Beat in food coloring, vinegar and vanilla. In another bowl, whisk together flour, cocoa, baking soda and salt; add to creamed mixture alternately with buttermilk, beating well after each addition.

2. Pour into 2 greased and floured 9-in. round baking pans. Bake until a toothpick inserted in the center comes out clean, 20-25 minutes. Cool layers 10 minutes before removing from pans to wire racks to cool completely. Trim ¼ in. off top of each cake layer; crumble trimmings onto a baking sheet. Let crumbs stand at room temperature while making frosting.

3. For frosting, combine water and cornstarch in a small saucepan over medium heat. Stir until thickened and opaque, 2-3 minutes. Cool to room temperature. Cream butter and vanilla until light and fluffy, 3-4 minutes. Beat in cornstarch mixture. Gradually add confectioners' sugar; beat until light and fluffy. Spread between the layers and over top and side of cake. Press the reserved cake crumbs into side of cake.

1 PIECE 595 cal., 34g fat (21g sat. fat), 115mg chol., 564mg sod., 71g carb. (52g sugars, 1g fiber), 4g pro.

CHERRY HAND PIES

There's nothing better than a sweet, from-scratch delight like traditional cherry pie. These precious little hand pies always go fast when I sell them at my pie bakery!
—Allison Cebulla, Milwaukee, WI

PREP: 45 MIN. • **BAKE:** 25 MIN. + COOLING • **MAKES:** 8 SERVINGS

- 6 Tbsp. water, divided
- 2 Tbsp. sugar
- 2 Tbsp. cherry brandy
- 4½ tsp. cornstarch
- 1½ tsp. lemon juice
- 1 tsp. quick-cooking tapioca
- ¼ tsp. grated lemon zest
- Dash salt
- 2 cups fresh or frozen pitted tart cherries, thawed and halved
- 1 cup fresh or frozen pitted dark sweet cherries, thawed and halved
- Dough for double-crust pie
- 1 large egg, room temperature

ICING
- 2⅔ cups confectioners' sugar
- 3 to 4 Tbsp. hot water
- 2 Tbsp. butter, melted
- ½ tsp. almond extract
- ¼ tsp. vanilla extract
- Dash salt
- Freeze-dried strawberries, crushed, optional

Make your own Dough for Double-Crust Pie. Recipe on p. 218.

1. In a large saucepan, whisk 4 Tbsp. water, sugar, brandy, cornstarch, lemon juice, tapioca, lemon zest and salt until combined. Add cherries. Bring to a boil; cook and stir until thickened, 3-5 minutes. Remove from heat. Set aside to cool.

2. Preheat oven to 400°. On a lightly floured surface, roll half the dough to a 14x9-in. rectangle. Cut out eight 3½x4½-in. rectangles. Repeat with remaining dough.

3. Transfer 8 rectangles to baking sheets lined with parchment; spoon about 3 Tbsp. cherry mixture in center of each. Whisk egg and remaining 2 Tbsp. water. Brush edges of crust with egg wash. Top with the remaining 8 rectangles; press the edges with a fork to seal. Brush tops with egg wash; cut slits on tops.

4. Bake until crust is golden brown and slightly puffed, 25-30 minutes. Remove from pans to wire racks to cool. Combine confectioners' sugar, hot water, butter, extracts and salt; drizzle over the pies. Garnish with freeze-dried strawberries if desired. Let stand until set.

1 PIE 589 cal., 27g fat (16g sat. fat), 91mg chol., 380mg sod., 83g carb. (49g sugars, 2g fiber), 6g pro.

READER REVIEW

"My family loved these hand pies. Instead of freeze-dried strawberries, I topped the pies with toasted sliced almonds—delicious!"

—JELLYBUG, TASTEOFHOME.COM

CAKES & PIES

FRESH PUMPKIN PIE

In my opinion, there's no contest as to which pie is best. No matter how good your canned pumpkin is, it'll never match fresh pie filling made with traditional spices.
—Christy Harp, Massillon, OH

PREP: 30 MIN. + CHILLING • **BAKE:** 55 MIN. + COOLING • **MAKES:** 8 SERVINGS

Dough for single-crust pie
1 medium pie pumpkin
2 large eggs
¾ cup packed brown sugar
1 tsp. ground cinnamon
½ tsp. salt
½ tsp. ground ginger
¼ tsp. ground cloves
1 cup 2% milk
Whipped cream, optional

Make your own Dough for Single-Crust Pie. Recipe on p. 169.

Make your own Sweetened Whipped Cream. Recipe on p. 300.

NO TRICKS, JUST TREATS!
For the best puree, go for a pie pumpkin—the jack-o'-lantern variety just won't do. The seeds? Save them! Roast them for a tasty snack or crunchy garnish.

1. On a lightly floured surface, roll dough to a ⅛-in.-thick circle; transfer to a 9-in. pie plate. Trim crust to ½ in. beyond rim of plate; flute edge. Refrigerate while preparing filling.

2. Cut the pumpkin in half lengthwise; discard seeds. Place cut side down in a microwave-safe dish; add 1 in. water. Cover and microwave on high until very tender, 15-18 minutes.

3. Preheat oven to 425°. Drain pumpkin. When cool enough to handle, scoop out pulp and mash. Set aside 1¾ cups (save remaining pumpkin for another use). In a large bowl, combine mashed pumpkin, eggs, brown sugar, cinnamon, salt, ginger and cloves; beat until smooth. Gradually beat in milk. Pour into crust.

4. Bake for 15 minutes. Reduce the oven setting to 350°; bake until a knife inserted in the center comes out clean, 40-50 minutes longer. Cover the edge loosely with foil during last 30 minutes if needed to prevent overbrowning. Remove foil. Cool on a wire rack. If desired, serve with whipped cream. Refrigerate leftovers.

1 PIECE 303 cal., 14g fat (8g sat. fat), 79mg chol., 343mg sod., 41g carb. (24g sugars, 2g fiber), 5g pro.

CAKES & PIES

RUSTIC HONEY CAKE

When my boys were young, they couldn't drink milk but could have yogurt. This was a cake they could eat. And it's one dessert that isn't overly sweet, which is always a nice change of pace.
—Linda Leuer, Hamel, MN

PREP: 15 MIN. • **BAKE:** 30 MIN. + COOLING • **MAKES:** 12 SERVINGS

- ½ cup butter, softened
- 1 cup honey
- 2 large eggs, room temperature
- ½ cup plain yogurt
- 1 tsp. vanilla extract
- 2 cups all-purpose flour
- 2 tsp. baking powder
- ½ tsp. salt
- Assorted fresh fruit and additional honey
- Chopped pistachios, optional

1. Preheat oven to 350°. Grease a 9-in. cast-iron skillet.

2. In a large bowl, beat butter and honey until blended. Add the eggs, 1 at a time, beating well after each addition. Beat in yogurt and vanilla. In another bowl, whisk flour, baking powder and salt; add to the butter mixture. Transfer batter to prepared skillet.

3. Bake until a toothpick inserted in the center comes out clean, 30-35 minutes. Cool completely in pan on a wire rack. Serve with fruit, additional honey and, if desired, chopped pistachios.

FREEZE OPTION Securely wrap cooled cake in foil; freeze. To use, thaw at room temperature and top as directed.

1 PIECE 248 cal., 9g fat (5g sat. fat), 53mg chol., 257mg sod., 40g carb. (24g sugars, 1g fiber), 4g pro.

FROST IT IF YOU MUST!
This cake is delicious on its own, with a tender crumb and rich flavor. But if you like a little extra indulgence, serve the cake warm with a dollop of fresh whipped cream or a sprinkle of shredded coconut.

COCONUT PIE

I grew up watching my mother cook and bake from scratch, so premade foods were a novelty to me after I left home. One of Mom's best desserts is her creamy old-fashioned coconut pie. A rich slice is true comfort food.
—*Mary McGuire, Graham, NC*

PREP: 10 MIN. • **BAKE:** 45 MIN. + COOLING • **MAKES:** 8 SERVINGS

Dough for single-crust pie
1½ cups whole milk
1 cup sugar
¾ cup sweetened shredded coconut
2 large eggs, lightly beaten
3 Tbsp. all-purpose flour
1 Tbsp. butter, melted
¼ tsp. vanilla extract

Make your own Dough for Single-Crust Pie. Recipe on p. 169.

1. Preheat oven to 350°. On a lightly floured surface, roll the dough to a ⅛-in.-thick circle; transfer to a 9-in. pie plate. Trim crust to ½ in. beyond rim of plate; flute edge.

2. In a large bowl, combine the milk, sugar, coconut, eggs, flour, butter and vanilla. Pour into crust.

3. Bake until a knife inserted in center comes out clean, 45-50 minutes. Cool to room temperature on a wire rack. Refrigerate leftovers.

1 PIECE 382 cal., 19g fat (12g sat. fat), 85mg chol., 227mg sod., 49g carb. (32g sugars, 1g fiber), 6g pro.

GRANDMA'S BLACKBERRY CAKE

A lightly seasoned spice cake lets the wonderful flavor of blackberries shine through in this delectable treat.
—*Diana Martin, Moundsville, WV*

PREP: 15 MIN. • **BAKE:** 45 MIN. • **MAKES:** 9 SERVINGS

1 cup fresh blackberries
2 cups all-purpose flour, divided
½ cup butter, softened
1 cup sugar
2 large eggs, room temperature
1 tsp. baking soda
1 tsp. ground cinnamon
1 tsp. ground nutmeg
½ tsp. salt
¼ tsp. ground cloves
¼ tsp. ground allspice
¾ cup buttermilk
Optional: Whipped cream and confectioners' sugar

Make your own Sweetened Whipped Cream. Recipe on p. 300.

1. Preheat the oven to 350°. Toss the blackberries with ¼ cup flour; set aside. In a large bowl, cream the butter and sugar until light and fluffy, 5-7 minutes. Beat in eggs. Combine the baking soda, cinnamon, nutmeg, salt, cloves, allspice and remaining 1¾ cups flour; add to the creamed mixture alternately with the buttermilk, beating well after each addition. Fold in the blackberries.

2. Pour into a greased and floured 9-in. square baking pan. Bake until a toothpick inserted in the center comes out clean, 45-50 minutes. Cool on a wire rack. If desired, serve with whipped cream and top with confectioners' sugar and additional fresh blackberries.

1 PIECE 312 cal., 12g fat (7g sat. fat), 75mg chol., 410mg sod., 47g carb. (24g sugars, 2g fiber), 5g pro.

CAKES & PIES 225

BEST ANGEL FOOD CAKE

For our daughter's wedding, a friend made this lovely, airy cake from a recipe she's used for decades.
It really is one of the best angel food cake recipes I've found. Serve slices plain or dress them up with fresh fruit.
—*Marilyn Niemeyer, Doon, IA*

PREP: 15 MIN. + STANDING • **BAKE:** 35 MIN. + COOLING • **MAKES:** 16 SERVINGS

1¼ cups egg whites (about 9 large)
1½ cups sugar, divided
1 cup cake flour
1¼ tsp. cream of tartar
1 tsp. vanilla extract
¼ tsp. almond extract
¼ tsp. salt
   Optional: Whipped cream and
   fresh berries

Make your own Sweetened Whipped Cream. Recipe on p. 300.

1. Place egg whites in a large bowl; let stand at room temperature 30 minutes. Sift ½ cup sugar and flour together twice; set aside.

2. Place oven rack in the lowest position. Preheat oven to 350°. Add the cream of tartar, extracts and salt to egg whites; beat on medium speed until soft peaks form. Gradually add remaining sugar, about 2 Tbsp. at a time, beating on high until stiff peaks form. Gradually fold in flour mixture, about ½ cup at a time.

3. Gently spoon into an ungreased 10-in. tube pan. Cut through batter with a knife to remove air pockets. Bake until lightly browned and the entire top appears dry, 35-40 minutes. Immediately invert pan; cool completely, about 1 hour.

4. Run a knife around side and center tube of pan. Remove cake to a serving plate. If desired, serve with whipped cream and fresh berries.

1 PIECE 115 cal., 0 fat (0 sat. fat), 0 chol., 68mg sod., 26g carb. (19g sugars, 0 fiber), 3g pro. **DIABETIC EXCHANGES** 1½ starch.

made from scratch HOMEMADE STRAWBERRY SYRUP

This recipe is a spin-off of my dad's homemade syrup. Our son requests it with fluffy pancakes whenever he and his family come to visit.
—*Nancy Dunaway, Springfield, IL*

TAKES: 20 MIN.
MAKES: ABOUT 2½ CUPS

1 cup sugar
1 cup water
1½ cups mashed unsweetened
   strawberries

In a saucepan, bring sugar and water to a boil. Gradually add strawberries; return to a boil. Reduce heat; simmer, uncovered, 10 minutes, stirring occasionally. Serve over pancakes, waffles or ice cream.

2 TBSP. 43 cal., 0 fat (0 sat. fat), 0 chol., 0 sod., 11g carb. (11g sugars, 0 fiber), 0 pro.

CLASSIC LEMON MERINGUE PIE

Love lemon meringue pie? This is the only recipe you'll ever need. The flaky, tender, made-from-scratch crust is worth the effort.
—Lee Bremson, Kansas City, MO

PREP: 30 MIN. + STANDING • **BAKE:** 25 MIN. + CHILLING • **MAKES:** 8 SERVINGS

- 1⅓ cups all-purpose flour
- ½ tsp. salt
- ½ cup shortening
- 1 to 3 Tbsp. cold water

FILLING
- 1¼ cups sugar
- ¼ cup cornstarch
- 3 Tbsp. all-purpose flour
- ¼ tsp. salt
- 1½ cups water
- 3 large egg yolks, lightly beaten
- 2 Tbsp. butter
- 1½ tsp. grated lemon zest
- ⅓ cup lemon juice

MERINGUE
- 4 large egg whites
- ¾ tsp. vanilla extract
- ½ cup sugar, divided
- 1 Tbsp. cornstarch
- ½ cup cold water

1. In a small bowl, combine the flour and salt; cut in the shortening until crumbly. Gradually add 3 Tbsp. cold water, tossing with a fork until dough forms a ball.

2. Roll out dough to fit a 9-in. pie plate. Transfer crust to pie plate. Trim to ½ in. beyond rim of plate; flute edge. Bake at 425° for 12-15 minutes or until lightly browned.

3. Meanwhile, in a large saucepan, combine the sugar, cornstarch, flour and salt. Gradually stir in water until smooth. Cook and stir over medium-high heat until thickened and bubbly. Reduce heat; cook and stir 2 minutes longer.

4. Remove from the heat. Stir a small amount of hot filling into the egg yolks; return all to the pan, stirring constantly. Bring to a gentle boil; cook and stir for 2 minutes longer. Remove from the heat. Gently stir in the butter and lemon zest. Gradually stir in lemon juice just until combined. Pour into the crust.

5. Place egg whites in a large bowl; let stand at room temperature for 30 minutes. For meringue, in a saucepan, combine 2 Tbsp. sugar and cornstarch. Gradually stir in cold water. Cook and stir over medium heat until the mixture is clear. Transfer to a bowl; cool.

6. Beat egg whites and vanilla until soft peaks form. Gradually beat in the remaining sugar, 1 Tbsp. at a time. Beat in cornstarch mixture on high until stiff peaks form and the sugar is dissolved (meringue will not be smooth). Spread evenly over hot filling, sealing edge to the crust.

7. Bake at 350° for 25 minutes or until the meringue is golden brown. Cool on a wire rack for 1 hour. Refrigerate for at least for 3 hours before serving. Refrigerate leftovers.

1 PIECE 444 cal., 17g fat (5g sat. fat), 87mg chol., 282mg sod., 68g carb. (43g sugars, 1g fiber), 5g pro.

OLIVE OIL CAKE

A good olive oil cake isn't overly sweet, so it can just as easily be a breakfast treat or an afternoon snack as a dessert.
—Lisa Kaminski, Wauwatosa, WI

PREP: 15 MIN. • **BAKE:** 45 MIN. + COOLING • **MAKES:** 16 SERVINGS

- 3 large eggs, room temperature
- 1½ cups sugar
- ¾ cup extra virgin olive oil
- ¾ cup ground almonds
- ½ cup 2% milk
- 4 tsp. grated orange zest
- 1 tsp. vanilla extract
- 1¾ cups all-purpose flour
- 2 tsp. baking powder
- ½ tsp. salt
- ¾ cup confectioners' sugar
- 2 to 3 Tbsp. orange juice
  Sliced almonds, toasted, optional

1. Preheat oven to 350°. Grease and flour a 10-in. fluted tube pan. In a large bowl, beat the eggs on high speed 3 minutes. Gradually add sugar, beating until thick and lemon-colored. Gradually beat in oil. Beat in the ground almonds, milk, orange zest and vanilla.

2. In another bowl, whisk flour, baking powder and salt; fold into egg mixture. Transfer the batter to the prepared pan, spreading evenly. Bake until a toothpick inserted in the center comes out clean, 45-50 minutes. Cool in pan 15 minutes before removing to a wire rack to cool completely.

3. For icing, in a small bowl, whisk the confectioners' sugar and enough orange juice to reach a drizzling consistency. Drizzle over cake. If desired, sprinkle with almonds.

1 PIECE 279 cal., 14g fat (2g sat. fat), 35mg chol., 152mg sod., 37g carb. (25g sugars, 1g fiber), 4g pro.

CAKES & PIES

YELLOW LAYER CAKE WITH CHOCOLATE BUTTERCREAM

This will become your go-to recipe for celebrating birthdays. The tender yellow cake with flavorful chocolate buttercream is perfect for any occasion.
—Taste of Home *Test Kitchen*

PREP: 15 MIN. • **BAKE:** 25 MIN. + COOLING • **MAKES:** 16 SERVINGS

- ⅔ cup butter, softened
- 1¾ cups sugar
- 2 large eggs, room temperature
- 1½ tsp. vanilla extract
- 2½ cups all-purpose flour
- 2½ tsp. baking powder
- ½ tsp. salt
- 1¼ cups 2% milk

CHOCOLATE BUTTERCREAM
- 2 cups butter, softened
- 4 cups confectioners' sugar, sifted
- ½ cup Dutch-processed cocoa, sifted
- 1½ tsp. vanilla extract
- ⅛ tsp. salt
- ⅓ cup 2% milk

1. Preheat oven to 350°. Grease and flour two 9-in. round baking pans. In a large bowl, cream butter and sugar until light and fluffy, 5-7 minutes. Add eggs, 1 at a time, beating well after each addition. Beat in vanilla. In another bowl, whisk flour, baking powder and salt; add to creamed mixture alternately with milk, beating well after each addition.

2. Transfer to prepared pans. Bake until a toothpick inserted in the center comes out clean, 25-30 minutes. Cool in pans for 10 minutes before removing to wire racks to cool completely.

3. For the buttercream, in a large bowl, beat butter until creamy. Gradually beat in confectioners' sugar and cocoa until smooth. Add vanilla and salt. Add the milk; beat until light and fluffy, about 5 minutes.

4. Spread buttercream between layers and over top and sides of cake.

1 PIECE 593 cal., 33g fat (21g sat. fat), 107mg chol., 432mg sod., 72g carb. (53g sugars, 4g fiber), 5g pro.

CAKES & PIES

GOOEY BUTTER CAKE

A friend once shared a quick cake mix version of this recipe, but I prefer baking from scratch, so I made my own version. My family can't get enough! The center will sink a little—that's normal. It's just as enjoyable warm as it's chilled.
—Cheri Foster, Vail, AZ

PREP: 20 MIN. • **BAKE:** 40 MIN. + COOLING • **MAKES:** 16 SERVINGS

- 2½ cups all-purpose flour
- 1¾ cups sugar
- 2½ tsp. baking powder
- ½ tsp. salt
- 1 cup butter, melted
- 1 large egg, room temperature
- 1½ tsp. vanilla extract

TOPPING
- 1 pkg. (8 oz.) cream cheese, softened
- 2 large eggs, beaten, room temperature
- 2 cups confectioners' sugar

1. Preheat oven to 325°. In a large bowl, combine the flour, sugar, baking powder and salt. In another bowl, whisk together butter, egg and vanilla; add to the flour mixture and stir to combine. Press onto bottom of a greased 13x9-in. baking dish.

2. For topping, in a large bowl, beat cream cheese and eggs until smooth. Add confectioners' sugar and stir to combine. Pour over crust. Bake until center is almost set and edges start to brown, 40-45 minutes. Cool 1 hour on a wire rack. Sprinkle with additional confectioners' sugar if desired.

1 PIECE 381 cal., 17g fat (10g sat. fat), 80mg chol., 299mg sod., 53g carb. (37g sugars, 1g fiber), 4g pro.

BANANA BREAD SNACK CAKES

This snack cake doesn't need any frosting—just a dusting of powdered sugar. Guests are amazed how easy it is to make the treat from scratch. Just before serving, top with sliced bananas if you'd like.
—*Denise Loewenthal, Hinckley, OH*

PREP: 10 MIN. • **BAKE:** 30 MIN. + COOLING • **MAKES:** 9 SERVINGS

1⅔ cups all-purpose flour
1 tsp. baking soda
1 cup packed brown sugar
½ cup water
⅓ cup mashed ripe bananas (about 1 small)
⅓ cup canola oil
½ tsp. vanilla extract
Confectioners' sugar

Preheat oven to 350°. In a bowl, combine flour and baking soda. In another bowl, whisk brown sugar, water, banana, oil and vanilla. Stir into dry ingredients just until moistened. Transfer to a greased 8-in. square baking pan. Bake until a toothpick inserted in center comes out clean, 30-35 minutes. Cool on a wire rack. Dust the cake with confectioners' sugar. Cut into 9 pieces.

1 PIECE 259 cal., 9g fat (1g sat. fat), 0 chol., 147mg sod., 44g carb. (25g sugars, 1g fiber), 3g pro.

NOTES

_____
_____
_____
_____
_____

CAKES & PIES   233

CREAM CHEESE BLUEBERRY PIE

This delightful old-fashioned pie is a great finale to any meal. Best of all, it's far easier than you might think!
—Lisieux Bauman, Cheektowaga, NY

PREP: 40 MIN. + CHILLING • **COOK:** 10 MIN. + CHILLING • **MAKES:** 8 SERVINGS

Dough for single-crust pie
- 4 oz. cream cheese, softened
- ½ cup confectioners' sugar
- ½ cup heavy whipping cream, whipped
- ⅔ cup sugar
- ¼ cup cornstarch
- ½ cup water
- ¼ cup lemon juice
- 3 cups fresh or frozen blueberries

Make your own Dough for Single-Crust Pie. Recipe on p. 169.

1. On a lightly floured surface, roll dough to a ⅛-in.-thick circle; transfer to a 9-in. pie plate. Trim to ½ in. beyond rim of the plate; flute edge. Refrigerate 30 minutes. Preheat oven to 425°.

2. Line crust with a double thickness of foil. Fill with pie weights, dried beans or uncooked rice. Bake on a lower oven rack until edge is golden brown, 20-25 minutes. Remove foil and weights; bake until the bottom is golden brown, 3-6 minutes longer. Cool on a wire rack.

3. In a small bowl, beat cream cheese and confectioners' sugar until smooth. Fold in whipped cream. Spread into the pie shell.

4. In a large saucepan, combine sugar, cornstarch, water and lemon juice until smooth; stir in blueberries. Bring to a boil over medium heat; cook and stir for 2 minutes or until thickened. Cool. Spread over the cream cheese layer. Refrigerate until serving.

1 PIECE 414 cal., 22g fat (14g sat. fat), 61mg chol., 205mg sod., 52g carb. (31g sugars, 2g fiber), 4g pro.

SPICED APPLE CAKE WITH CARAMEL ICING

Easy to prepare and popular with my friends and family, this apple cake is one of my all-time favorite recipes. A slice of this soft treat is delicious with a hot cup of coffee or tea.
—Monica Burns, Fort Worth, TX

PREP: 45 MIN. • **BAKE:** 1¼ HOURS + COOLING • **MAKES:** 16 SERVINGS

- 3 cups chopped peeled Gala or Braeburn apples (about 3 medium)
- ½ cup bourbon
- 2 cups sugar
- 1½ cups canola oil
- 3 large eggs, room temperature
- 2 tsp. vanilla extract
- 3 cups all-purpose flour
- 2 tsp. apple pie spice
- 1 tsp. salt
- 1 tsp. baking soda
- 1 cup chopped walnuts, toasted

ICING
- ¼ cup butter, cubed
- ½ cup packed brown sugar
- 1 Tbsp. 2% milk
- 1 Tbsp. bourbon
  Dash salt
- ⅛ tsp. vanilla extract

1. Preheat oven to 350°. Grease and flour a 10-in. tube pan. In a large bowl, toss the apples with bourbon.

2. In a large bowl, beat sugar, oil, eggs and vanilla until well blended. In another bowl, whisk the flour, pie spice, salt and baking soda; gradually beat into sugar mixture. Stir in the apple mixture and walnuts.

3. Transfer to prepared pan. Bake until a toothpick inserted in the center comes out clean, 1¼-1½ hours. Cool in pan for 10 minutes before removing to wire rack.

4. In a small heavy saucepan, combine butter, brown sugar, milk, bourbon and salt. Bring to a boil over medium heat, stirring occasionally; cook and stir 3 minutes. Remove from heat; stir in vanilla. Drizzle over warm cake. Cool completely.

NOTE To toast nuts, bake in a shallow pan in a 350° oven for 5-10 minutes or cook in a skillet over low heat until lightly browned, stirring occasionally. To remove the cakes easily, use solid shortening to grease plain and fluted tube pans.

1 PIECE 499 cal., 30g fat (4g sat. fat), 43mg chol., 275mg sod., 54g carb. (34g sugars, 2g fiber), 5g pro.

CLASSIC ALMOND RICOTTA CAKE

After I started making homemade ricotta cheese, I was inspired to use it in desserts, not just savory dishes. This almond-flavored treat has a smooth texture and is versatile enough for dinner parties or a casual snack. Missing a stand mixer? Just use a hand mixer. For a change of pace, try adding lemon zest or fresh blueberries.
—*Carrie Dault, Harriman, TN*

PREP: 20 MIN. • **BAKE:** 45 MIN. + COOLING • **MAKES:** 12 SERVINGS

- ½ cup unsalted butter, softened
- 1 cup sugar
- 2 large eggs, room temperature
- 1¼ tsp. almond extract
- 1 tsp. vanilla extract
- 1½ cups all-purpose flour
- 1¼ tsp. baking powder
- ¼ tsp. salt
- 1 carton (15 oz.) whole-milk ricotta cheese
- ¾ cup sliced almonds
  Confectioners' sugar, optional

1. Preheat oven to 350°. In a large bowl, cream butter and sugar until light and fluffy, 5-7 minutes. Add eggs, 1 at a time, beating well after each addition. Beat in extracts. Sift flour, baking powder and salt together; gradually add to creamed mixture alternately with ricotta. Spread into a greased 9-in. springform pan. Sprinkle with almonds.

2. Bake until a toothpick inserted near the center comes out with moist crumbs, 45-50 minutes. Cool on a wire rack for 15 minutes. Loosen sides from pan with a knife; remove rim from pan. Allow cake to cool completely. If desired, dust with confectioners' sugar before serving.

1 PIECE 289 cal., 15g fat (8g sat. fat), 66mg chol., 155mg sod., 32g carb. (19g sugars, 1g fiber), 8g pro.

CAKES & PIES   237

OLD-TIME BUTTERMILK PIE

This recipe is more than a 100 years old! My mother and grandmother made this pie with buttermilk and eggs from our farm, serving it at church meetings and social gatherings. I did the same, and now our children make it too!
—*Kate Mathews, Shreveport, LA*

PREP: 15 MIN. • **BAKE:** 45 MIN. + COOLING • **MAKES:** 10 SERVINGS

CRUST
- 1½ cups all-purpose flour
- 1 tsp. salt
- ½ cup shortening
- ¼ cup cold 2% milk
- 1 large egg, lightly beaten

FILLING
- ½ cup butter, softened
- 2 cups sugar
- 3 Tbsp. all-purpose flour
- 3 large eggs
- 1 cup buttermilk
- 1 tsp. vanilla extract
- 1 tsp. ground cinnamon
- ¼ cup lemon juice
- Optional: Whipped cream and fresh berries

Make your own Sweetened Whipped Cream. Recipe on p. 300.

1. Preheat oven to 350°. In a large bowl, mix flour and salt. Cut in shortening until crumbly. Gradually stir in milk and egg. On a lightly floured surface, roll dough to a ⅛-in.-thick circle; transfer to a 9-in. pie plate. Trim crust to ½ in. beyond rim of plate; flute edge.

2. For filling, in a large bowl, cream butter and sugar; beat in flour. Add eggs, 1 at a time, beating well after each addition. Stir in the buttermilk, vanilla, cinnamon and lemon juice; mix well. Pour into crust.

3. Bake until center is set, 45-50 minutes. Cool completely on a wire rack. Serve or refrigerate within 2 hours. If desired, top servings with whipped cream and fresh berries.

1 PIECE 448 cal., 21g fat (9g sat. fat), 100mg chol., 388mg sod., 59g carb. (42g sugars, 1g fiber), 6g pro.

CAKES & PIES

BLUE-RIBBON BUTTER CAKE

I found this recipe in an old cookbook I bought at a garage sale, and I couldn't wait to try it. I knew it had been someone's favorite because of the well-worn page.
—*Joan Gertz, Palmetto, FL*

PREP: 20 MIN. • **BAKE:** 55 MIN. + COOLING • **MAKES:** 16 SERVINGS

1   cup butter, softened
2   cups sugar
4   large eggs, room temperature
2   tsp. vanilla extract
3   cups all-purpose flour
1   tsp. baking powder
½   tsp. baking soda
½   tsp. salt
1   cup buttermilk

BUTTER SAUCE
1   cup sugar
½   cup butter, cubed
¼   cup water
1½ tsp. almond extract
1½ tsp. vanilla extract

1. In a large bowl, cream butter and sugar until light and fluffy. Add eggs, 1 at a time, beating well after each addition. Beat in vanilla. Combine flour, baking powder, baking soda and salt; add to creamed mixture alternately with buttermilk, beating well after each addition.

2. Pour into a greased and floured 10-in. tube pan. Bake at 350° until a toothpick inserted in the center comes out clean, 55-70 minutes. Cool 10 minutes. Run a knife around edge and center tube of pan. Invert cake onto a wire rack over waxed paper.

3. For sauce, combine sugar, butter and water in a small saucepan. Cook over medium heat just until butter is melted and sugar is dissolved. Remove from heat; stir in extracts.

4. Poke holes in top of the warm cake; spoon ¼ cup sauce over cake. Let stand until sauce is absorbed. Repeat twice. Poke holes into sides of the cake; brush the remaining sauce over sides. Cool completely.

1 PIECE 410 cal., 19g fat (11g sat. fat), 100mg chol., 344mg sod., 56g carb. (38g sugars, 1g fiber), 5g pro.

---

made from scratch
EASY BLUEBERRY SAUCE

Looking for a blueberry sauce recipe for cheesecake? Look no further! This luscious blueberry topping is perfectly sweetened to put on anything from a scoop of vanilla ice cream to a slice of angel food or pound cake.
—*Doris Dezur, Eugene, OR*

TAKES: 20 MIN. • **MAKES:** ¾ CUP

¼   cup sugar
1   tsp. cornstarch
    Dash salt
¼   cup water
1   cup fresh or frozen blueberries
½   tsp. grated lemon zest
1½ tsp. lemon juice
    Vanilla ice cream

In a small saucepan, combine the sugar, cornstarch and salt. Gradually whisk in the water until mixture is smooth. Add the blueberries, lemon zest and juice; bring to a boil over medium heat, stirring constantly. Cook and stir until thickened, 2-3 minutes (some berries will remain whole). Serve warm or chilled over vanilla ice cream.

¼ CUP 97 cal., 0 fat (0 sat. fat), 0 chol., 50mg sod., 25g carb. (22g sugars, 1g fiber), 0 pro.

ITALIAN CREAM CHEESE CAKE

Buttermilk makes every bite of this awesome Italian cream cheese cake moist and flavorful. I rely on this recipe year-round.
—*Joyce Lutz, Centerview, MO*

PREP: 40 MIN. • **BAKE:** 20 MIN. + COOLING • **MAKES:** 16 SERVINGS

- ½ cup butter, softened
- ½ cup shortening
- 2 cups sugar
- 5 large eggs, separated, room temperature
- 1 tsp. vanilla extract
- 2 cups all-purpose flour
- 1 tsp. baking soda
- 1 cup buttermilk
- 1½ cups sweetened shredded coconut
- 1 cup chopped pecans

CREAM CHEESE FROSTING

- 11 oz. cream cheese, softened
- ¾ cup butter, softened
- 6 cups confectioners' sugar
- 1½ tsp. vanilla extract
- ¾ cup chopped pecans

1. Preheat oven to 350°. Grease and flour three 9-in. round baking pans. In a large bowl, cream the butter, shortening and sugar until light and fluffy, 5-7 minutes. Beat in egg yolks and vanilla. Combine flour and baking soda; add to creamed mixture alternately with the buttermilk. Beat until just combined. Stir in coconut and pecans.

2. In another bowl, beat egg whites with clean beaters until stiff but not dry. Fold a fourth of the egg whites into the batter, then fold in the remaining whites. Pour into the prepared pans.

3. Bake until a toothpick inserted in the center comes out clean, 20-25 minutes. Cool 10 minutes before removing from pans to wire racks to cool completely.

4. For frosting, beat cream cheese and butter until smooth. Beat in the confectioners' sugar and vanilla until fluffy. Stir in pecans. Spread frosting between layers and over top and side of cake. Store cake in the refrigerator.

1 PIECE 736 cal., 41g fat (19g sat. fat), 117mg chol., 330mg sod., 90g carb. (75g sugars, 2g fiber), 7g pro.

BEYOND THE CARTON

Instead of buying buttermilk, you can place 1 Tbsp. white vinegar or lemon juice in a liquid measuring cup and add enough milk to measure 1 cup. Stir, let sit for 5 minutes. Alternatively, substitute 1 cup plain yogurt for the buttermilk.

CAKES & PIES 241

STRAWBERRY CUPCAKES

These cupcakes are the perfect use for fresh strawberries. Instead of strawberry jam or Jell-O powder, they feature the natural color and flavor of vibrant, fresh berries. Pair them with a pale pink strawberry frosting or use your favorite—either way, they're sure to impress!
—Molly Allen, Hood River, OR

PREP: 20 MIN. + CHILLING • **BAKE:** 20 MIN. + COOLING • **MAKES:** 1 DOZEN

- 1½ lbs. fresh strawberries, hulled
- ½ cup unsalted butter, softened
- 1 cup sugar
- 1 large egg, room temperature
- 1 large egg white, room temperature
- 1 tsp. vanilla extract
- 1⅓ cups all-purpose flour
- ½ tsp. baking powder
- ½ tsp. baking soda
- ½ tsp. salt
- ⅓ cup 2% milk
- ¼ cup sour cream
- Red food coloring, optional

FROSTING
- ½ cup unsalted butter, softened
- 5½ to 6 cups confectioners' sugar, divided
- 2 Tbsp. 2% milk
- 1 tsp. vanilla extract
- ⅛ tsp. salt

1. Place strawberries in a food processor. Process until pureed. Transfer to a small saucepan. Bring to a boil over medium heat. Reduce heat; simmer, uncovered, until reduced to 1¼ cups, 20-25 minutes, stirring occasionally. Transfer to a bowl. Cover and refrigerate until chilled.

2. Preheat oven to 350°. Line 12 muffin cups with paper liners. In a large bowl, cream butter and sugar until light and fluffy, 5-7 minutes. Beat in the egg, egg white and vanilla. In a bowl, whisk flour, baking powder, baking soda and salt. In a small bowl, whisk milk and sour cream until blended. Add dry ingredients to the creamed mixture alternately with milk mixture. Fold in ¾ cup cooled strawberry puree. If desired, add food coloring. Fill prepared cups half full with batter. Bake until a toothpick inserted in the center comes out clean, 20-25 minutes. Cool in pan 10 minutes before removing to wire rack to cool completely.

3. For frosting, in a large bowl, cream butter and 2 cups confectioners' sugar until light and fluffy, 3-4 minutes. Beat in the milk, vanilla, salt and remaining ½ cup strawberry puree. Gradually beat in enough remaining confectioners' sugar until frosting reaches desired consistency. Pipe or spread frosting over cooled cupcakes.

1 CUPCAKE 507 cal., 17g fat (10g sat. fat), 60mg chol., 216mg sod., 87g carb. (74g sugars, 2g fiber), 3g pro.

from scratch BROWNIES, BARS & COOKIES

MILLIONAIRE SHORTBREAD BARS, PAGE 254

FUDGE BROWNIE PIE

Here's a fun and festive way to serve brownies. Family and friends will love topping their pieces with whipped cream and strawberries.
—*Johnnie McLeod, Bastrop, LA*

PREP: 15 MIN. • **BAKE:** 25 MIN. • **MAKES:** 6 SERVINGS

- 1 cup sugar
- ½ cup butter, melted
- 2 large eggs, room temperature
- 1 tsp. vanilla extract
- ½ cup all-purpose flour
- ⅓ cup baking cocoa
- ¼ tsp. salt
- ½ cup chopped pecans
  Optional: Ice cream, whipped cream or strawberries

1. In a large bowl, beat sugar and butter. Add eggs and vanilla; mix well. Add flour, cocoa and salt. Stir in pecans.

2. Pour into a greased 9-in. pie pan or ovenproof skillet. Bake at 350° until almost set, 25-30 minutes. If desired, serve with optional toppings.

1 PIECE 409 cal., 24g fat (11g sat. fat), 112mg chol., 274mg sod., 46g carb. (33g sugars, 2g fiber), 5g pro.

NOTES

KEY LIME BLONDIE BARS

Here's my tropical take on a beloved treat. These Key lime bars combine the taste of the classic pie with a blondie batter and cream cheese frosting. You can make a thicker crust if desired.
—Kristin LaBoon, Austin, TX

PREP: 35 MIN. + CHILLING • **BAKE:** 25 MIN. + COOLING • **MAKES:** 16 SERVINGS

- 1⅓ cups graham cracker crumbs, divided
- ⅓ cup plus 2 Tbsp. melted butter, divided
- 3 Tbsp. plus ¼ cup packed brown sugar, divided
- ⅔ cup butter, softened
- 1 cup plus 1 Tbsp. sugar, divided
- 2 large eggs, room temperature
- 1 large egg white, room temperature
- 3 Tbsp. Key lime juice
- 4½ tsp. grated Key lime zest
- 1 cup all-purpose flour
- ½ tsp. plus ⅛ tsp. salt, divided
- 1 tsp. vanilla extract
- ⅛ tsp. ground cinnamon

FROSTING
- ¼ cup butter, softened
- ¼ cup cream cheese, softened
- 4 cups confectioners' sugar
- 2 Tbsp. 2% milk
- 1 tsp. vanilla extract
- Key lime slices, optional

1. Preheat oven to 350°. Line a 9-in. square baking pan with parchment, letting ends extend up sides. Combine 1 cup cracker crumbs, ⅓ cup melted butter and 3 Tbsp. brown sugar; press onto bottom of prepared pan. Bake 10 minutes. Cool on a wire rack.

2. For the blondie layer, in a large bowl, cream softened butter and 1 cup sugar until light and fluffy, 5-7 minutes. Beat in the eggs, egg white and lime juice and zest. In a small bowl, mix flour and ½ tsp. salt; gradually add to creamed mixture, mixing well.

3. Spread over the crust. Bake until a toothpick inserted in center comes out clean, 25-30 minutes (do not overbake). Cool completely in pan on a wire rack.

4. For streusel, combine the remaining ⅓ cup cracker crumbs, 2 Tbsp. melted butter, ¼ cup brown sugar, 1 Tbsp. sugar and ⅛ tsp. salt, along with the vanilla and cinnamon, until crumbly. Reserve ½ cup for topping.

5. In a large bowl, combine butter, cream cheese, confectioners' sugar, milk and vanilla extract; beat until smooth. Stir in remaining ½ cup streusel. Spread over bars. Sprinkle with the reserved topping. Refrigerate for at least 4 hours before cutting. Lifting with parchment, remove from the pan. Cut into bars. Store in an airtight container in refrigerator. Garnish with sliced Key limes if desired.

1 BLONDIE 422 cal., 19g fat (11g sat. fat), 69mg chol., 283mg sod., 62g carb. (51g sugars, 1g fiber), 3g pro.

READER REVIEW

"These are absolutely delicious! I used 2 cups sugar for the frosting, and it was perfect. Thanks for the wonderful recipe!"
—TAMMY2225, TASTEOFHOME.COM

SNICKERDOODLES

The history of these whimsically named treats is widely disputed, but their popularity is undeniable! Help yourself to one of our soft cinnamon-sugared cookies and see for yourself.
—Taste of Home *Test Kitchen*

PREP: 20 MIN. • **BAKE:** 10 MIN./BATCH • **MAKES:** 2½ DOZEN

½ cup butter, softened
1 cup sugar
1 large egg, room temperature
½ tsp. vanilla extract
1½ cups all-purpose flour
¼ tsp. salt
¼ tsp. baking soda
¼ tsp. cream of tartar

CINNAMON SUGAR
2 Tbsp. sugar
2 tsp. ground cinnamon

1. Preheat oven to 375°. Cream butter and sugar until light and fluffy, 5-7 minutes; beat in the egg and vanilla. In another bowl, whisk flour, salt, baking soda and cream of tartar; gradually beat into the creamed mixture.

2. In a small bowl, combine sugar and cinnamon. Shape dough into 1-in. balls; roll in the cinnamon sugar. Place 2 in. apart on ungreased baking sheets.

3. Bake until light brown, 10-12 minutes. Remove from pans to wire racks to cool.

1 COOKIE 82 cal., 3g fat (2g sat. fat), 14mg chol., 57mg sod., 13g carb. (8g sugars, 0 fiber), 1g pro.

BROWNIES, BARS & COOKIES   249

THICK SUGAR COOKIES

Thicker than the norm, this sugar cookie is like one you might find at a good bakery. My children often request these for their birthdays and are always happy to help decorate.
—*Heather Biedler, Martinsburg, WV*

PREP: 25 MIN. + CHILLING • **BAKE:** 10 MIN./BATCH + COOLING • **MAKES:** ABOUT 3 DOZEN

- 1 cup butter, softened
- 1 cup sugar
- 2 large eggs, room temperature
- 3 large egg yolks, room temperature
- 1½ tsp. vanilla extract
- ¾ tsp. almond extract
- 3½ cups all-purpose flour
- 1½ tsp. baking powder
- ¼ tsp. salt

FROSTING
- 4 cups confectioners' sugar
- ½ cup butter, softened
- ½ cup shortening
- 1 tsp. vanilla extract
- ½ tsp. almond extract
- 2 to 3 Tbsp. 2% milk
- Assorted colored sprinkles, optional

Make your own DIY Colored Sugar. Recipe on p. 278.

1. In a large bowl, cream butter and sugar until light and fluffy, 5-7 minutes. Beat in eggs, egg yolks and extracts. In another bowl, whisk flour, baking powder and salt; gradually beat into creamed mixture. Shape into a disk; wrap and refrigerate 1 hour or until firm enough to roll.

2. Preheat oven to 375°. On a lightly floured surface, roll dough to ½-in. thickness. Cut with a floured 2-in. cookie cutter. Place the cutouts 1 in. apart on ungreased baking sheets.

3. Bake until edges begin to brown, 10-12 minutes. Cool on pans 5 minutes. Remove to wire racks to cool completely.

4. For frosting, in a large bowl, beat confectioners' sugar, butter, shortening, extracts and enough milk to reach desired consistency. Spread over cookies. If desired, top cookies with sprinkles.

1 FROSTED COOKIE 220 cal., 11g fat (6g sat. fat), 46mg chol., 103mg sod., 28g carb. (19g sugars, 0 fiber), 2g pro.

CLASSIC LEMON BARS

These bars are simple enough for no-fuss dinners yet elegant enough for special celebrations.
Regardless of when you serve them, I'm sure they'll be a hit at your home.
—*Melissa Mosness, Loveland, CO*

PREP: 15 MIN. • **BAKE:** 25 MIN. + COOLING • **MAKES:** 9 SERVINGS

½ cup butter, softened
¼ cup sugar
1 cup all-purpose flour

FILLING
¾ cup sugar
2 large eggs
3 Tbsp. lemon juice
2 Tbsp. all-purpose flour
1 tsp. grated lemon zest
¼ tsp. baking powder
   Confectioners' sugar

1. Preheat oven to 350°. In a small bowl, cream the butter and sugar until light and fluffy, 5-7 minutes; gradually beat in flour until blended.

2. Press into an ungreased 8-in. square baking dish. Bake 15-20 minutes or until the edges are lightly browned.

3. For filling, in a small bowl, beat the sugar, eggs, lemon juice, flour, lemon zest and baking powder until frothy. Pour over crust.

4. Bake 10-15 minutes longer or until set and lightly browned. Cool on a wire rack. Sprinkle with confectioners' sugar. Cut into squares.

1 PIECE 250 cal., 11g fat (7g sat. fat), 74mg chol., 99mg sod., 35g carb. (23g sugars, 0 fiber), 3g pro.

COOKIE JAR GINGERSNAPS

My grandma kept two cookie jars in her pantry. One of the jars, which I now have, always had these crisp and chewy gingersnaps in it. They're still my favorite cookie recipe. My daughter, Becky, used this recipe for a 4-H fair and won a blue ribbon.
—*Deb Handy, Pomona, KS*

PREP: 20 MIN. • **BAKE:** 15 MIN./BATCH • **MAKES:** 3 DOZEN

¾ cup shortening
1 cup plus 2 Tbsp. sugar, divided
1 large egg, room temperature
¼ cup molasses
2 cups all-purpose flour
2 tsp. baking soda
1½ tsp. ground ginger
1 tsp. ground cinnamon
½ tsp. salt

1. Preheat the oven to 350°. Cream the shortening and 1 cup sugar until light and fluffy, 5-7 minutes. Beat in egg and molasses. In another bowl, combine the next 5 ingredients; gradually add to the creamed mixture and mix well.

2. Shape level tablespoons of dough into balls. Dip each ball halfway into remaining sugar; place 2 in. apart, sugary side up, on greased baking sheets. Bake until lightly browned and crinkly, 12-15 minutes. Remove to wire racks to cool.

1 COOKIE 92 cal., 4g fat (1g sat. fat), 5mg chol., 106mg sod., 13g carb. (7g sugars, 0 fiber), 1g pro.

ALMOND BISCOTTI

I've learned to bake a double batch of these crisp dunking cookies because one batch goes too fast!
—H. Michaelsen, St. Charles, IL

PREP: 15 MIN. • **BAKE:** 35 MIN. + COOLING • **MAKES:** 3 DOZEN

- ½ cup butter, softened
- 1¼ cups sugar, divided
- 3 large eggs, room temperature
- 1 tsp. anise extract
- 2 cups all-purpose flour
- 2 tsp. baking powder
- Dash salt
- ½ cup chopped almonds
- 2 tsp. 2% milk

1. Preheat oven to 375°. In a large bowl, cream butter and 1 cup sugar until light and fluffy, 5-7 minutes. Add eggs, 1 at a time, beating well after each addition. Beat in extract. Combine dry ingredients; gradually add to creamed mixture and mix well. Stir in almonds.

2. Line a baking sheet with foil and grease foil. Divide the dough in half; on the foil, shape each portion into a 12x3-in. rectangle. Brush with milk; sprinkle with remaining ¼ cup sugar.

3. Bake until golden brown and firm to touch, 15-20 minutes. Lift foil with rectangles onto a wire rack; cool for 15 minutes. Reduce oven heat to 300°.

4. Transfer rectangles to a cutting board; cut diagonally with a serrated knife into ½-in. slices. Place cut side down on ungreased baking sheets.

5. Bake for 10 minutes. Turn and bake until firm, 10 minutes longer. Remove to wire racks to cool. Store cookies in an airtight container.

1 COOKIE 207 cal., 9g fat (4g sat. fat), 50mg chol., 129mg sod., 29g carb. (16g sugars, 1g fiber), 4g pro.

BROWNIES, BARS & COOKIES

MILLIONAIRE SHORTBREAD BARS

This three-in-one bar brings together the delectable flavors of buttery shortbread, sweet caramel and rich chocolate for a treat worth a million bucks. Cut it easily into any size bar you wish.
—Taste of Home *Test Kitchen*

PREP: 40 MIN. + CHILLING • **BAKE:** 20 MIN. + COOLING • **MAKES:** 2 DOZEN

- 1 cup unsalted butter, softened
- ⅓ cup sugar
- 1½ tsp. vanilla extract
- 1 large egg yolk, room temperature
- 2 cups all-purpose flour
- ½ tsp. salt

CARAMEL FILLING
- 1 can (14 oz.) sweetened condensed milk
- 1 cup packed brown sugar
- ¾ cup unsalted butter, cubed
- ¼ cup light corn syrup
- 1 tsp. vanilla extract
- ¼ tsp. salt

TOPPING
- 1½ cups 60% cacao bittersweet chocolate baking chips
- ⅔ cup heavy whipping cream
- Flaked sea salt, optional

1. Line a 13x9-in. pan with parchment, letting ends extend up sides. In a large bowl, cream butter, sugar and vanilla until light and fluffy, 5-7 minutes. Beat in egg yolk. In another bowl, whisk flour and salt; gradually beat into creamed mixture.

2. Spread into prepared pan (dough will be sticky). Refrigerate for 30 minutes. Preheat oven to 350°. Bake until edges are lightly browned and center is dry, 20-25 minutes. Cool completely on a wire rack.

3. Meanwhile, in a large heavy saucepan, combine caramel filling ingredients. Bring to a boil over medium heat, stirring occasionally. Reduce heat to maintain a low boil; cook and stir until mixture is amber-colored and reaches 225°, 20-25 minutes. Remove from heat; quickly pour over cooled crust. Let cool 15 minutes; refrigerate until chilled, about 1 hour.

4. For ganache topping, place chocolate in a small bowl. In a small saucepan, bring cream just to a boil. Pour over the chocolate; let stand 5 minutes. Stir with a whisk until smooth. Pour over caramel layer. If desired, sprinkle with sea salt. Refrigerate until set, at least 2 hours. Lifting with the parchment, remove the shortbread from pan. Cut into bars. Store in an airtight container in refrigerator.

1 BAR 351 cal., 21g fat (13g sat. fat), 53mg chol., 103mg sod., 41g carb. (32g sugars, 1g fiber), 4g pro.

GIANT MOLASSES COOKIES

My family always requests these soft and deliciously chewy cookies. The cookies are also great for shipping as holiday gifts or to troops overseas.
—*Kristine Chayes, Smithtown, NY*

PREP: 30 MIN. • **BAKE:** 15 MIN./BATCH • **MAKES:** 2 DOZEN

- 1½ cups butter, softened
- 2 cups sugar
- 2 large eggs, room temperature
- ½ cup molasses
- 4½ cups all-purpose flour
- 4 tsp. ground ginger
- 2 tsp. baking soda
- 1½ tsp. ground cinnamon
- 1 tsp. ground cloves
- ¼ tsp. salt
- ¼ cup chopped pecans
- ¾ cup coarse sugar

1. Preheat oven to 350°. In a large bowl, cream the butter and sugar until light and fluffy, 5-7 minutes. Beat in the eggs and molasses. Combine the flour, ginger, baking soda, cinnamon, cloves and salt; gradually add to creamed mixture and mix well. Fold in pecans.

2. Shape into 2-in. balls and roll in coarse sugar. Place 2½ in. apart on ungreased baking sheets. Bake until the tops are cracked, 13-15 minutes. Remove to wire racks to cool.

1 COOKIE 310 cal., 13g fat (7g sat. fat), 48mg chol., 219mg sod., 46g carb. (27g sugars, 1g fiber), 3g pro.

BIG & BUTTERY CHOCOLATE CHIP COOKIES

My take on the classic cookie is inspired by a bakery in California called Hungry Bear. It's big, thick and chewy—truly the best chocolate chip cookie recipe.
—Irene Yeh, Mequon, WI

PREP: 35 MIN. + CHILLING • **BAKE:** 10 MIN./BATCH • **MAKES:** ABOUT 2 DOZEN

- 1 cup butter, softened
- 1 cup packed brown sugar
- ¾ cup sugar
- 2 large eggs, room temperature
- 1½ tsp. vanilla extract
- 2⅔ cups all-purpose flour
- 1¼ tsp. baking soda
- 1 tsp. salt
- 1 pkg. (12 oz.) semisweet chocolate chips
- 2 cups coarsely chopped walnuts, toasted

1. In a large bowl, beat the butter and sugars until blended. Beat in eggs and vanilla. In a small bowl, whisk the flour, baking soda and salt; gradually beat into the butter mixture. Stir in the chocolate chips and walnuts.

2. Shape ¼ cupfuls of dough into balls. Flatten each to ¾-in. thickness (2½-in. diameter), smoothing edge as necessary. Place in an airtight container, separating layers with waxed paper or parchment; refrigerate, covered, overnight.

3. To bake, place the dough portions 2 in. apart on parchment-lined baking sheets; let stand at room temperature 30 minutes before baking. Preheat oven to 400°.

4. Bake until the edges are golden brown (centers will be light), 10-12 minutes. Cool on pans 2 minutes. Remove to wire racks to cool completely.

NOTE To toast nuts, bake in a shallow pan in a 350° oven for 5-10 minutes or cook in a skillet over low heat until lightly browned, stirring occasionally.

1 COOKIE 311 cal., 19g fat (8g sat. fat), 38mg chol., 229mg sod., 35g carb. (23g sugars, 2g fiber), 4g pro.

ALMOND CHOCOLATE CHIP COOKIES Reduce vanilla to 1 tsp. and add ¼ tsp. almond extract. Substitute toasted almonds for the walnuts.

BIG & BUTTERY WHITE CHIP COOKIES Substitute white baking chips for the chocolate chips and toasted hazelnuts for the walnuts.

BIG & BUTTERY CRANBERRY NUT COOKIES Substitute dried cranberries for the chocolate chips.

BIG & BUTTERY CHERRY CHOCOLATE CHIP COOKIES Substitute 1 cup chopped dried cherries for 1 cup walnuts.

BROWNIES, BARS & COOKIES

ZUCCHINI BROWNIES

A fast peanut butter and chocolate frosting tops these cakelike brownies. What a sweet way to use up your garden bounty!
—*Allyson Wilkins, Amherst, NH*

PREP: 20 MIN. • **BAKE:** 35 MIN. • **MAKES:** 1½ DOZEN

- 1 cup butter, softened
- 1½ cups sugar
- 2 large eggs, room temperature
- ½ cup plain yogurt
- 1 tsp. vanilla extract
- 2½ cups all-purpose flour
- ¼ cup baking cocoa
- 1 tsp. baking soda
- ½ tsp. salt
- 2 cups shredded zucchini

FROSTING
- ⅔ cup semisweet chocolate chips
- ½ cup creamy peanut butter

Make your own Homemade Peanut Butter. Recipe on p. 270.

1. Preheat oven to 350°. In a large bowl, cream butter and sugar until light and fluffy, 5-7 minutes. Add eggs, 1 at a time, beating well after each addition. Beat in the yogurt and vanilla. In another bowl, combine flour, cocoa, baking soda and salt; gradually add to creamed mixture. Stir in zucchini.

2. Pour into a greased 13x9-in. baking pan. Bake until a toothpick inserted in the center comes out clean, 35-40 minutes.

3. For frosting, in a small saucepan, combine chocolate chips and peanut butter. Cook and stir over low heat until smooth. Spread over warm brownies. Cool on a wire rack. Cut into bars.

1 BROWNIE 307 cal., 17g fat (8g sat. fat), 52mg chol., 283mg sod., 37g carb. (21g sugars, 2g fiber), 5g pro.

NOTES

_____
_____
_____
_____
_____

BROWNIES, BARS & COOKIES

RHUBARB CUSTARD BARS

Once I tried these rich, gooey bars, I just had to have the recipe. The shortbread-like crust and the rhubarb and custard layers inspire everyone to seek out rhubarb and bake a batch themselves.
—*Shari Roach, South Milwaukee, WI*

PREP: 25 MIN. • **BAKE:** 50 MIN. + CHILLING • **MAKES:** 3 DOZEN

- 2 cups all-purpose flour
- ¼ cup sugar
- 1 cup cold butter

FILLING
- 2 cups sugar
- 7 Tbsp. all-purpose flour
- 1 cup heavy whipping cream
- 3 large eggs, beaten
- 5 cups finely chopped fresh or frozen rhubarb, thawed and drained

TOPPING
- 6 oz. cream cheese, softened
- ½ cup sugar
- ½ tsp. vanilla extract
- 1 cup heavy whipping cream, whipped

1. In a bowl, combine flour and sugar; cut in butter until the mixture resembles coarse crumbs. Press into a greased 13x9-in. baking pan. Bake at 350° for 10 minutes.

2. Meanwhile, for filling, combine sugar and flour in a bowl. Whisk in cream and eggs. Stir in the rhubarb. Pour over the crust. Bake at 350° until custard is set, 40-45 minutes. Cool.

3. For topping, beat cream cheese, sugar and vanilla until smooth; fold in whipped cream. Spread over the top. Cover and refrigerate until firm enough to cut, about 1 hour. Cut into bars. Store in the refrigerator.

1 BAR 198 cal., 11g fat (7g sat. fat), 52mg chol., 70mg sod., 23g carb. (16g sugars, 1g fiber), 2g pro.

READER REVIEW

"These are wonderful just as written. After freezing them for 4 months, they were still perfect! My husband, who doesn't even like rhubarb, insisted we keep this recipe."
—DIANEM1955, TASTEOFHOME.COM

OATMEAL RAISIN COOKIES

A friend shared this recipe with me years ago, and these cookies are as delicious as Mom used to make.
The secret is to measure exactly (no guessing the amounts) and not overbake.
—*Wendy Coalwell, Abbeville, GA*

TAKES: 30 MIN. • **MAKES:** ABOUT 3½ DOZEN

1 cup shortening
1 cup sugar
1 cup packed light brown sugar
3 large eggs, room temperature
1 tsp. vanilla extract
2½ cups all-purpose flour
2 tsp. baking soda
1 tsp. salt
1 tsp. ground cinnamon
2 cups old-fashioned oats
1 cup raisins
1 cup coarsely chopped pecans, optional

1. In a large bowl, cream shortening and sugars until light and fluffy, 5-7 minutes. Beat in the eggs, 1 at a time, beating well after each addition. Beat in the vanilla. Combine the flour, baking soda, salt and cinnamon. Add to the creamed mixture, stirring just until combined. Stir in the oats, raisins and, if desired, pecans.

2. Shape into 1-in. balls. Place 2 in. apart on ungreased baking sheets. Flatten with a greased glass bottom.

3. Bake at 350° until golden brown, 10-11 minutes. Do not overbake. Remove to a wire rack to cool.

1 COOKIE 138 cal., 5g fat (1g sat. fat), 13mg chol., 123mg sod., 21g carb. (12g sugars, 1g fiber), 2g pro.

GIRL SCOUT COOKIES

To commemorate the anniversary of the first nationwide sale, the Girl Scouts are pleased
to share the original sugar cookie recipe used when the troops made their own cookies.
—*Girl Scout Council*

PREP: 15 MIN. + CHILLING • **BAKE:** 10 MIN./BATCH • **MAKES:** 4 DOZEN (2½-IN. COOKIES)

1 cup butter, softened
1 cup sugar
2 large eggs, room temperature
2 Tbsp. milk
1 tsp. vanilla extract
2½ cups all-purpose flour
2 tsp. baking powder
Decorator's sugar, optional

***Make your own DIY Colored Sugar.
Recipe on p. 278.***

1. In a bowl, cream the butter and sugar until light and fluffy, 5-7 minutes. Add the eggs, 1 at a time, beating well after each addition. Beat in milk and vanilla. Whisk together the flour and baking powder; gradually add to creamed mixture and mix well. Chill for at least 2 hours or overnight.

2. Preheat the oven to 350°. On a lightly floured surface, roll the dough to ¼-in. thickness. Cut with a trefoil cookie cutter or cutter of your choice. Place cookies on ungreased baking sheets. Sprinkle with decorator's sugar if desired.

3. Bake until lightly browned, 8-10 minutes. Cool on wire racks.

1 COOKIE 78 cal., 4g fat (3g sat. fat), 18mg chol., 54mg sod., 9g carb. (4g sugars, 0 fiber), 1g pro.

BROWNIES, BARS & COOKIES

WYOMING COWBOY COOKIES

These cookies are very popular here in Wyoming. Mix up a batch for your crew and see why.
—Patsy Steenbock, Shoshoni, WY

PREP: 25 MIN. • **BAKE:** 15 MIN. • **MAKES:** 6 DOZEN

- 1 cup sweetened shredded coconut
- ¾ cup chopped pecans
- 1 cup butter, softened
- 1½ cups packed brown sugar
- ½ cup sugar
- 2 large eggs, room temperature
- 1½ tsp. vanilla extract
- 2 cups all-purpose flour
- 1 tsp. baking soda
- ½ tsp. salt
- 2 cups old-fashioned oats
- 2 cups chocolate chips

1. Preheat oven to 350°. Place coconut and pecans on a 15x10x1-in. baking pan. Bake for 6-8 minutes or until toasted, stirring every 2 minutes. Set aside to cool.

2. In a large bowl, cream the butter and sugars until light and fluffy, 5-7 minutes. Add the eggs and vanilla; beat well. In another bowl, combine flour, baking soda and salt. Add to creamed mixture; beat well. Stir in the oats, chocolate chips, toasted coconut and toasted pecans.

3. Drop by rounded teaspoonfuls onto greased baking sheets. Bake at 350° for 12 minutes or until browned. Remove to wire racks to cool.

1 COOKIE 105 cal., 6g fat (3g sat. fat), 12mg chol., 61mg sod., 14g carb. (9g sugars, 1g fiber), 1g pro.

DOUBLE THE SIZE, DOUBLE THE FUN!

For heartier appetites, double the size of these cookies. Just make sure to increase the oven time and keep an eye on them until they're golden brown. The larger size makes them ideal for sharing too!

BUTTERY COCONUT BARS

My coconut bars are an American version of a Filipino coconut cake called bibingka. These are a crispier, sweeter take on the Christmas tradition I grew up with.
—Denise Nyland, Panama City, FL

PREP: 20 MIN. + COOLING • **BAKE:** 40 MIN. + COOLING • **MAKES:** 3 DOZEN

- 2 cups all-purpose flour
- 1 cup packed brown sugar
- ½ tsp. salt
- 1 cup butter, melted

FILLING
- 3 large eggs
- 1 can (14 oz.) sweetened condensed milk
- ½ cup all-purpose flour
- ¼ cup packed brown sugar
- ¼ cup butter, melted
- 3 tsp. vanilla extract
- ½ tsp. salt
- 4 cups sweetened shredded coconut, divided

1. Preheat oven to 350°. Line a 13x9-in. baking pan with parchment, letting ends extend up sides.

2. In a large bowl, mix flour, brown sugar and salt; stir in 1 cup melted butter. Press onto bottom of the prepared pan. Bake until light brown, 12-15 minutes. Cool for 10 minutes on a wire rack. Reduce oven setting to 325°.

3. In a large bowl, whisk the first 7 filling ingredients until blended; stir in 3 cups coconut. Pour over the crust; sprinkle with the remaining 1 cup coconut. Bake until light golden brown, 25-30 minutes. Cool in pan on a wire rack. Lifting with parchment, remove from the pan. Cut into bars.

1 BAR 211 cal., 12g fat (8g sat. fat), 36mg chol., 166mg sod., 25g carb. (18g sugars, 1g fiber), 3g pro.

CHOCOLATE CHIP COOKIE BROWNIES

Experimenting with this brownie recipe was so much fun. When my daughter tasted the final version, she told me they were the best brownies ever! Now, that sure makes a mom feel good.
—Dion Frischer, Ann Arbor, MI

PREP: 15 MIN. • **BAKE:** 50 MIN. + COOLING • **MAKES:** 1 DOZEN

- ¾ cup butter
- 1½ cups sugar
- ½ cup baking cocoa
- 3 large eggs, room temperature
- ¾ cup all-purpose flour
- ½ cup chopped walnuts

CHOCOLATE CHIP LAYER

- ½ cup butter
- 1 cup packed brown sugar
- 1 large egg, room temperature
- 1 cup all-purpose flour
- ½ tsp. baking soda
- 1 cup semisweet chocolate chips

1. Preheat oven to 350°. Line a 9-in. square baking pan with foil, letting ends extend up sides; grease foil.

2. In a microwave, melt butter in a large microwave-safe bowl. Stir in sugar and cocoa. Add eggs, 1 at a time, whisking to blend after each addition. Add flour; stir just until combined. Stir in nuts. Spread into prepared pan. Bake 15 minutes.

3. Meanwhile, for cookie layer, melt the butter in another microwave-safe bowl. Stir in brown sugar. Whisk in the egg. In a small bowl, whisk the flour and baking soda; stir into butter mixture just until combined. Stir in the chocolate chips.

4. Spoon mixture over hot brownie layer. Bake until a toothpick inserted in center comes out with moist crumbs, 35-40 minutes longer. Cool completely in pan on a wire rack. Lifting foil, remove the brownies from pan. Cut into bars.

1 BROWNIE 536 cal., 29g fat (15g sat. fat), 113mg chol., 236mg sod., 69g carb. (51g sugars, 2g fiber), 6g pro.

READER REVIEW

"These are rich, chewy and hard to resist. I love that I don't have to choose between a brownie and a cookie—I get both!"
—BETH, TASTEOFHOME.COM

BROWNIES, BARS & COOKIES

SWEDISH BUTTER COOKIES

It's impossible to eat just one of these treats. Naturally, they're a favorite with my Swedish husband and children, but anyone with a sweet tooth will appreciate them. My recipe is well-traveled among our friends and neighbors.
—*Sue Soderland, Elgin, IL*

PREP: 10 MIN. • **BAKE:** 25 MIN./BATCH • **MAKES:** ABOUT 6 DOZEN

1 cup butter, softened
1 cup sugar
2 tsp. maple syrup
2 cups all-purpose flour
1 tsp. baking soda
  Confectioners' sugar

1. Preheat oven to 300°. In a large bowl, cream butter and sugar until light and fluffy, 5-7 minutes. Add syrup. Combine flour and baking soda; gradually add to the creamed mixture and mix well.

2. Divide dough into 8 portions. Roll each portion into a 9-in. log. Place 3 in. apart on ungreased baking sheets. Bake until lightly browned, 25 minutes. Cut into 1-in. slices. Remove to wire racks. Dust with confectioners' sugar.

1 COOKIE 47 cal., 3g fat (2g sat. fat), 7mg chol., 38mg sod., 6g carb. (3g sugars, 0 fiber), 0 pro.

CAN YOU MAKE SWEDISH COOKIES AHEAD OF TIME?

Yes, you easily can! Prepare the dough and refrigerate it for 2-4 days before dividing it into 8 portions and rolling them into logs.

HAZELNUT MADELEINE COOKIES

These soft, cakelike cookies have a delicate hazelnut flavor—perfect for making great memories! They're baked in the distinctive shell-shaped madeleine pan, available in kitchen specialty stores.
—Taste of Home *Test Kitchen*

PREP: 30 MIN. • **BAKE:** 20 MIN. + COOLING • **MAKES:** 2 DOZEN

- ½ cup whole hazelnuts, toasted
- 1 Tbsp. confectioners' sugar
- 1 Tbsp. plus ½ cup butter, divided
- 2 Tbsp. plus 1 cup all-purpose flour, divided
- 2 large eggs, separated, room temperature
- ⅔ cup sugar
- ¼ tsp. vanilla extract
- 1 tsp. baking powder
- ⅛ tsp. salt
- Additional confectioners' sugar, optional

1. In a food processor, combine the hazelnuts and confectioners' sugar; cover and process until nuts are finely chopped. Set aside. Melt 1 Tbsp. butter; brush two 12-shell madeleine pans with butter. Dust with 2 Tbsp. flour; tap pans to remove excess flour and set aside. Place the remaining ½ cup butter in a saucepan; melt over low heat until it turns a light amber color, 4-5 minutes. Set aside to cool.

2. In a large bowl, beat the egg yolks and sugar until thick and a pale lemon color. Stir in the melted butter and vanilla. Combine the baking powder, salt and remaining flour; stir into butter mixture just until combined. In a small bowl, beat the egg whites on high speed until stiff peaks form; fold into batter. Gently fold in reserved nut mixture.

3. With a tablespoon, fill prepared pans two-thirds full. Bake at 325° until golden brown, 18-20 minutes. Cool for 2 minutes before inverting pans onto wire racks to remove cookies. Cool completely. Lightly dust with additional confectioners' sugar if desired.

1 COOKIE 103 cal., 6g fat (3g sat. fat), 29mg chol., 78mg sod., 11g carb. (6g sugars, 0 fiber), 1g pro.

APPLE CRUMB BARS

This has been a favorite recipe of mine for many years. I've made these apple bars for parties and for family, and they're always a hit.
—*Barbara Pickard, Union Lake, MI*

PREP: 15 MIN. • **BAKE:** 35 MIN. • **MAKES:** 3 DOZEN

- 3 cups all-purpose flour
- 1½ cups old-fashioned oats
- 1½ cups packed brown sugar
- ¾ tsp. baking soda
- 1¼ cups cold butter, divided
- 5 to 6 cups thinly sliced peeled apples
- 1 cup sugar
- 3 Tbsp. cornstarch
- 1 cup cold water
- 1 tsp. vanilla extract
- Vanilla ice cream, optional

1. Preheat oven to 350°. In a large bowl, combine flour, oats, brown sugar and baking soda; cut in 1 cup plus 2 Tbsp. butter until mixture resembles coarse crumbs. Set aside 2 cups for topping. Press the remaining oat mixture into a greased 13x9-in. baking pan. Arrange apples over the top.

2. In a small saucepan, combine sugar, cornstarch, water, vanilla and remaining 2 Tbsp. butter. Bring to a boil. Cook and stir until thickened, 1-2 minutes; pour over apples. Sprinkle with reserved oat mixture.

3. Bake until top is lightly browned, 35-45 minutes. Cool in pan on a wire rack. If desired, serve with vanilla ice cream.

1 BAR 174 cal., 7g fat (4g sat. fat), 17mg chol., 94mg sod., 28g carb. (16g sugars, 1g fiber), 2g pro.

HONEY-PEANUT BUTTER COOKIES

It's not unusual for my husband to request these cookies by name. You'll love 'em.

—Lucile Proctor, Panguitch, UT

PREP: 15 MIN. • **BAKE:** 10 MIN./BATCH • **MAKES:** 5 DOZEN

½ cup shortening
1 cup creamy peanut butter
1 cup honey
2 large eggs, room temperature, lightly beaten
3 cups all-purpose flour
1 cup sugar
1½ tsp. baking soda
1 tsp. baking powder
½ tsp. salt

1. Preheat oven to 350°. In a bowl, mix shortening, peanut butter and honey. Add eggs; mix well. Combine flour, sugar, baking soda, baking powder and salt; add to the peanut butter mixture and mix well.

2. Roll into 11½-in. balls and place on ungreased baking sheets. Flatten with a fork dipped in flour. Bake until set, 8-10 minutes. Remove to wire racks to cool.

1 COOKIE 95 cal., 4g fat (1g sat. fat), 6mg chol., 80mg sod., 14g carb. (8g sugars, 0 fiber), 2g pro.

made from scratch

HOMEMADE PEANUT BUTTER

We eat a lot of peanut butter, so I decided to make my own. My homemade version is easier on my wallet, and I know what ingredients are in it. It's also a lot tastier!

—Marge Austin, North Pole, AK

TAKES: 15 MIN.
MAKES: ABOUT 1 CUP

2 cups unsalted dry roasted peanuts
½ tsp. salt
1 Tbsp. honey

Process the peanuts and salt in a food processor until desired consistency, about 5 minutes, scraping down side as needed. Add honey; process just until blended. Store in an airtight container in refrigerator.

1 TBSP. 111 cal., 9g fat (1g sat. fat), 0 chol., 75mg sod., 5g carb. (2g sugars, 2g fiber), 4g pro.
DIABETIC EXCHANGES 2 fat.

CINNAMON SUGAR COOKIES

My mom always had these cookies on hand. They're so good with a cup of hot chocolate, coffee or milk.
—Leah Costigan, Otto, NC

PREP: 25 MIN. + CHILLING • **BAKE:** 10 MIN. • **MAKES:** 8 DOZEN

- 1 cup butter, softened
- 1 cup sugar
- 1 cup confectioners' sugar
- 1 cup vegetable oil
- 2 large eggs, room temperature
- 1 tsp. vanilla extract
- 4 1/3 cups all-purpose flour
- 1 tsp. salt
- 1 tsp. baking soda
- 1 tsp. cream of tartar
- 1 tsp. ground cinnamon
- 1 cup finely chopped pecans, optional
- Cinnamon sugar, optional

1. In a large bowl, cream butter, sugars and oil. Add eggs and vanilla; mix well. Add the flour, salt, baking soda, cream of tartar and cinnamon. Stir in pecans if desired. Cover and refrigerate 3 hours or until easy to handle.

2. Roll into 1-in. balls. Place 2 in. apart on greased baking sheets; flatten with the bottom of a glass dipped in sugar. If desired, sprinkle with cinnamon sugar.

3. Bake at 375° for 7-9 minutes or until set.

1 COOKIE 73 cal., 4g fat (2g sat. fat), 9mg chol., 55mg sod., 8g carb. (3g sugars, 0 fiber), 1g pro.

COPYCAT STARBUCKS CRANBERRY BLISS BARS

These beloved coffeehouse blondies are studded with tangy cranberries and white chocolate and topped with a luscious cream cheese frosting brightened with orange zest.
—Molly Allen, Hood River, OR

PREP: 25 MIN. + CHILLING • **BAKE:** 20 MIN. + COOLING • **MAKES:** 24 BLONDIES

BLONDIE LAYER
- ¾ cup butter, melted
- 2 cups packed brown sugar
- 2 large eggs, room temperature
- 1 tsp. vanilla extract
- 2 cups all-purpose flour
- ½ tsp. baking powder
- ½ tsp. salt
- ¼ tsp. ground ginger
- ½ cup dried cranberries
- 2 oz. white baking chocolate, chopped

FROSTING
- 1 block (8 oz.) cream cheese, softened
- ¼ cup butter, softened
- 2 Tbsp. whole milk
- 5 cups confectioners' sugar
- 2 Tbsp. grated orange zest
- ½ cup dried cranberries
- 2 oz. white baking chocolate, chopped

1. Preheat oven to 350°. Line a 13x9-in. baking dish with parchment paper; set aside.

2. In a large mixing bowl, beat melted butter and brown sugar on medium speed until combined. Add eggs, 1 at a time, until combined; beat in vanilla extract.

3. In a separate bowl, whisk flour, baking powder, salt and ginger. Gradually add dry ingredients into butter mixture; stir until combined. Stir in dried cranberries and half the white chocolate. Transfer batter into prepared baking dish; use a spatula to spread into 1 even layer. Bake 20-25 minutes or until the edges are golden brown. Let completely cool; use parchment to pull blondie layer out of the pan. Transfer to a cutting board.

4. Meanwhile, in a large bowl, beat cream cheese and butter until smooth. Alternate mixing milk and confectioners' sugar, beating until fluffy, 2-3 minutes. Beat in orange zest.

5. Spread frosting on cooled blondie layer. Sprinkle evenly with dried cranberries.

6. In a small microwave-safe bowl, microwave white chocolate in 30 second increments, stirring each time, until melted. Drizzle white chocolate over bars. Allow to cool and set in refrigerator at least 30 minutes; slice and serve.

1 BLONDIE 716 cal., 26g fat (16g sat. fat), 91mg chol., 332mg sod., 121g carb. (101g sugars, 1g fiber), 5g pro.

PECAN PIE BROWNIES

Chopped pecans top these chewy, chocolaty brownies for an irresistible dessert. The nutty pie topping has a gooey texture that ties this treat together.
—Molly Allen, Hood River, OR

PREP: 10 MIN. + CHILLING • **COOK:** 40 MIN. + CHILLING • **MAKES:** 12 BROWNIES

BROWNIES
- 1 cup sugar
- ¾ cup all-purpose flour
- ⅓ cup baking cocoa
- ½ tsp. baking powder
- ½ tsp. salt
- ¾ cup canola oil
- 3 large eggs, room temperature
- 1 Tbsp. light corn syrup
- 1 tsp. vanilla extract
- ¼ cup hot water

TOPPING
- ½ cup packed brown sugar
- 4 Tbsp. light corn syrup
- 1 tsp. vanilla extract
- ¼ cup butter, melted
- 2 large eggs, room temperature, beaten
- 2 cups chopped pecans

1. Preheat oven to 350°. In a large bowl, whisk sugar, flour, cocoa, baking powder and salt until combined. Whisk in the oil, eggs, corn syrup, vanilla extract and hot water until a thick batter forms. Pour the batter into a parchment paper-lined 8-in. square baking pan. Bake 20-25 minutes or until batter is set.

2. Meanwhile, in a large bowl, whisk the brown sugar, corn syrup, vanilla extract, butter and eggs until incorporated. Fold in the pecans. Pour mixture on top of the brownies and spread into an even layer. Bake an additional 20-25 minutes or until the pecan mixture is set. Let completely cool. Cover; refrigerate 1 hour. Slice into squares.

1 BROWNIE 476 cal., 33g fat (5g sat. fat), 88mg chol., 187mg sod., 43g carb. (34g sugars, 2g fiber), 6g pro.

READER REVIEW

"These brownies were delicious—two of my favorite desserts in one! I used gluten-free flour and dairy-free butter with great success and can't wait to make them again!"

—LPHJKITCHEN, TASTEOFHOME.COM

BROWNIES, BARS & COOKIES

TRIPLE CHOCOLATE CHEESECAKE BARS

What could be better than a brownie crust layered with chocolate cheesecake and topped with ganache? These cheesecake bars will satisfy even the biggest chocolate lovers.
—Andrea Price, Grafton, WI

PREP: 35 MIN. • **BAKE:** 25 MIN. + CHILLING • **MAKES:** 2½ DOZEN

- ¼ cup butter, cubed
- ½ cup sugar
- 3 Tbsp. baking cocoa
- ½ tsp. vanilla extract
- 1 large egg, room temperature
- ¼ cup all-purpose flour
- ⅛ tsp. baking powder
- ⅛ tsp. salt

CHEESECAKE LAYER
- 2 pkg. (8 oz. each) cream cheese, softened
- ½ cup sugar
- 1½ tsp. vanilla extract
- ¾ cup semisweet chocolate chips, melted and cooled
- 2 large eggs, room temperature, lightly beaten

GANACHE
- 1½ cups semisweet chocolate chips
- ½ cup heavy whipping cream
- 1 tsp. vanilla extract

1. Preheat oven to 350°. Line a 13x9-in. pan with foil, letting ends extend up the sides; grease foil. In a microwave, melt butter in a large microwave-safe bowl. Stir in sugar, cocoa and vanilla. Add egg; blend well. Add flour, baking powder and salt; stir just until combined. Spread as a thin layer in prepared pan. Bake until top appears dry, 6-8 minutes.

2. Meanwhile, in a large bowl, beat cream cheese, sugar and vanilla until smooth. Beat in chocolate chips. Add eggs; beat on low speed just until combined. Spread over brownie layer. Bake until the filling is set, 25-30 minutes. Cool 10 minutes on a wire rack.

3. For ganache, place chocolate chips in a small bowl. In a saucepan, bring cream just to a boil. Pour over the chocolate; let stand 5 minutes. Stir with a whisk until smooth. Stir in the vanilla; cool slightly, stirring occasionally. Pour over the cheesecake layer; cool in pan on a wire rack 1 hour. Refrigerate at least 2 hours. Lifting with foil, remove brownies from pan. Cut into bars.

1 BAR 180 cal., 13g fat (7g sat. fat), 42mg chol., 81mg sod., 17g carb. (14g sugars, 1g fiber), 2g pro.

READER REVIEW

"I rarely write reviews, but this recipe was phenomenal! I made it for New Year's, and it was a hit—just like something from a bakery. The layers take some time, but they're well worth it."

—PHYLLIS705, TASTEOFHOME.COM

CHOCOLATE CHUNK WALNUT BLONDIES

Put a stack of these beauties out at a potluck, and you'll find only crumbs on your platter when it's time to head home. Everyone will be asking for the recipe, so bring a few copies to share!
—Peggy Woodward, Shullsburg, WI

PREP: 15 MIN. • **BAKE:** 30 MIN. + COOLING • **MAKES:** 2 DOZEN

1 cup butter, melted
2 cups packed brown sugar
2 tsp. vanilla extract
2 large eggs, room temperature
2 cups all-purpose flour
½ cup ground walnuts
1 tsp. baking powder
½ tsp. salt
⅛ tsp. baking soda
1 cup chopped walnuts, toasted
1 cup semisweet chocolate chunks

1. Preheat oven to 350°. Line a greased 13x9-in. pan with parchment, letting ends extend up sides; grease paper.

2. In a large bowl, mix the butter, brown sugar and vanilla until blended. Add the eggs, 1 at a time, whisking to blend after each addition. In another bowl, mix flour, ground walnuts, baking powder, salt and baking soda; stir into the butter mixture. Fold in walnuts and chocolate chunks.

3. Spread into prepared pan. Bake until a toothpick inserted in center comes out clean, 30-35 minutes (do not overbake). Cool completely in pan on a wire rack. Lifting with parchment, remove from pan. Cut into bars. Store in an airtight container.

1 BAR 260 cal., 15g fat (7g sat. fat), 38mg chol., 140mg sod., 32g carb. (22g sugars, 1g fiber), 3g pro.

HOMEMADE HONEY GRAHAMS

The way my boys eat them, I would spend a fortune on honey graham crackers at the grocery store. So I created this homemade version—less processed, more affordable and absolutely wonderful!
—Crystal Jo Bruns, Iliff, CO

PREP: 15 MIN. + CHILLING • **BAKE:** 10 MIN./BATCH • **MAKES:** 32 CRACKERS

1 cup whole wheat flour
¾ cup all-purpose flour
½ cup toasted wheat germ
2 Tbsp. dark brown sugar
1 tsp. baking powder
1 tsp. ground cinnamon
½ tsp. salt
½ tsp. baking soda
6 Tbsp. cold butter, cubed
¼ cup honey
4 Tbsp. ice water

1. In a bowl, whisk the first 8 ingredients; cut in the butter until crumbly. In another bowl, whisk honey and water; gradually add to the dry ingredients, tossing with a fork until the dough holds together when pressed.

2. Divide dough in half. Shape each into a disk; cover and refrigerate until firm enough to roll, about 30 minutes.

3. Preheat oven to 350°. On a lightly floured surface, roll each portion of dough to an 8-in. square. Using a knife or fluted pastry wheel, cut each portion into sixteen 2-in. squares. If desired, prick holes with a fork. Place 1 in. apart on parchment-lined baking sheets.

4. Bake until edges are light brown, 10-12 minutes. Remove from pans to wire racks to cool. Store in an airtight container.

1 CRACKER 60 cal., 2g fat (1g sat. fat), 6mg chol., 89mg sod., 9g carb. (3g sugars, 1g fiber), 1g pro. **DIABETIC EXCHANGES** ½ starch, ½ fat.

AMISH SUGAR COOKIES

These melt-in-your-mouth cookies are so easy to make, they've become a favorite among my friends.
After I gave the recipe to my sister, she entered the cookies in a local fair and won the best of show prize!
—*Sylvia Ford, Kennett, MO*

PREP: 10 MIN. • **BAKE:** 10 MIN./BATCH • **MAKES:** ABOUT 5 DOZEN

1 cup butter, softened
1 cup canola oil
1 cup sugar
1 cup confectioners' sugar
2 large eggs, room temperature
1 tsp. vanilla extract
4½ cups all-purpose flour
1 tsp. baking soda
1 tsp. cream of tartar

1. Preheat oven to 375°. In a large bowl, beat butter, oil and sugars. Beat in the eggs until well blended. Beat in vanilla. Combine flour, baking soda and cream of tartar; gradually add to the creamed mixture.

2. Drop by small teaspoonfuls onto ungreased baking sheets. Bake until lightly browned, 8-10 minutes. Remove to wire racks to cool.

1 COOKIE 117 cal., 7g fat (2g sat. fat), 14mg chol., 48mg sod., 13g carb. (5g sugars, 0 fiber), 1g pro.

MAKE YOUR COOKIES POP!

Looking to add more flavor? Add salted butter and a splash of your favorite extract—try almond, orange or lemon! If you like your treats on the sweeter side, top them with a pinch of coarse sugar.

made from scratch
DIY COLORED SUGAR

Creating your own colored sugar is so simple and easy. It adds a distinctive pop of color to cookies, cupcakes and other baked treats.
—*Sarah Farmer, Waukesha, WI*

PREP: 5 MIN. + STANDING
MAKES: ¼ CUP

¼ cup sugar
1 to 3 drops assorted food coloring

In a small resealable bag, combine sugar and a few drops food coloring. Seal bag and shake to tint sugar. Allow sugar to dry on flat surface for 15-20 minutes before using.

1 TBSP 49 cal., 0 fat (0 sat. fat), 0 chol., 0 sod., 13g carb. (13g sugars, 0 fiber), 0 pro.

from scratch DESSERTS & SWEETS

RHUBARB CRUMBLE, PAGE 287

CONTEST-WINNING
BUTTER PECAN ICE CREAM

This rich buttery ice cream sure beats store-bought versions. With its pretty color
and plentiful pecan crunch, it's nice enough to serve guests at a summer party.
—*Jenny White, Glen, MS*

PREP: 45 MIN. + CHILLING • **PROCESS:** 20 MIN. + FREEZING • **MAKES:** 1 QT.

½ cup chopped pecans
1 Tbsp. butter
1½ cups half-and-half cream
¾ cup packed brown sugar
2 large eggs, lightly beaten
½ cup heavy whipping cream
1 tsp. vanilla extract
Optional: Caramel sauce and chopped pecans or toppings of your choice

1. In a small skillet, toast pecans in butter for 5-6 minutes or until lightly browned. Cool.

2. In a heavy saucepan, heat half-and-half to 175°; stir in the brown sugar until dissolved. Whisk a small amount of hot cream mixture into eggs; return all to pan, whisking constantly. Cook and stir over low heat until the mixture reaches at least 160° and coats back of a metal spoon. Do not allow to boil. Remove from heat immediately.

3. Quickly transfer to a small bowl; place bowl in a pan of ice water. Stir gently and occasionally 2 minutes. Stir in whipping cream and vanilla. Press plastic wrap onto the surface of custard. Refrigerate for several hours or overnight. Stir in toasted pecans.

4. Fill cylinder of the ice cream maker no more than two-thirds full; freeze according to manufacturer's directions. Transfer ice cream to freezer containers, allowing headspace for expansion. Freeze until firm, 2-4 hours. Serve with toppings if desired.

½ CUP 269 cal., 17g fat (8g sat. fat), 90mg chol., 62mg sod., 23g carb. (22g sugars, 1g fiber), 4g pro.

---

made from scratch
SALTED CARAMEL SAUCE

Rich and delicious, this sauce is the perfect blend of sweet, salty and creamy all in one. I like to make a big batch and refrigerate it for up to 2 weeks.
—*Angie Stewart, Memphis, TN*

TAKES: 20 MIN. • **MAKES:** 1¼ CUPS

1 cup sugar
1 cup heavy whipping cream
3 Tbsp. butter, cubed
1½ tsp. salt
1 tsp. almond extract

In a large heavy saucepan, spread sugar; cook, without stirring, over medium-low heat until it begins to melt. Gently drag the melted sugar to center of pan, so sugar melts evenly. Cook, without stirring, until the melted sugar turns a medium-dark amber, 5-10 minutes. Immediately remove from heat, then slowly stir in cream, butter, salt and almond extract.

2 TBSP. 191 cal., 12g fat (8g sat. fat), 36mg chol., 388mg sod., 21g carb. (21g sugars, 0 fiber), 1g pro.

RICH HOT CHOCOLATE

Each February, my friends and I gather for an outdoor show called Mittenfest. We skip the Bloody Marys and fill our thermoses with this hot cocoa instead. Try the variations too.
—*Gina Nistico, Denver, CO*

TAKES: 15 MIN. • **MAKES:** 2 SERVINGS

- ⅔ cup heavy whipping cream
- 1 cup 2% milk
- 4 oz. dark chocolate candy bar, chopped
- 3 Tbsp. sugar
- Vanilla rum, optional
- Sweetened heavy whipping cream, whipped

In a small saucepan, heat the heavy whipping cream, milk, chocolate and sugar over medium heat just until the mixture comes to a simmer, stirring constantly. Remove from heat; stir until smooth. If desired, add rum. Pour mixture into 2 mugs; top with the sweetened whipped cream.

1 CUP 653 cal., 49g fat (32g sat. fat), 107mg chol., 79mg sod., 60g carb. (56g sugars, 4g fiber), 9g pro.

PUMPKIN-SPICED COCOA Heat ⅔ cup heavy cream, 1 cup milk, ½ cup white baking chips, 2 Tbsp. canned pumpkin and 1 tsp. pumpkin pie spice over medium heat just until mixture comes to a simmer, stirring constantly. Remove from heat; stir until smooth. If desired, add 3 oz. RumChata liqueur.

TOASTED COCONUT COCOA Heat 1 can coconut milk, ½ cup milk, ⅔ cup chocolate chips and 2 Tbsp. sugar over medium heat just until mixture comes to a simmer, stirring constantly. Remove from heat; stir until smooth. If desired, add 3 oz. Malibu rum.

SPICY CINNAMON COCOA Heat ⅔ cup heavy cream, 1 cup milk, ⅔ cup chocolate chips, 2 Tbsp. sugar, 1 tsp. ground cinnamon and ⅛ tsp. cayenne pepper over medium heat just until the mixture comes to a simmer, stirring constantly. Remove from heat; stir until smooth. If desired, add 3 oz. cinnamon whiskey.

CHOCOLATE-ORANGE COCOA Heat ⅔ cup heavy cream, 1 cup milk, ⅔ cup chocolate chips, 2 Tbsp. sugar and 1 tsp. grated orange zest over medium heat just until the mixture comes to a simmer, stirring constantly. Remove from heat; stir until smooth. If desired, add 3 oz. Cointreau liqueur.

BANANA BREAD PUDDING

With its crusty golden top, custardlike inside and smooth vanilla sauce, this bread pudding from my grandmother is a real homespun dessert. I enjoy making it for my grandchildren.
—Mary Detweiler, Middlefield, OH

PREP: 10 MIN. • **BAKE:** 40 MIN. • **MAKES:** 6 SERVINGS

- 4 cups cubed day-old French or sourdough bread (1-in. pieces)
- ¼ cup butter, melted
- 3 large eggs, room temperature
- 2 cups whole milk
- ½ cup sugar
- 2 tsp. vanilla extract
- ½ tsp. ground cinnamon
- ½ tsp. ground nutmeg
- ½ tsp. salt
- 1 cup sliced firm bananas (¼-in. pieces)

SAUCE
- 3 Tbsp. butter
- 2 Tbsp. sugar
- 1 Tbsp. cornstarch
- ¾ cup whole milk
- ¼ cup light corn syrup
- 1 tsp. vanilla extract

1. Place the bread cubes in a greased 2-qt. casserole; pour butter over top and toss to coat. In a medium bowl, lightly beat eggs; add milk, sugar, vanilla, cinnamon, nutmeg and salt. Stir in bananas.

2. Pour over the bread cubes and stir to coat. Bake, uncovered, at 375° for about 40 minutes or until a knife inserted in the center comes out clean.

3. Meanwhile, for sauce, melt butter in a small saucepan. Combine sugar and cornstarch; add to the butter. Stir in the milk and corn syrup. Cook and stir over medium heat until mixture comes to a full boil. Boil for 1 minute. Remove from heat; stir in vanilla. Serve warm sauce over warm pudding.

1 SERVING 439 cal., 21g fat (12g sat. fat), 157mg chol., 561mg sod., 56g carb. (38g sugars, 1g fiber), 9g pro.

READER REVIEW

"Very good—especially the sauce! I love that it doesn't use a full stick of butter, keeping it light and not greasy."
—DESTINE, TASTEOFHOME.COM

DESSERTS & SWEETS

RHUBARB CRUMBLE

To tell you the truth, I'm not sure how well my crumble keeps—we usually eat it all in a day! You can make this with all rhubarb, but apples and strawberries make this dessert better.
—*Linda Enslen, Schuler, AB*

PREP: 20 MIN. • **BAKE:** 40 MIN. • **MAKES:** 8 SERVINGS

- 3 cups sliced fresh or frozen rhubarb (½-in. pieces)
- 1 cup diced peeled apples
- ½ to 1 cup sliced strawberries
- ⅓ cup sugar
- ½ tsp. ground cinnamon
- ½ cup all-purpose flour
- 1 tsp. baking powder
- ¼ tsp. salt
- 4 Tbsp. cold butter
- ⅔ cup packed brown sugar
- ⅔ cup quick-cooking oats
- Vanilla ice cream, optional

1. Preheat the oven to 350°. Combine the rhubarb, apples and strawberries; spoon into a greased 8-in. square baking dish. Combine the sugar and cinnamon; sprinkle over rhubarb mixture. Set aside.

2. In a bowl, combine the flour, baking powder and salt. Cut in the butter until the mixture resembles coarse crumbs. Stir in brown sugar and oats. Sprinkle over rhubarb mixture.

3. Bake at 350° for 40-50 minutes or until lightly browned. Serve warm or cold, with a scoop of ice cream if desired.

1 SERVING 227 cal., 6g fat (4g sat. fat), 15mg chol., 191mg sod., 41g carb. (29g sugars, 2g fiber), 2g pro.

POTS DE CREME

Looking for an easy dessert recipe that's guaranteed to impress?
Served in pretty stemmed glasses, this classic chocolate custard really sets the tone.
—*Connie Dreyfoos, Cincinnati, OH*

PREP: 15 MIN. + CHILLING • **MAKES:** 5 SERVINGS

1 large egg
2 Tbsp. sugar
Dash salt
¾ cup half-and-half cream
1 cup semisweet chocolate chips
1 tsp. vanilla extract
Optional: Whipped cream and assorted fresh fruit

Make your own Sweetened Whipped Cream. Recipe on p. 300.

1. In a small saucepan, combine the egg, sugar and salt. Whisk in cream. Cook and stir over medium heat until mixture reaches 160° and coats the back of a metal spoon.

2. Remove from heat; whisk in chocolate chips and vanilla until smooth. Pour into small dessert dishes. Cover and refrigerate, 8 hours or overnight. If desired, garnish with whipped cream and fruit.

⅓ CUP 246 cal., 15g fat (9g sat. fat), 55mg chol., 66mg sod., 28g carb. (25g sugars, 2g fiber), 4g pro.

BUTTERSCOTCH PEARS

This showstopping dessert simmers during dinner and impresses as soon as it hits the table. Serve as is or with vanilla ice cream and a slice of pound cake. If you have leftover pear nectar, mix it with sparkling wine or pour it over ice for a refreshing drink.
—*Theresa Kreyche, Tustin, CA*

PREP: 20 MIN. • **COOK:** 2 HOURS • **MAKES:** 8 SERVINGS

4 large firm pears
1 Tbsp. lemon juice
¼ cup packed brown sugar
3 Tbsp. butter, softened
2 Tbsp. all-purpose flour
½ tsp. ground cinnamon
¼ tsp. salt
½ cup chopped pecans
½ cup pear nectar
2 Tbsp. honey

1. Cut pears in half lengthwise; remove cores. Brush pears with lemon juice. In a small bowl, combine the brown sugar, butter, flour, cinnamon and salt; stir in pecans. Spoon into the pears; place in a 4-qt. slow cooker.

2. Combine the pear nectar and honey; drizzle over the pears. Cover and cook on low for 2-3 hours or until the pears are tender. Serve warm.

1 STUFFED PEAR HALF 209 cal., 10g fat (3g sat. fat), 11mg chol., 109mg sod., 33g carb. (24g sugars, 4g fiber), 1g pro.

READER REVIEW

"This recipe has the perfect balance and really lets the pear flavor shine—sweet but not too heavy."

—CHRISTINEHALE, TASTEOFHOME.COM

CONTEST-WINNING WHITE CHOCOLATE CHEESECAKE

This is my all-time favorite cheesecake recipe, and I have a lot of them! I've made this delicious cake so many times over the years—it's frequently requested as birthday cake.
—Janet Gill, Taneytown, MD

PREP: 40 MIN. • **BAKE:** 45 MIN. + CHILLING • **MAKES:** 12 SERVINGS

- 7 whole cinnamon graham crackers, crushed
- ¼ cup sugar
- ⅓ cup butter, melted

FILLING
- 4 pkg. (8 oz. each) cream cheese, softened
- ½ cup plus 2 Tbsp. sugar
- 1 Tbsp. all-purpose flour
- 1 tsp. vanilla extract
- 4 large eggs, room temperature, lightly beaten
- 2 large egg yolks, room temperature, lightly beaten
- 8 oz. white baking chocolate, melted and cooled

STRAWBERRY SAUCE
- ½ cup sugar
- 2 Tbsp. cornstarch
- ½ cup water
- 1½ cups chopped fresh strawberries
- Red food coloring, optional
- Melted white chocolate

1. In a small bowl, combine the cracker crumbs and sugar; stir in butter. Press onto the bottom and 1 in. up the side of a greased 10-in. springform pan.

2. In a large bowl, beat the cream cheese, sugar, flour and vanilla until well blended. Add eggs and egg yolks; beat on low speed just until combined. Stir in white chocolate. Pour over crust. Place pan on a baking sheet.

3. Bake at 350° for 45-50 minutes or until center is just set. Cool on a wire rack for 10 minutes. Carefully run a knife around edge of pan to loosen; cool 1 hour longer. Refrigerate overnight.

4. For the sauce, in a large saucepan, combine sugar, cornstarch and water until smooth. Add strawberries. Bring to a boil; cook and stir until thickened. Remove from heat; stir in a few drops of food coloring if desired. Cool.

5. Spread strawberry sauce over top of the cheesecake; drizzle with melted white chocolate. Refrigerate leftovers.

1 PIECE 572 cal., 41g fat (25g sat. fat), 205mg chol., 348mg sod., 46g carb. (38g sugars, 1g fiber), 10g pro.

DESSERTS & SWEETS 289

MINT CHIP ICE CREAM

We have a milk cow, so homemade ice cream is a regular dessert in our household. This creamy version has a mild mint flavor.
—*Farrah McGuire, Springdale, WA*

PREP: 15 MIN. + CHILLING • **PROCESS:** 20 MIN./BATCH + FREEZING • **MAKES:** 1½ QT.

1¾ cups whole milk
¾ cup sugar
Pinch salt
3 large eggs, lightly beaten
1¾ cups heavy whipping cream
1 tsp. vanilla extract
¼ tsp. peppermint extract
4 drops green food coloring, optional
½ cup miniature semisweet chocolate chips

1. In a small saucepan, heat the milk to 175°; stir in sugar and salt until dissolved. Whisk in a small amount of hot mixture to eggs. Return all to the pan, whisking constantly. Cook and stir over low heat until mixture coats the back of a metal spoon and reaches at least 160°, 2-3 minutes. Remove from heat.

2. Cool quickly by placing pan in a bowl of ice water; stir for 2 minutes. Stir in the whipping cream, extracts and, if desired, food coloring. Press plastic wrap onto the surface of custard. Refrigerate for several hours or overnight.

3. Stir in chocolate chips. Fill the ice cream maker cylinder two-thirds full; freeze according to the manufacturer's directions. Refrigerate the remaining mixture until ready to freeze. Transfer the ice cream to a freezer container; freeze for 2-4 hours before serving.

½ CUP 243 cal., 17g fat (10g sat. fat), 90mg chol., 56mg sod., 20g carb. (19g sugars, 0 fiber), 4g pro.

made from scratch
ICE CREAM BOWLS

Once you sample these homemade waffle ice cream bowls, you'll want to serve them time and again! You can prepare them either with pretty designs in a special pizzelle cookie maker or without designs in the oven.
—Taste of Home *Test Kitchen*

PREP: 15 MIN. • **BAKE:** 35 MIN. • **MAKES:** 16 SERVINGS

3 large eggs, room temperature
¾ cup sugar
½ cup butter, melted
2 tsp. vanilla extract
1½ cups all-purpose flour
2 tsp. baking powder

1. In a small bowl, beat the eggs on medium speed until blended. Gradually beat in sugar until thick and lemon colored. Add butter and vanilla. Combine the flour and baking powder; gradually add to egg mixture. Invert two 6-oz. custard cups on paper towels; coat with cooking spray.

2. Prepare cookies in a preheated pizzelle cookie maker according to the manufacturer's directions, using 2 Tbsp. batter for each cookie. Immediately remove pizzelles and drape over inverted custard cups. To shape cookies into bowls, place another custard cup coated with cooking spray over each pizzelle. Let stand until set. Remove from the custard cups and set aside. Repeat with remaining batter.

3. To make ice cream bowls in the oven, line a baking sheet with parchment. Draw two 7-in. circles on the paper. Spread 2 Tbsp. batter over each circle. Bake at 400° for 4-5 minutes or until edges are golden brown. Immediately remove cookies and drape over inverted custard cups. Shape into bowls as directed. Store in an airtight container.

1 BOWL 145 cal., 7g fat (4g sat. fat), 50mg chol., 119mg sod., 19g carb. (10g sugars, 0 fiber), 2g pro.

IVA'S PEACH COBBLER

My mother received this recipe from a friend of hers many years ago, and fortunately, she shared it with me. Boise is situated right between two large fruit-producing areas in our state, so peaches are plentiful in the summer.
—Ruby Ewart, Boise, ID

PREP: 15 MIN. • **BAKE:** 45 MIN. • **MAKES:** 12 SERVINGS

- 6 to 8 large ripe peaches, peeled and sliced
- 2½ Tbsp. cornstarch
- ¾ to 1 cup sugar

CRUST
- 1 cup all-purpose flour
- 1 cup sugar
- 1 tsp. baking powder
- 2 large egg yolks, room temperature
- ¼ cup butter, melted
- 2 large egg whites, room temperature, stiffly beaten
- Vanilla ice cream, optional

Preheat oven to 375°. Combine peaches, cornstarch and sugar; place in a greased 13x9-in. baking dish. For crust, in a bowl, whisk flour, sugar and baking powder. Stir in egg yolks and butter. Gently fold in egg whites. Spread over the peaches. Bake until the fruit is bubbling around the edges and the top is golden, about 45 minutes. If desired, serve with ice cream.

½ CUP 224 cal., 5g fat (3g sat. fat), 46mg chol., 83mg sod., 44g carb. (33g sugars, 1g fiber), 3g pro.

PEACH PERFECT
For baking, stick to yellow peaches (the kind you're most likely to find at the supermarket), Babcock peaches, snow peaches or Belle of Georgia peaches. White and doughnut peaches don't work quite as well. If you can't find peaches, go ahead with nectarines or plums.

DARK CHOCOLATE TRUFFLES

I learned to make these truffles at a local cooking class and made them for my parents' 50th wedding anniversary, garnishing with smoked salt and colored coarse sugars. The original recipe called for dipping them in dark chocolate, but I learned that dusting with powdered sugar before rolling in cocoa powder makes shaping easier and sweetens the cocoa.
—*Shelly Bevington, Hermiston, OR*

PREP: 25 MIN. + CHILLING • **MAKES:** 5 DOZEN

- 1 lb. dark chocolate chips
- 1 cup heavy whipping cream
- 2 Tbsp. light corn syrup
- 2 Tbsp. butter, softened
- ¾ cup baking cocoa

1. Place the chocolate in a small bowl. In a small heavy saucepan, heat cream and corn syrup just to a boil. Pour over the chocolate; stir until smooth. Stir in the butter. Cool to room temperature, stirring occasionally. Refrigerate until firm enough to shape, about 3 hours.

2. Place cocoa in a small bowl. Shape chocolate mixture into 1-in. balls; roll in cocoa. Store in an airtight container in the refrigerator.

1 TRUFFLE 56 cal., 4g fat (3g sat. fat), 6mg chol., 5mg sod., 5g carb. (5g sugars, 1g fiber), 1g pro.

NOTES

DESSERTS & SWEETS 293

ARROZ CON LECHE (RICE PUDDING)

Sweet and simple, this creamy dessert is comfort food in any language.
You'll love the warm raisin and cinnamon flavors. It's great served cold too.
—*Marina Castle Kelley, Canyon Country, CA*

PREP: 5 MIN. • **COOK:** 30 MIN. • **MAKES:** 4 SERVINGS

1½ cups water
½ cup uncooked long grain rice
1 cinnamon stick (3 in.)
1 cup sweetened condensed milk
3 Tbsp. raisins

READER REVIEW

"My 5-year-old and I tried it tonight—awesome! Though a bit sweet, it's definitely a make-again recipe. I'm bringing it to my 'Sister Tuesday' taco night for dessert. Thanks for the wonderful recipe!"
—PEAPOD0114, TASTEOFHOME.COM

1. In a small saucepan, combine the water, rice and cinnamon. Bring to a boil. Reduce heat; simmer, uncovered, 15-20 minutes or until water is absorbed.

2. Stir in the milk and raisins. Bring to a boil. Reduce heat; simmer, uncovered, 10-15 minutes or until thick and creamy, stirring frequently. Discard cinnamon. Serve warm or cold.

½ CUP 351 cal., 7g fat (4g sat. fat), 26mg chol., 99mg sod., 65g carb. (46g sugars, 1g fiber), 8g pro.

DESSERTS & SWEETS

INDIAN KULFI ICE CREAM

Growing up near Little India in California, I loved baked goods and desserts from Indian sweet shops, especially *kulfi*—a spiced and nutty frozen custard in cone molds. Here, I use a shortcut method to make kulfi quickly, without any special equipment. You can also swap mango pulp for the milk to make mango kulfi.
—Justine Kmiecik, Crestview, FL

PREP: 30 MIN. + FREEZING • **MAKES:** 6 SERVINGS

- 1 can (14 oz.) sweetened condensed milk
- 1 cup whole milk
- 1 cup heavy whipping cream
- ¼ cup nonfat dry milk powder
- ½ tsp. ground cardamom
- ¼ tsp. sea salt
- 1 pinch saffron threads or ¼ tsp. ground turmeric, optional
- ¼ cup chopped cashews, toasted
- ¼ cup chopped shelled pistachios
- ¼ tsp. almond extract

1. In a large heavy saucepan, whisk milks, cream, milk powder, cardamom, sea salt and, if desired, saffron until blended. Cook over low heat until the mixture thickens slightly, about 15 minutes, stirring constantly. Do not allow to boil. Remove from heat. Strain through a fine-mesh strainer into a small bowl; cool.

2. Stir in the cashews, pistachios and extract. Transfer to six 4-oz. ramekins. Cover and freeze 8 hours or overnight. If desired, serve with additional nuts.

½ CUP 446 cal., 27g fat (14g sat. fat), 72mg chol., 266mg sod., 44g carb. (41g sugars, 1g fiber), 11g pro.

SOUTHERN PRALINES

These are a real southern specialty that I've used to fill many holiday gift tins!
—*Bernice Eberhart, Fort Payne, AL*

PREP: 35 MIN. • **MAKES:** ABOUT 3½ DOZEN

3 cups packed brown sugar
1 cup heavy whipping cream
2 Tbsp. light corn syrup
¼ tsp. salt
1½ cups chopped pecans
¼ cup butter, cubed
1¼ tsp. vanilla extract

1. In a large heavy saucepan, combine brown sugar, cream, corn syrup and salt. Bring to a boil over medium heat, stirring constantly. Cook until a candy thermometer reads 230° (thread stage), stirring occasionally.

2. Carefully stir in the pecans and butter. Cook, stirring occasionally, until a candy thermometer reads 236° (soft-ball stage).

3. Remove from the heat; stir in vanilla. Beat with a wooden spoon until candy thickens and begins to lose its gloss, 4-5 minutes.

4. Quickly drop by heaping tablespoonfuls onto waxed paper; spread to form 2-in. patties. Let stand until set. Store in an airtight container.

NOTE We recommend you test your candy thermometer before each use by bringing water to a boil; the thermometer should read 212°. Adjust your recipe temperature up or down based on your test.

1 PIECE 121 cal., 6g fat (2g sat. fat), 11mg chol., 31mg sod., 17g carb. (16g sugars, 0 fiber), 1g pro.

CLASSIC CREME BRULEE

Creme brulee is my favorite dessert, so I quickly learned how to make it at home. Recently, I was at a party where the guests used small torches to broil the sugar on their portions. What a clever way to finish off the dessert!
—*Joylyn Trickel, Helendale, CA*

PREP: 30 MIN. • **BAKE:** 25 MIN. + CHILLING • **MAKES:** 8 SERVINGS

4 cups heavy whipping cream
9 large egg yolks
¾ cup sugar
1 tsp. vanilla extract
Brown sugar

1. Preheat the oven to 325°. In a small saucepan, heat cream until bubbles form around side of pan; remove from heat. In a large bowl, whisk egg yolks and sugar until blended but not foamy. Slowly stir in hot cream. Stir in vanilla.

2. Place eight 6-oz. broiler-safe ramekins in a baking pan large enough to hold them without touching. Pour egg mixture into ramekins. Place pan on oven rack; add very hot water to pan to within ½ in. of top of ramekins. Bake until centers are just set (egg mixture will jiggle),

25-30 minutes. Immediately remove the ramekins from water bath to a wire rack; cool 10 minutes. Refrigerate until cold.

3. Place ramekins on a baking sheet; let stand at room temperature 15 minutes. Preheat broiler. Sprinkle custards evenly with 1-2 tsp. brown sugar each. Broil 8 in. from heat until the sugar is caramelized, 4-7 minutes. Refrigerate leftovers.

1 SERVING 551 cal., 50g fat (29g sat. fat), 402mg chol., 53mg sod., 22g carb. (22g sugars, 0 fiber), 6g pro.

DESSERTS & SWEETS

CHOCOLATE BREAD PUDDING

This is a fun recipe because the chocolate makes it different from traditional bread pudding. It's a rich, comforting dessert.
—*Mildred Sherrer, Fort Worth, TX*

PREP: 15 MIN. + STANDING • **BAKE:** 30 MIN. • **MAKES:** 2 SERVINGS

- 2 oz. semisweet chocolate
- ½ cup half-and-half cream
- ⅔ cup sugar
- ½ cup 2% milk
- 1 large egg, room temperature
- 1 tsp. vanilla extract
- ¼ tsp. salt
- 4 slices day-old bread, crusts removed, cut into cubes (about 3 cups)
- Optional toppings: Confectioners' sugar and whipped cream

Make your own Sweetened Whipped Cream. Recipe on p. 300.

1. In a small microwave-safe bowl, melt the chocolate; stir until smooth. Stir in cream; set aside.

2. In a large bowl, whisk the sugar, milk, egg, vanilla and salt. Stir in chocolate mixture. Add the bread cubes and toss to coat. Let stand for 15 minutes.

3. Spoon into 2 greased 2-cup souffle dishes. Bake at 350° until a knife inserted in the center comes out clean, 30-35 minutes.

4. If desired, sprinkle with confectioners' sugar and top with a dollop of whipped cream.

1 SERVING 622 cal., 17g fat (9g sat. fat), 145mg chol., 656mg sod., 105g carb. (79g sugars, 2g fiber), 12g pro.

STRAWBERRY SHORTCAKE CUPS

Back when store-bought shortcake was an unheard-of thing, my grandmother passed this recipe down to my mother. Mother later shared it with me, and I've since given it to my daughter.
—Althea Heers, Jewell, IA

PREP: 15 MIN. • **BAKE:** 15 MIN. + COOLING • **MAKES:** 8 SERVINGS

1 qt. fresh strawberries
4 Tbsp. sugar, divided
1½ cups all-purpose flour
1 Tbsp. baking powder
½ tsp. salt
¼ cup cold butter, cubed
1 large egg, room temperature
½ cup whole milk
   Whipped cream

1. Mash or slice the strawberries; place in a large bowl. Add 2 Tbsp. sugar and set aside. In another bowl, combine the flour, baking powder, salt and remaining 2 Tbsp. sugar; cut in butter until crumbly. In a small bowl, beat egg and milk; stir into flour mixture just until moistened.

2. Fill 8 greased muffin cups two-thirds full. Bake at 425° until golden brown, about 12 minutes. Remove from pan to cool on a wire rack.

3. Just before serving, split shortcakes in half horizontally. Spoon the berries and whipped cream between layers and over tops of shortcakes.

1 SHORTCAKE 202 cal., 7g fat (4g sat. fat), 40mg chol., 390mg sod., 30g carb. (11g sugars, 2g fiber), 4g pro. **DIABETIC EXCHANGES** 1½ starch, 1½ fat, ½ fruit.

made from scratch SWEETENED WHIPPED CREAM

Sometimes a dollop of sweetened whipped cream is all you need to top your favorite cake or other dessert. To make ahead, slightly underwhip the cream, then cover and refrigerate for several hours. Beat briefly just before using.
—Taste of Home *Test Kitchen*

TAKES: 10 MIN. • **MAKES:** 2 CUPS

1 cup heavy whipping cream
3 Tbsp. confectioners' sugar
½ tsp. vanilla extract

In a chilled small glass bowl and using chilled beaters, beat cream until it begins to thicken. Add the confectioners' sugar and vanilla; beat until soft peaks form. Store in the refrigerator.

2 TBSP. 57 cal., 6g fat (3g sat. fat), 20mg chol., 6mg sod., 2g carb. (2g sugars, 0 fiber), 0 pro.

PEAR PANDOWDY

I pulled out this recipe one night when my husband was craving something sweet, and it was a big hit with both of us. It's a superb last-minute dessert that almost melts in your mouth.
—Jennifer Class, Snohomish, WA

PREP: 20 MIN. • **BAKE:** 20 MIN. • **MAKES:** 2 SERVINGS

- 2 medium firm pears, peeled and sliced
- 2 Tbsp. brown sugar
- 4½ tsp. butter
- 1½ tsp. lemon juice
- ⅛ tsp. ground cinnamon
- ⅛ tsp. ground nutmeg

TOPPING
- ½ cup all-purpose flour
- 2 Tbsp. plus ½ tsp. sugar
- ½ tsp. baking powder
- ⅛ tsp. salt
- ¼ cup cold butter, cubed
- 2 Tbsp. water
- Vanilla ice cream, optional

1. In a small saucepan, combine the first 6 ingredients. Cook and stir over medium heat until pears are tender, about 5 minutes. Pour into a greased 3-cup baking dish.

2. In a small bowl, combine flour, 2 Tbsp. sugar, baking powder and salt; cut in butter until crumbly. Stir in the water. Sprinkle over pear mixture. Sprinkle with remaining sugar.

3. Bake, uncovered, at 375° until a toothpick inserted into topping comes out clean and topping is lightly browned, 20-25 minutes. Serve warm, with ice cream if desired.

1 SERVING 594 cal., 32g fat (20g sat. fat), 84mg chol., 572mg sod., 76g carb. (45g sugars, 5g fiber), 4g pro.

NOTES

DESSERTS & SWEETS   301

APPLE DUMPLINGS WITH SAUCE

These warm and comforting apple dumplings are incredible by themselves or served with ice cream. You can decorate each dumpling by cutting 1-in. leaves and a ½-in. stem from the leftover dough.
—Robin Lendon, Cincinnati, OH

PREP: 1 HOUR + CHILLING • **BAKE:** 50 MIN. • **MAKES:** 8 SERVINGS

- 3 cups all-purpose flour
- 1 tsp. salt
- 1 cup shortening
- ⅓ cup cold water
- 8 medium tart apples, peeled and cored
- 8 tsp. butter
- 9 tsp. cinnamon sugar, divided

SAUCE
- 1½ cups packed brown sugar
- 1 cup water
- ½ cup butter, cubed

1. In a large bowl, combine flour and salt; cut in shortening until crumbly. Gradually add water, tossing with a fork until dough forms a ball. Divide into 8 portions. Cover and refrigerate for at least 30 minutes or until easy to handle.

2. Preheat oven to 350°. Roll out each portion of dough between 2 lightly floured sheets of waxed paper into a 7-in. square. Place an apple on each square. Place 1 tsp. butter and 1 tsp. cinnamon sugar in center of each apple.

3. Gently bring up corners of dough to each center, trimming any excess; pinch edges to seal. If desired, cut out apple leaves and stems from dough scraps; attach to dumplings with water. Place dumplings in a greased 13x9-in. baking dish. Sprinkle with half the remaining 1 tsp. cinnamon sugar.

4. In a large saucepan, combine sauce ingredients. Bring just to a boil, stirring until blended. Pour over apples; sprinkle with remaining cinnamon sugar.

5. Bake until the apples are tender and pastry is golden brown, 50-55 minutes, basting occasionally with sauce. Serve them warm.

1 DUMPLING 764 cal., 40g fat (16g sat. fat), 41mg chol., 429mg sod., 97g carb. (59g sugars, 3g fiber), 5g pro.

GET-WELL CUSTARD

Whenever a friend or relative was ailing, my mother-in-law would bake some fresh custard and take it along when she visited. Because she took folks this special treat so often, our family began calling it Get-Well Custard!
—Ruth Van Dyke, Traverse City, MI

PREP: 15 MIN. • **BAKE:** 55 MIN. + CHILLING • **MAKES:** 10 SERVINGS

- 4 cups whole milk
- 4 large eggs
- ½ cup sugar
- ¼ tsp. salt
- 1 tsp. vanilla extract
  Ground nutmeg
  Fresh berries, optional

1. Preheat the oven to 350°. In a small saucepan, heat milk until bubbles form around sides of pan; remove from heat. In a large bowl, whisk eggs, sugar and salt until blended but not foamy. Slowly stir in hot milk. Stir in vanilla.

2. Pour egg mixture through a strainer into a 1½-qt. round baking dish; sprinkle with nutmeg. Place round baking dish in a larger baking pan. Place pan on oven rack; add very hot water to pan to within ½ in. of top of round baking dish. Bake until a knife inserted near center comes out clean, 55-60 minutes. Centers will be soft and jiggle even after chilling. Remove baking dish from water bath immediately to a wire rack; cool for 30 minutes. Refrigerate until cold. If desired, serve with fresh berries.

½ CUP 128 cal., 5g fat (2g sat. fat), 84mg chol., 130mg sod., 15g carb. (15g sugars, 0 fiber), 6g pro.

PUDDING OR CUSTARD: WHAT'S IN YOUR BOWL?
Custard and pudding may seem similar, but their textures and thickening agents set them apart. Custard is typically firmer because it has eggs as the thickening agent, while pudding has a softer texture, thickened with starch.

EASY COOKIE DOUGH ICE CREAM

Ice cream is easier to make than you might think. If you love cookie dough, you'll definitely want to try this chocolate treat.
—Taste of Home Test Kitchen

PREP: 20 MIN. • **PROCESS:** 15 MIN. + FREEZING • **MAKES:** 16 SERVINGS (2 QT.)

- ¼ cup butter, softened
- 3 Tbsp. sugar
- 3 Tbsp. brown sugar
- ½ tsp. vanilla extract
- ½ cup all-purpose flour
- ¼ cup miniature semisweet chocolate chips

ICE CREAM
- 1½ cups whole milk
- ¾ cup sugar
- 2 cups heavy whipping cream
- 3 tsp. vanilla extract
- ½ cup miniature semisweet chocolate chips

1. In a large bowl, beat butter and sugars until light and fluffy, 5-7 minutes. Beat in vanilla. Gradually beat in flour. Fold in the chocolate chips. Press into a 15x10x1-in. pan lined with parchment to ½-in. thickness. Freeze while making ice cream.

2. In a large bowl, whisk milk and sugar until sugar is dissolved. Whisk in cream and vanilla.

3. Fill cylinder of ice cream maker no more than two-thirds full. (Refrigerate any remaining mixture until ready to freeze.) Freeze according to the manufacturer's directions, adding chocolate chips during last minute of processing. Chop the cookie dough into small pieces; stir into ice cream.

4. Transfer the ice cream to freezer containers, allowing headspace for expansion. Freeze until firm, 2-4 hours.

NOTE Eating uncooked flour may cause foodborne illness.

½ CUP 253 cal., 17g fat (11g sat. fat), 44mg chol., 80mg sod., 25g carb. (21g sugars, 1g fiber), 2g pro.

DESSERTS & SWEETS

CLASSIC BLUEBERRY BUCKLE

This blueberry buckle recipe came from my grandmother. As children, my sister and I remember going to Pennsylvania for blueberry picking. Mother taught us to pick only perfect berries, and those gems went into this wonderful recipe.
—*Carol Dolan, Mt. Laurel, NJ*

PREP: 20 MIN. • **BAKE:** 40 MIN. • **MAKES:** 9 SERVINGS

- ¼ cup butter, softened
- ¾ cup sugar
- 1 large egg, room temperature
- 2 cups all-purpose flour
- 2 tsp. baking powder
- ¼ tsp. salt
- ½ cup 2% milk
- 2 cups fresh blueberries

TOPPING
- ⅔ cup sugar
- ½ cup all-purpose flour
- ½ tsp. ground cinnamon
- ⅓ cup cold butter, cubed
- Whipped cream, optional

Make your own Sweetened Whipped Cream. Recipe on p. 300.

1. Preheat oven to 375°. In a small bowl, cream butter and sugar until light and fluffy, 5-7 minutes. Add egg; beat well. In another bowl, combine flour, baking powder and salt; add to creamed mixture alternately with the milk, beating well after each addition. Fold in blueberries. Spread into a greased 9-in. square baking pan.

2. For topping, in a small bowl, combine sugar, flour and cinnamon; cut in butter until crumbly. Sprinkle over blueberry mixture.

3. Bake until a toothpick inserted in the center comes out clean, 40-45 minutes. Cool on a wire rack. If desired, serve with whipped cream and additional blueberries.

NOTE If using frozen blueberries, use without thawing to avoid discoloring the batter.

1 PIECE 390 cal., 13g fat (8g sat. fat), 54mg chol., 282mg sod., 64g carb. (36g sugars, 2g fiber), 5g pro.

PERFECT PEPPERMINT PATTIES

I make lots of candy at Christmas to give as gifts. It can be time-consuming, but it's worth it seeing the delight it brings people. Calling for just a few ingredients, this is one candy that's simple to prepare.
—*Joanne Adams, Bath, ME*

PREP: 20 MIN. + CHILLING • **MAKES:** 5 DOZEN

- 4 cups confectioners' sugar
- 3 Tbsp. butter, softened
- 2 tsp. peppermint extract
- ½ tsp. vanilla extract
- ¼ cup evaporated milk
- 2 cups semisweet chocolate chips
- 2 Tbsp. shortening

1. In a large bowl, combine the first 4 ingredients. Add milk and mix well. Roll into 1-in. balls and place them on a baking sheet lined with waxed paper or parchment paper. Flatten with a glass to ¼-in. thickness. Cover and freeze for 30 minutes.

2. Microwave the chocolate chips and shortening on high until melted; stir until smooth. Dip patties, allowing excess to drip off. Place on waxed paper; let stand until set.

1 PATTY 69 cal., 3g fat (2g sat. fat), 2mg chol., 6mg sod., 12g carb. (11g sugars, 0 fiber), 0 pro.

MICHIGAN CHERRY JAPANESE-STYLE CHEESECAKE

Michigan is known for its amazing tart cherries, which inspired this twist on the traditional American cheesecake. I combined their unique flavor with the light, melt-in-your-mouth texture of a Japanese-style cheesecake to create something truly special.
—*Laura Kurella, Wellston, MI*

PREP: 1 HOUR + COOLING • **BAKE:** 1 HOUR 20 MIN. • **MAKES:** 12 SERVINGS

- 6 Tbsp. butter, cubed
- 4 oz. reduced-fat cream cheese
- 2/3 cup heavy whipping cream
- 1/4 cup all-purpose flour
- 1/4 cup cornstarch
- 6 large egg yolks, room temperature
- 2 tsp. vanilla extract
- 1½ to 2 tsp. grated lemon zest
- 12 large egg whites, room temperature
- 3/4 cup sugar

TOPPING
- 1/2 cup sugar
- 2 Tbsp. cornstarch
- 1/4 tsp. cayenne pepper, optional
- 1/2 cup water
- 2 cups fresh or frozen pitted tart cherries
- 1 Tbsp. butter
  Confectioners' sugar

1. Preheat oven to 325°. Place a 9-in. springform pan on a double thickness of heavy-duty foil (about 18 in. square). Wrap foil securely around pan. Line bottom and inside of the pan with parchment; set aside.

2. In a small saucepan, cook and stir butter and cream cheese over medium heat until melted. Remove from heat; whisk in cream until smooth. Let cool completely.

3. Sift flour and cornstarch together twice; place in a large bowl. In a small bowl, whisk the egg yolks, vanilla, zest and cooled cream cheese mixture until smooth. Add to flour mixture; beat until well blended.

4. In a large bowl with clean beaters, beat egg whites on medium speed until foamy. Gradually add sugar, 1 Tbsp. at a time, beating on high after each addition until sugar is dissolved. Continue beating until soft glossy peaks form. Fold a fourth of the whites into batter, then fold in remaining whites. Gently transfer to prepared pan. Place springform pan in a larger baking pan; add 1 in. hot water to larger pan.

5. Bake for 25 minutes. Reduce oven setting to 280°. Bake until the top is puffed and springs back when lightly touched and the center appears set, 55-65 minutes longer.

6. Meanwhile, for the topping, in a small saucepan, mix the sugar, cornstarch and, if desired, cayenne. Whisk in water until smooth. Add cherries; cook and stir over medium heat until thickened and bubbly, about 5 minutes. Remove from heat; whisk in butter. Cool completely.

7. Remove springform pan from water bath. Loosen rim from pan with a knife; remove foil. Remove rim from the pan; remove paper. Serve cheesecake warm with confectioners' sugar and cherry topping. Refrigerate leftovers.

1 PIECE 294 cal., 16g fat (9g sat. fat), 132mg chol., 157mg sod., 31g carb. (24g sugars, 1g fiber), 7g pro.

DESSERTS & SWEETS

BEST EVER VANILLA ICE CREAM

This ice cream is technically a custard because it contains eggs. I've found that eggs are key to making a smooth and creamy treat that rivals premium store-bought ice cream.
—Peggy Woodward, Shullsburg, WI

PREP: 15 MIN. + CHILLING • **PROCESS:** 25 MIN./BATCH + FREEZING • **MAKES:** 4½ CUPS

- 2 cups heavy whipping cream
- 2 cups 2% milk
- ¾ cup sugar
- ⅛ tsp. salt
- 1 vanilla bean
- 6 large egg yolks

Make your own Homemade Strawberry Syrup. Recipe on p. 226.

1. In a large heavy saucepan, combine cream, milk, sugar and salt. Split vanilla bean in half lengthwise. With a sharp knife, scrape seeds into pan; add bean. Heat cream mixture over medium heat until bubbles form around side of pan, stirring to dissolve sugar.

2. In a small bowl, whisk a small amount of the hot mixture into egg yolks; return all to the pan, whisking constantly. Cook over low heat until mixture is just thick enough to coat a metal spoon and temperature reaches 180°, stirring constantly. Do not allow to boil. Immediately transfer to a bowl.

3. Place bowl in a pan of ice water. Stir gently and occasionally for 2 minutes; discard vanilla bean. Press waxed paper onto surface of mixture. Refrigerate several hours or overnight.

4. Fill the cylinder of ice cream maker two-thirds full; freeze according to the manufacturer's directions. (Refrigerate remaining mixture until ready to freeze.) Transfer the ice cream to a freezer container; freeze until firm, 4-6 hours. Repeat with remaining mixture.

½ CUP 310 cal., 23g fat (14g sat. fat), 188mg chol., 78mg sod., 21g carb. (21g sugars, 0 fiber), 5g pro.

made from scratch HOT FUDGE ICE CREAM TOPPING

Hot fudge sundaes make for an elegant yet easy dessert. This rich, dark chocolate sauce drapes beautifully and is delicious on peppermint, coffee, butter pecan and lots of other ice cream flavors!
—Paula Zsiray, Logan, UT

TAKES: 20 MIN. • **MAKES:** 2 CUPS

- 2 cups sugar
- ¼ cup baking cocoa
- 1 can (5 oz.) evaporated milk
- ½ cup butter, cubed
- 1 tsp. vanilla extract

1. In a small saucepan, combine sugar and cocoa. Stir in milk; add butter. Bring to a boil over medium heat, stirring constantly. Reduce heat; cook and stir 1 minute or until slightly thickened. Remove from heat; stir in vanilla. Serve warm. Refrigerate leftovers.

2. To reheat, place the sauce in a small saucepan and bring to a boil, stirring until smooth.

2 TBSP. 163 cal., 6g fat (4g sat. fat), 18mg chol., 67mg sod., 27g carb. (25g sugars, 0 fiber), 1g pro.

VERY BLUEBERRY CLAFOUTIS

A French dessert traditionally made with cherries, clafoutis is somewhere between a fruit-filled pancake and a fruity egg custard. It's a quick and easy alternative to pie, easily adapted to any berry or cut fruit. Even kids can make it with some help moving the pan to and from the oven. Out of fresh berries? Use frozen berries thawed in a colander and discard the juice.
—*Ken Hulme, Venice, FL*

PREP: 10 MIN. • **BAKE:** 30 MIN. + STANDING • **MAKES:** 8 SERVINGS

- 2 tsp. butter
- 16 oz. fresh or frozen unsweetened blueberries
- 3 large eggs, room temperature
- ¾ cup all-purpose flour
- ¾ cup whole milk
- ⅓ cup sugar
- 1 tsp. vanilla extract
- ½ tsp. ground cinnamon

DON'T HAVE A CAST-IRON SKILLET?
Any 10-to-12-in. ovenproof skillet will work well. If all else fails, use a large pie pan. Don't use a plastic handled or nonstick skillet, as either can produce unhealthy vapors at high oven temperatures and during long cooking times.

1. Preheat oven to 400°. Place butter in a 12-in. cast-iron or other ovenproof skillet. Place skillet in the oven until the butter is melted, 1-2 minutes. Carefully tilt pan to coat bottom and side with butter. Spread blueberries in bottom of pan. In a large bowl, whisk the eggs, flour, milk, sugar, vanilla and cinnamon. Pour egg mixture over blueberries.

2. Bake until center is puffed and edge is browned, 30-35 minutes. Sprinkle with additional cinnamon if desired. Let stand 15 minutes before cutting.

1 PIECE 188 cal., 4g fat (2g sat. fat), 75mg chol., 46mg sod., 34g carb. (20g sugars, 3g fiber), 5g pro. **DIABETIC EXCHANGES** 2 starch, 1 fat.

VANILLA WHITE CHOCOLATE MOUSSE

I needed a quick dessert for my daughter's bridal shower, and a co-worker gave
me this vanilla mousse recipe. It's so pretty with almonds and raspberries on top.
—*Marina Castle Kelley, Canyon Country, CA*

PREP: 20 MIN. + CHILLING • **MAKES:** 4 SERVINGS

1¼ cups heavy whipping cream, divided
2 Tbsp. sugar
2 large egg yolks
7 oz. white baking chocolate, chopped
2 vanilla beans
  Toasted sliced almonds, optional

1. In a small saucepan, combine ¼ cup cream and sugar; cook over medium heat until bubbles form around side of pan.

2. In a small bowl, whisk a small amount of hot mixture into egg yolks; return all to pan, whisking constantly. Cook over low heat until mixture is just thick enough to coat a metal spoon and a thermometer reads at least 160°, stirring constantly. Do not allow to boil. Immediately remove from heat. Stir in chocolate until smooth.

3. Split vanilla beans lengthwise. Using the tip of a sharp knife, scrape the seeds from center into chocolate mixture; stir. Transfer to a large bowl; cool 10 minutes.

4. In a small bowl, beat the remaining 1 cup cream until soft peaks form; fold into the chocolate mixture. Spoon into 4 dessert dishes. Refrigerate, covered, 1 hour before serving. If desired, sprinkle with almonds.

½ CUP 555 cal., 43g fat (29g sat. fat), 177mg chol., 60mg sod., 41g carb. (40g sugars, 0 fiber), 7g pro.

COCONUT MILK STRAWBERRY-BANANA POPS

These four-ingredient freezer pops are a delicious way to use up a pint of fresh strawberries.
You'll love the hint of tropical flavor, thanks to the coconut milk.
—Taste of Home *Test Kitchen*

PREP: 10 MIN. + FREEZING • **MAKES:** 12 POPS

1 can (13.66 oz.) coconut milk
1 pint fresh strawberries, chopped, divided
1 medium banana, sliced
2 Tbsp. maple syrup
12 freezer pop molds or 12 paper cups (3 oz. each) and wooden pop sticks

In a blender, place coconut milk, 1½ cups strawberries, banana and syrup; cover and process until smooth. Divide the remaining strawberries among 12 molds or paper cups. Pour pureed mixture into molds or cups, filling three-fourths full. Top molds with holders. If using cups, top with foil and insert pop sticks through foil. Freeze until firm, at least 4 hours.

1 POP 51 cal., 3g fat (3g sat. fat), 0 chol., 5mg sod., 7g carb. (5g sugars, 1g fiber), 1g pro.

DESSERTS & SWEETS

CREAMY CARAMELS

I discovered this recipe in a local newspaper years ago and have made these soft buttery caramels ever since. I make them for Christmas, picnics and charity auctions—they're so much better than the store-bought version.
—Marcie Wolfe, Williamsburg, VA

PREP: 10 MIN. • **COOK:** 30 MIN. + COOLING • **MAKES:** 64 PIECES (2½ LBS.)

- 1 tsp. plus 1 cup butter, divided
- 1 cup sugar
- 1 cup dark corn syrup
- 1 can (14 oz.) sweetened condensed milk
- 1 tsp. vanilla extract

DEPTH OF DELICIOUSNESS
Dark corn syrup may contain molasses and/or caramel color and flavor. Use it for a more robust and complex taste.

1. Line an 8-in. square pan with foil; grease the foil with 1 tsp. butter.

2. In a large heavy saucepan, combine sugar, corn syrup and remaining 1 cup butter; bring to a boil over medium heat, stirring constantly. Boil for 4 minutes without stirring.

3. Remove from heat; stir in milk. Reduce the heat to medium-low and cook until a candy thermometer reads 238° (soft-ball stage), stirring constantly. Remove from heat; stir in vanilla.

4. Pour into prepared pan (do not scrape saucepan). Cool. Using foil, lift candy out of pan. Discard foil; cut candy into 1-in. squares. Wrap individually in waxed paper; twist ends.

NOTE We recommend you test your candy thermometer before each use by bringing water to a boil; the thermometer should read 212°. Adjust your recipe temperature up or down based on your test.

1 PIECE 72 cal., 3g fat (2g sat. fat), 10mg chol., 45mg sod., 10g carb. (8g sugars, 0 fiber), 1g pro.

INDEX

A

Air-Fryer Eggplant Fries 57
Air-Fryer Mozzarella Sticks 45
Air-Fryer Sweet Potato Fries..................... 148
All-American Turkey Potpie 113
Almond Biscotti 253
Amish Sugar Cookies 278
Apple Crumb Bars 269
Apple Dumplings with Sauce 303
Apple Pie... 215
Applesauce Bread 199
Arroz Con Leche (Rice Pudding)................. 295
Aunt Betty's Blueberry Muffins 26

B

Back Porch Meatballs 60
Bacon Cheddar Potato Skins 44
Baked Chorizo Corn Dip............................. 52
Baked Mac & Cheese 162
Baked Teriyaki Salmon............................... 128
Baked Tilapia.. 121
Banana Bread Pudding............................... 285
Banana Bread Snack Cakes....................... 233
Basic Crepes.. 39
Basic Homemade Bread 183
Beer-Battered Fish 123
Beer-Braised Stew 91
Best Angel Food Cake 226
Best Bacon-Wrapped Shrimp 63
Best Cinnamon Rolls 29

Best Deviled Eggs....................................... 66
Best Ever Vanilla Ice Cream....................... 311
Best Lasagna 126
Best-Ever Banana Bread............................ 182
Big & Buttery Chocolate Chip Cookies....... 257
Bistro Mac & Cheese.................................. 129
Blue-Ribbon Butter Cake 240
Braised Short Ribs with Gravy................... 120
Brioche French Toast 32
Bubble & Squeak Leftover Potato Cakes..... 31
Burgoo 76
Buttermilk Pancakes 21
Butterscotch Pears 288
Buttery Coconut Bars................................. 264
Buttery Cornbread 174
Buttery Croissants 186

C

Caesar Salad 159
Caramelized Onion Spinach Dip 72
Challah.. 188
Cheese Puffs 71
Cheesy Bacon & Grits Casserole 27
Cherry Hand Pies.. 221
Chewy Soft Pretzels 58
Chicago-Style Deep-Dish Pizza 117
Chicken Tamales 116
Chili con Carne 95
Chocolate Bread Pudding 298
Chocolate Chip Cookie Brownies................ 265

316   TASTEOFHOME.COM

Chocolate Chunk Walnut Blondies 277

Chocolate Ganache 210

Chunky Tomato Salsa.. 61

Cinnamon Coffee Cake.. 34

Cinnamon Roll Biscuits.. 18

Cinnamon Spiced Pecans 50

Cinnamon Sugar Cookies.. 272

Cinnamon Sugar Doughnuts.. 23

Cinnamon Swirl Breakfast Bread 185

Classic Almond Ricotta Cake.. 237

Classic Blueberry Buckle.. 306

Classic Cottage Pie... 142

Classic Creme Brulee... 297

Classic French Onion Soup 84

Classic Irish Soda Bread 204

Classic Lemon Bars... 252

Classic Lemon Meringue Pie 228

Classic Tartar Sauce.. 123

Coconut Milk Strawberry-Banana Pops.......................... 313

Coconut Pie 225

Contest-Winning Butter Pecan Ice Cream 282

Contest-Winning White Chocolate Cheesecake 289

Cookie Jar Gingersnaps 252

Copycat Bloomin' Onion.. 55

Copycat Blooming Onion Sauce..................................... 55

Copycat Honey Baked Ham 139

Copycat McDonald's Sweet & Sour Sauce...................... 124

Copycat Starbucks Cranberry Bliss Bars 273

Copycat Starbucks Egg Bites 19

Copycat Starbucks Pumpkin Bread 206

Courtside Caramel Corn.. 64

Cranberry Wild Rice... 156

Cream Cheese Blueberry Pie 234

Creamy Caramels... 314

Creamy Corn Crab Soup... 92

D

Dad's Greek Salad 154

Dark Chocolate Truffles.. 293

Delectable Granola... 15

DIY Colored Sugar 278

Dough for Double-Crust Pie.. 218

Dough for Single-Crust Pie 169

Dutch Apple Loaf 202

E

Easy & Elegant Tenderloin Roast 129

Easy Blueberry Sauce 240

Easy Cheese-Stuffed Jalapenos 53

Easy Cheesy Biscuits... 203

Easy Cookie Dough Ice Cream 305

Easy Shrimp Cocktail 49

Eddie's Favorite Fiesta Corn 149

Effortless Guacamole 49

Eggs Benedict Casserole 10

F

Favorite Hamburger Stew 98

Feta & Chive Muffins.. 207

Flourless Chocolate Cake 210

Fluffy Waffles.. 11

Focaccia 172

Fresh Pumpkin Pie 223

Fudge Brownie Pie 246

G

Garlic Basil Butter 207

Garlic Mashed Red Potatoes... 168

Garlic Rosemary Pull-Apart Bread 198

German Chocolate Cake.. 217

Get-Well Custard 304

INDEX **317**

Giant Molasses Cookies.. 256

Ginger Dressing 164

Girl Scout Cookies 261

Gooey Butter Cake... 232

Grandma's Blackberry Cake 225

Grandma's Oxtail Stew 94

Grandma's Red Velvet Cake 220

Green Shakshuka 35

Grilled Bruschetta 69

Gruyere Spinach Quiche 24

H

Hazelnut Madeleine Cookies... 268

Hearty Pasta Fajioli.. 103

Hearty Ragu Bolognese... 140

Heavenly Cheese Danish... 15

Herbed Onion Salad Dressing.. 156

Home Fries 22

Homemade Beef Broth 103

Homemade Biscuits & Maple Sausage Gravy 38

Homemade Cajun Seasoning... 81

Homemade Cheez-Its 48

Homemade Chicken Broth 92

Homemade Frosted Strawberry Toaster Pastries 16

Homemade Honey Grahams 277

Homemade Mayonnaise.. 13

Homemade Pasta Dough... 134

Homemade Peanut Butter... 270

Homemade Pierogi 165

Homemade Pizza Sauce 141

Homemade Potato Chips 72

Homemade Potato Gnocchi 157

Homemade Spicy Hot Sauce... 180

Homemade Strawberry Syrup 226

Homemade Tater Tots.. 146

Homemade Tortilla Chips 42

Homemade Tortillas 187

Homemade Vegetable Broth 87

Honey Bagels 193

Honey Chipotle Vinaigrette... 152

Honey Cinnamon Butter 26

Honey-Kissed Savory Shortbread Crackers.................. 178

Honey-Mustard Chicken Wings 68

Honey-Peanut Butter Cookies....................................... 270

Hot Fudge Ice Cream Topping 311

Hungarian Goulash 102

I

Ice Cream Bowls 290

Indian Kulfi Ice Cream 296

Italian Cream Cheese Cake 241

Iva's Peach Cobbler... 292

J

Jen's Baked Beans 149

Josh's Marbled Rye Bread... 175

K

Kentucky Spoon Bread 151

Key Lime Blondie Bars.. 248

L

Lemon & Coriander Greek Yogurt................................... 22

Loaded Breakfast Burger 13

Louisiana Red Beans & Rice 97

Loukoumades (Greek Doughnuts with Honey)................ 14

M

Mama's Potato Salad.. 167

Manchester Stew... 86

Mango & Coconut Chicken Soup................................ 106
Mediterranean Rack of Lamb.................................... 131
Michigan Cherry Japanese-Style Cheesecake........... 309
Millionaire Shortbread Bars 254
Mint Chip Ice Cream... 290
Mint Lamb Stew 79
Mint Sauce for Lamb.. 131
Mom's Italian Bread 191
Mom's Pickled Carrots.. 57
Mother's Walnut Cake 213
Mughlai Chicken 121

N

Naan Bread 187
Nacho Cheese Sauce... 42

O

Oatmeal Raisin Cookies... 261
Old-Fashioned Applesauce 199
Old-Time Buttermilk Pie 239
Olive Oil Cake.. 229
Orzo with Parmesan & Basil.................................... 153
Oven-Baked Brisket 115

P

Pancake Syrup.. 21
Panko Chicken Tenders 124
Pear Pandowdy 301
Pecan Pie Brownies.. 275
Peppy Peach Salsa 73
Perfect Peppermint Patties 308
Pico de Gallo 100
Pico de Gallo Black Bean Soup................................ 100
Pimiento Cheese 65
Pizza Rustica (Easter Pie) 8

Pork Chops & Mushrooms....................................... 137
Portobello Pizzas... 141
Potluck Fried Chicken.. 132
Pots de Crème 288

Q

Quick & Healthy Turkey Veggie Soup....................... 99
Quick Bean & Rice Burritos 112
Quick Cream of Mushroom Soup 78
Quick Ham & Bean Soup 90
Quick Jalapeno Hush Puppies................................. 180

R

Ranch Dressing 146
Red Wine Cranberry Sauce...................................... 118
Refreshing Key Lime Pie 216
Rhubarb Crumble 287
Rhubarb Custard Bars 260
Rhubarb Rosemary Flatbread 179
Rich Hot Chocolate 284
Roasted Chicken with Rosemary 136
Roasted Tomato Soup with Fresh Basil..................... 90
Rolled Buttermilk Biscuits....................................... 195
Rustic Honey Cake... 224
Rustic Tomato Pie 169

S

Salad Croutons 159
Salted Caramel Sauce 282
Sea Salt Sticks.. 195
Seafood Gumbo.. 81
Shaker Lemon Pie 218
Sheet-Pan Yellow Bells & Eggs................................. 30
Shortbread Lemon Tart.. 212
Shrimp Alfredo 136

Snickerdoodles... 249
Sour Cream Peach Kuchen 216
Sour Cream Rolls with Walnut Filling 194
Southern Pralines 297
Southern Vinegar Slaw 161
Spanish Rice... 168
Spiced Apple Cake with Caramel Icing 236
Spicy Ketchup 115
Steak Stir-Fry... 110
Strawberry Cupcakes 242
Strawberry Salad with Poppy Seed Dressing.............. 160
Strawberry Shortcake Cups.................................... 300
Sunday Pork Roast.. 125
Swedish Butter Cookies 267
Sweet Curry Roasted Pistachios............................... 64
Sweet Potato Biscuits with Honey Butter 177
Sweetened Whipped Cream 300

T

Tangy Macaroni Salad.. 153
Tasty Salmon Croquettes 69
Teriyaki Beef Jerky... 56
The Best Beef Stew.. 105
The Best Chicken & Dumplings.................................. 82
The Best Hummus... 47
The Best Marinara Sauce 133
The Ultimate Chicken Noodle Soup............................. 89

Thick Sugar Cookies 251
Thin Crust Pizza Dough 182
Traditional New England Clam Chowder...................... 107
Traditional Scones... 201
Triple-Chocolate Cheesecake Bars 276
Turkey Breakfast Sausage 38
Turkey Cabbage Stew... 83
Turkey in Cream Sauce... 118
Tuscan Cornbread with Asiago Butter 190

V

Vanilla White Chocolate Mousse 313
Vegan Carrot Soup 87
Very Blueberry Clafoutis... 312

W

Wonderful English Muffins...................................... 196
Wyoming Cowboy Cookies 262

Y

Yellow Layer Cake with Chocolate Buttercream 231

Z

Zucchini Brownies... 259
Zucchini Frittata... 37
Zucchini Nut Bread.. 202